MEXICAN AMERICAN BASEBALL IN SACRAMENTO

PELOTEROS IN PARADISE

Echoes of a past time. Sounds in the air, trapped in a memory, flickering moments that last forever.

WHACK! The crack of a bat. WHOMP! The sound of leather hitting leather.

La pelota, baseball, *los peloteros*, the players, the games played in the sleepy town streets and open spaces in little *pueblitos* all throughout Mexico.

And when they came here, they brought the game with them. *Cruzando la liña*, the border. *El Norte*, they came here in waves, *la onda*, and they brought the game with them. All aboard, *nos vamos al Norte*!

The *engancho*. The hook! The trains that carried them to the farms and fields in California's Central Valley to the Midwest, to the Golden State capital in Sacramento, to the stockyards in Kansas City and Omaha.

They played the game in unplowed fields and dirt roads, in empty lots and patches of green that would become parks, in Sacramento, Stockton, Merced, Modesto, Tracy, Woodland, the Bay Area, even at *el prisión de Folsom*! *No somos Yanquis, pero somos peloteros.*

And they played in English, Spanish, and Spanglish.

¡Dame la pelota! *¡Hechalo*! *¡Honrun*! Throw me the ball, eh!

The Octubre Club, El Club Atlético Mexicano, Los Gallos, Chicanos and Chicanas. They were far from the homeland but they wore their pride on their chests. Baseball, the American game, played by Mexicanos and Mexicanas.

They settled into their new homes, creating *barrios* etched out of farm worker camps, or neighborhoods in the shadows of downtown buildings and centers.

And they played their game. On Sundays, all day, at night, on sandlots and open fields, or self-made diamonds laid out in the streets. *Peloteros* in paradise!

—Tomas J. Benítez

ON THE FRONT COVER: Born in Sacramento on June 20, 1932, Facundo "Cuno" Barragán is one of six children of Mexican immigrant parents. Cuno played baseball at Sacramento High School and Sacramento City College and is widely recognized as the first Mexican American from Sacramento to make it into the major leagues, playing for the Chicago Cubs from 1961 to 1963. (Courtesy of Cuno Barragán.)

COVER BACKGROUND: The Mexican Athletic Club (MAC) softball team played in one of the city leagues in Sacramento during the 1930s. These young women were the cream of the crop. This team had exceptional skills, and the majority of the women played together for nearly four years. (Courtesy of Mexican American Hall of Fame Sports Association.)

BACK COVER: This post–World War II Sacramento MAC team consists of players returning from the war. This picture was taken in front of the chapel at Folsom Prison prior to either an exhibition game or a game against the prisoners. (Courtesy of Mexican American Hall of Fame Sports Association.)

MEXICAN AMERICAN BASEBALL IN SACRAMENTO

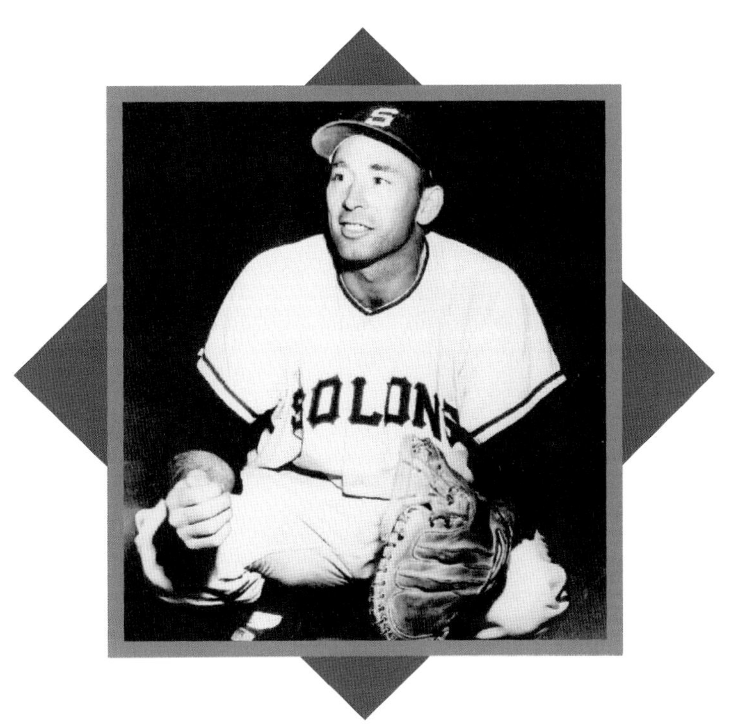

Mark A. Ocegueda, Christopher Docter, Richard A. Santillán, Ernie Cervantes Jr., and Cuno Barragán
Foreword by Juan Carrillo

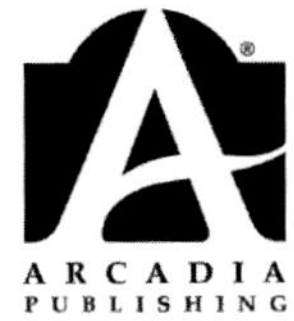

ISBN 978-1-4671-0269-8

Published by Arcadia Publishing
Charleston, South Carolina

Printed in the United States of America

Library of Congress Control Number: 2018965651

For all general information, please contact Arcadia Publishing:
Telephone 843-853-2070
Fax 843-853-0044
E-mail sales@arcadiapublishing.com
For customer service and orders:
Toll-Free 1-888-313-2665

Visit us on the Internet at www.arcadiapublishing.com

Dedicated to Monse and Chloe. I look forward to our new and exciting chapter in Sacramento. Also, for my students at Sacramento State. You continue to inspire and amaze me in so many ways.

—Mark

To my grandparents Robert Lloyd Docter and Dolores Diane Docter.

—Chris

Since 1965, I have been active in California politics, and I dedicate this book to the 1965 Farm Workers Union boycott, the 1968 Bobby Kennedy presidential campaign, the Peace and Freedom and La Raza Unida third parties, the 1982 Tom Bradley gubernatorial campaign, the Jesse Jackson Rainbow Coalition of the 1984 and 1988 presidential campaigns, and the struggle against racial gerrymandering and at-large district systems. I dedicate this book especially to my wife, Teresa—my political soulmate since 1979.

—Richard

All my contributions to this book are dedicated to the baseball bushers who made each weekend enjoyable to the Sacramento community when it was the only game in town.

—Ernie

Dedicated to my beloved friend, mentor, and father figure for over 60 years, Chuck Stevens. Chuck coached me and was responsible for furthering my baseball career.

—Cuno

CONTENTS

Acknowledgments 6

Foreword 7

Introduction 8

1. Barrio Baseball in Sacramento 9

2. Youth Baseball from Sandlots to University Diamonds 35

3. Mexican Americans and Professional Baseball 59

4. The Upper San Joaquin Valley 73

5. The Lower San Joaquin Valley 97

6. Field of Dreams 119

Latino Baseball History Project Advisory Board 126

Bibliography 127

ACKNOWLEDGMENTS

This book could not have been done without the commitment and enthusiasm of so many people. The Sacramento Mexican American Hall of Fame Sports Association served as the source for many of the historic images in this book. As such, we recognize the organization and current members, including Rudy Saenz, Eddie Cervantes, Ernie Cervantes Jr., Rosie Gayton, Jaime Delgadillo, Gerardo López, Paulette Cervantes, Nick Muñoz, Hank Torres, Ruth Torres, Albert Morales, Ralph García, Louise García, Ernie Martínez, Marie Antoinette Martínez, Rose María Vivier, Gil Luna, Gerold López, Ernie Hidalgo, Markos Egure, and Ruben Young. In addition, the authors are indebted to the many other organizations, players, community members, and families who provided remarkable images and stories on the ensuing pages: Juanita Ramírez-Evans, Diana Salgado Zúñiga, Lydia Ramírez Lofton, Karla Barragán, Pedro and Mercedes López, the Cervantes family, the Sacramento chapter of the Society for American Baseball Research, Alan O'Connor, Tom Crisp, William McPoil, Rick Cabral, the Sacramento Sports Hall of Fame, Juan Carrillo, and the Royal Chicano Air Force. We also thank the department of history at Sacramento State and the university archives for their assistance. We thank the Occidental College Special Collections and the Walter P. Reuther Library archives at Wayne State University for their help. The outstanding Sacramento State students Yosa Lagunas Guerrero and Yazmine Vargas Castañeda provided research assistance.

Contributions for the San Joaquin Valley chapters came from Roy Álvarez Jr., the Camacho family, Eddie Chapa, John Chávez, Bill Contreras, Dave Contreras Jr., Anita Delgado Betancourt, Danny Delgado, Isabel Delgado Ybarra, John Delgado, Margie Delgado Carrillo, Richard Delgado, the Dinuba Alta District Historical Society, Michael H. Estrada, Frank García, John Garza, Linda Garza Ávila, Evelyn Hernández Slater, Ester Hernández, Manny Hernández, the Kern County Museum, Sylvia Lovato, Teresa Martínez Vincent, David Monsibais, Ernie Morín, Margaret Morín, Raymond Olivarez, Rachel Ozuna Arias, Eddie Padilla, Juana Pérez, Rudy Trejo, Louis A. Valverde, Maxine Villalovoz Gonzáles, Steve Villalovoz, Virginia Villalovoz Vásquez, Lori Wear, and Randy Zaragoza.

Our appreciation also goes out to Anthony and Julie Luna; Alec Luna; Joe and Karl Soltero; the Latin American Citizens Association; Anthony and Irene C. González; Hector Meneses; Hilda Fried; Tonita's Restaurant; Eddie Navarro; Al Ramos; Joe Talaugon; Al De La Rosa; Eddie Corral; the Alhambra Historical Society; the Whittier College Institute for Baseball Studies; the Pasadena Baseball Reliquary; Terry Cannon; the Historical Society of Southern California; the Whittier College Wardman Library; the Peña family; Ray Lara; Gene T. Chávez; Rod Martínez; California State University, Dominguez Hills; Greg Williams; the North American Society for Sport History; Fernando Valenzuela; Dale Suchil; Teresa M. Santillán; Dianne Sánchez; Monse Segura; John Talamantes; Monica Fox; Lilia and George Van Dyke; Sergio Hernández; in-house editor Elisa Grajeda-Urmstom; longtime editor Jeff Ruetsche; and the Latino Baseball History Project at California State University, San Bernardino.

FOREWORD

The game of baseball has brought joy and drama to millions of fans across the years, while heroes and legends have been created and honored, promoting pure sportsmanship and a deep commitment to the sport.

Unfortunately, the game also took on the values and traditions of 19th- and 20th-century racism and exclusionary practices. For many years, the structural history of baseball segregated players along racial lines. As was true for African Americans, Mexican Americans were relegated to playing outside of established baseball organizations. But like many things in segregated life, baseball was approached with determination, pride, and festivity. Participation in the sport by the Mexican community has gone on for most of that time, and this book helps to reveal some of that hidden history by giving us a glimpse of the vast network of Mexican and Mexican American players, teams, and leagues in Sacramento and the surrounding Central Valley.

I grew up in San Francisco in the 1940s and 1950s, becoming a great fan of baseball and the Pacific Coast League (PCL) San Francisco Seals. Sacramento was the PCL home of the Sacramento Solons and has been my residence for the past 50 years. I recall my early family visits here and going to a neighborhood park to hit baseballs with my cousin in the 105-degree sun. Baseball season in Sacramento meant that the game was played during the hottest part of the year.

Who were those Mexicanos/Mexicanas who played the game here in Sacramento and the Central Valley? This book focuses on the communities of Sacramento, Roseville, Woodland, Stockton, Tracy, and even farther south to Fresno, Bakersfield, and other towns spread across the vast agricultural area of the state. We are introduced to the earliest of Sacramento teams, like the Octubre Club of the 1920s as well as El Club Atlético Mexicano and the Century Club of the 1930s. Women played by establishing softball clubs in these early years as well. This book introduces us to the great players of those times: Ernie Cervantes Sr., Manuel Ramírez, Consuelo Sánchez, and Cuno Barragán. We even learn of an entire family inducted into the Mexican American Hall of Fame Sports Association.

This book, along with the others in this series, brings us this largely unknown sports history. Railroad companies, the canneries, and the business community made possible a network of teams and leagues, enabling communities to play, cheer, and demonstrate their athletic best. While the segregation resulted in limited opportunities for players early on, Sacramento and the Central Valley can be proud of the later contributions made by Mexican American players who broke through to play in the major leagues. These stories and images bring us a remarkable documentation of the relationship of Mexicans and their long love of baseball.

—Juan Manuel Carrillo

INTRODUCTION

Organized baseball in California dates from the mid-19th century, and Mexican American baseball in the Golden State has been documented as far back as the 1870s. By the 1920s, as the Mexican Revolution transformed Mexican communities in the United States by spurring one of the largest waves of migration in world history, nearly every California barrio had at least one Mexican baseball team. These baseball and softball teams competed every weekend on makeshift community fields and municipal parks, attracting hundreds if not thousands of barrio residents to the games. In Sacramento, as Mexicans labored at the Southern Pacific Railroad, canneries, packing houses, and in the booming agricultural communities within the Central Valley, baseball served as the primary recreational and leisure activity. Moreover, baseball meant much more than just an entertaining and leisurely pursuit, as the sport served to reinforce a sense of community pride and ethnic identity for the men and women who played *pelota*.

Mexican American baseball teams traveled to nearby communities, crisscrossed counties, and crossed state borders, and some players even ventured into Mexico to play the game. These baseball trips established permanent networks that eventually merged into an interconnected maze of families, *compadres*, labor associations, and even political alliances. With the sport of baseball, Mexicans in Sacramento made connections with barrios in nearby communities like Woodland, Elk Grove, Stockton, Merced, Atwater, Turlock, Pittsburg, Martínez, and even into the San Francisco Bay Area. In many ways, the sport became a focal point and a crucial element of the social fabric that influenced the development of the Sacramento Mexican community.

This photo book chronicles the overlooked history of Sacramento's Mexican American sports community and connects those stories to a broader Mexican American history. While some attention is given to the rise of individual professional and major-league players, the emphasis rests on the celebration of ethnic identity and community solidarity that Mexican American baseball provided to Sacramento and surrounding communities. Although former players and their families in the region have not forgotten baseball's cultural and social significance, this book serves as one of the first efforts to present the history of Mexican American baseball and softball in Sacramento.

1 Barrio Baseball in Sacramento

Though Mexicans resided in Sacramento prior to the 1910s, the migration spurred by the Mexican Revolution during the first two decades of the 20th century led to a more centralized and cohesive Mexican community in the California capital. In the classic 1971 novel *Barrio Boy*, Ernesto Galarza described the journey that his family experienced when fleeing the violence of the revolution and eventually settling in Sacramento. Galarza recalled that his family first settled in a multiethnic immigrant community off Fifth and L Streets in front of what is now the Golden 1 Center. For thousands of other Mexican immigrants, the story told by Ernesto Galarza rings true to their own journeys to Sacramento during this era. These new migrants converged in the capital to work at the Southern Pacific Railroad, packing houses, and canneries and in farm labor and first settled in downtown's multiethnic communities. As the years passed, these immigrants and their progeny formed a vibrant Mexican community with their own organizations, churches, community centers, and of course, baseball teams.

This chapter looks at teams from the late 1920s, including the Octubre Club, which consisted of players like Julio Reséndez and Pete Benton, who went on to establish the Mexican Athletic Club (MAC) in 1931. The MAC served as a social and cultural lifeline for the Sacramento community for over 26 years and produced excellent barrio players like Ernie Cervantes Sr. and Manuel Ramírez. Women also played for the MAC, such as Consuelo "Chelo" Sánchez, Mary Dávila, and Babe Cervantes. Some of these players also played in the military while serving in World War II, the Korean War, and Vietnam. During and after World War II, another era of Mexican American players emerged and carried the torch, playing with pride for their community and bringing joy to Sacramento's baseball fanatics. Overall, these photographs and stories show Sacramento's Mexican American history through the lens of baseball and celebrate its positive impact in the community.

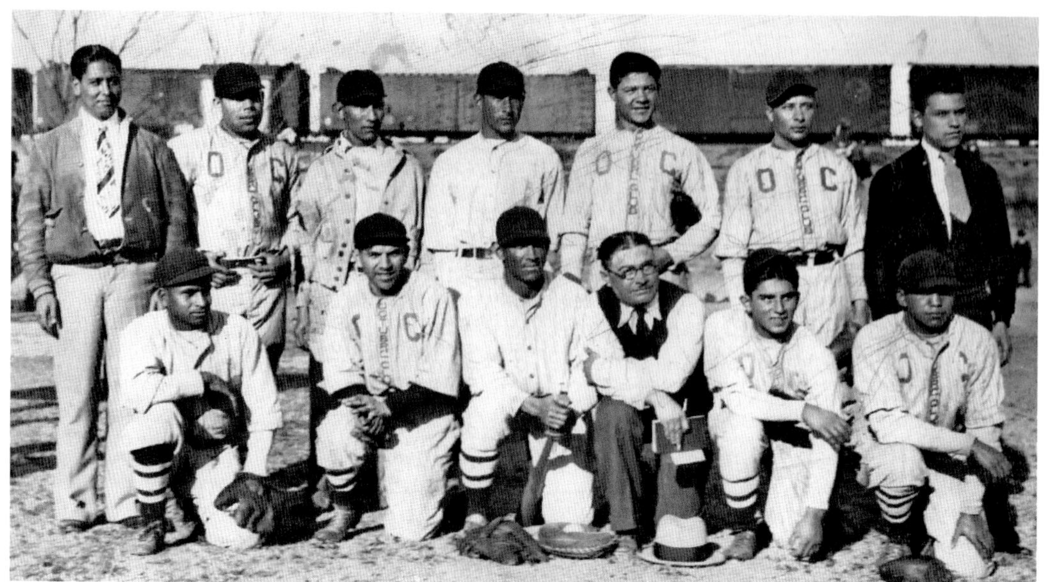

The Sacramento Mexican American Octubre Club baseball team, pictured in the late 1920s, was a social forerunner of the MAC, which formed in 1931. This picture was taken at the ballpark at Twenty-First and C Streets in Sacramento. The ballpark (now Ulysses S. Grant Park) and Southern Pacific train tracks are visible in the background. Many Mexicans in Sacramento during this period worked for the Southern Pacific. Hard-hitting outfielder Pete Benton is second from left in the second row. Julio Reséndez (second row, third from left) was an outstanding pitcher, once pitching a 20-inning game. Reséndez was also one of the founders of the MAC. (Courtesy of Julius Reséndez.)

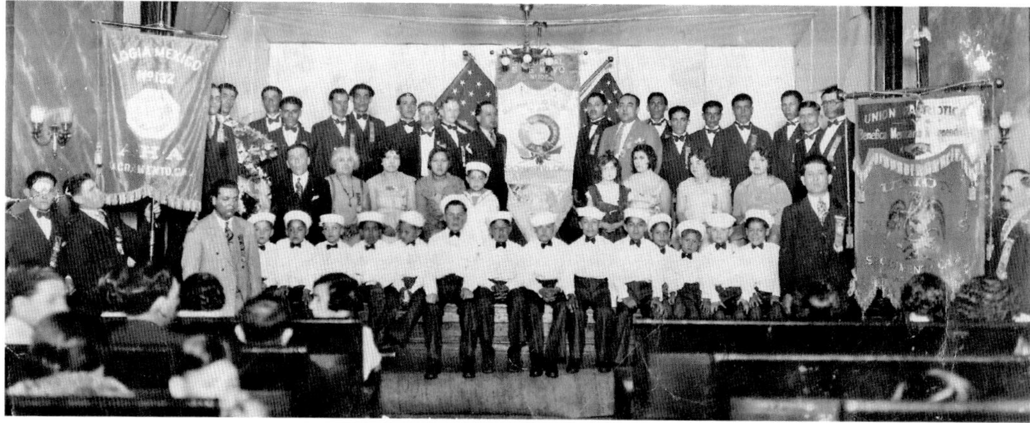

Sacramento's Mexican community thrived during the 1920s, as demonstrated by this image featuring the Alianza Hispano-Americana Logia No. 132. Founded in Tucson, Arizona, in 1894, Alianza was a *mutualista* (mutual aid society) meant to provide basic services and economic assistance to Mexican Americans in the face of discrimination. The organization grew to become the largest and most recognized mutual aid society in the Southwest and by 1939 had over 17,000 members. The Sacramento chapter was founded on May 10, 1928, and this image shows members celebrating their one-year anniversary in 1929. (Courtesy of Diana Salgado Zúñiga.)

Sacramento's Alianza hosted a variety of community events and celebrations, including annual Reina de Fiestas Patrias beauty pageants commemorating Mexican Independence Day. Popular in barrios throughout the Southwest in the late 19th and early 20th centuries, these pageants were exhibitions of national and ethnic pride for Mexican immigrants. They also represented an opportunity to display notions of a Mexican American identity. For example, this late 1920s image shows Sacramento's *reinas* in front of the Mexican and US flags. (Courtesy of Diana Salgado Zúñiga.)

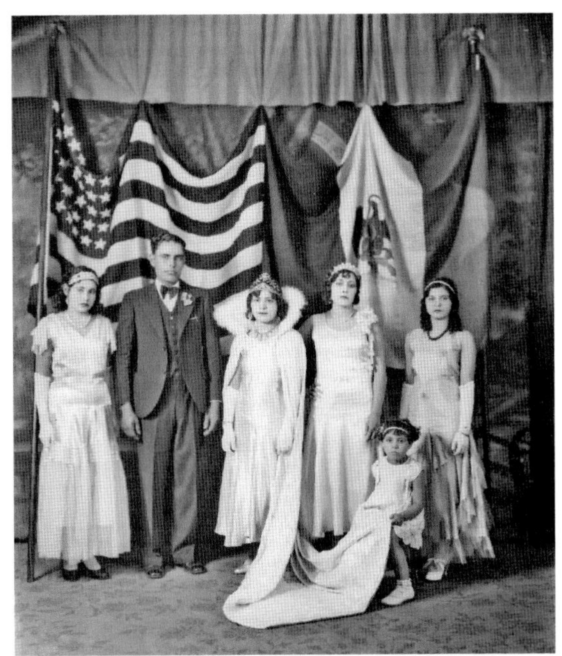

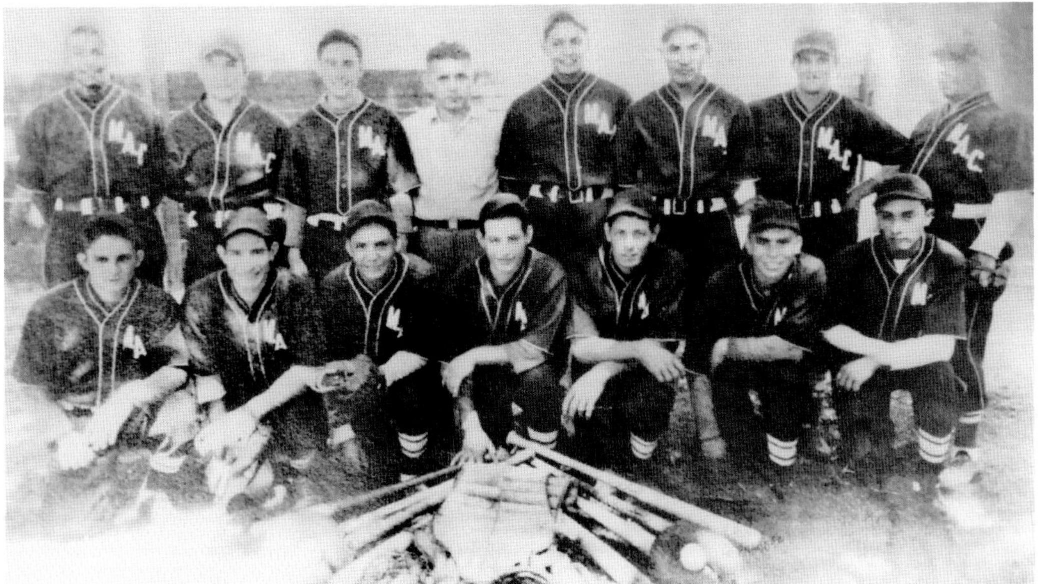

The renowned MAC of Sacramento spanned from 1931 to 1957. The organization was formed so that Mexicans in the city could have their own space for sport and recreation. It originally supported a baseball team but soon became a cultural force for the Mexican community by sponsoring other sports and social activities. From left to right are (first row) Ernie Cervantes Sr., Jim Herrera, Ken Sánchez, Lupe Cisneros, Soco Trujillo, Chon Hernández, and Joe Hernández; (second row) Ted Sánchez, Eddie Trujillo, Ray Lujan, Pete Benton (manager), Jess Sánchez, Julian Cisneros, Abe Salgado, and Pete Urías. The picture was taken at the ballpark at Twenty-First and C Streets in 1937. (Courtesy of Mexican American Hall of Fame Sports Association.)

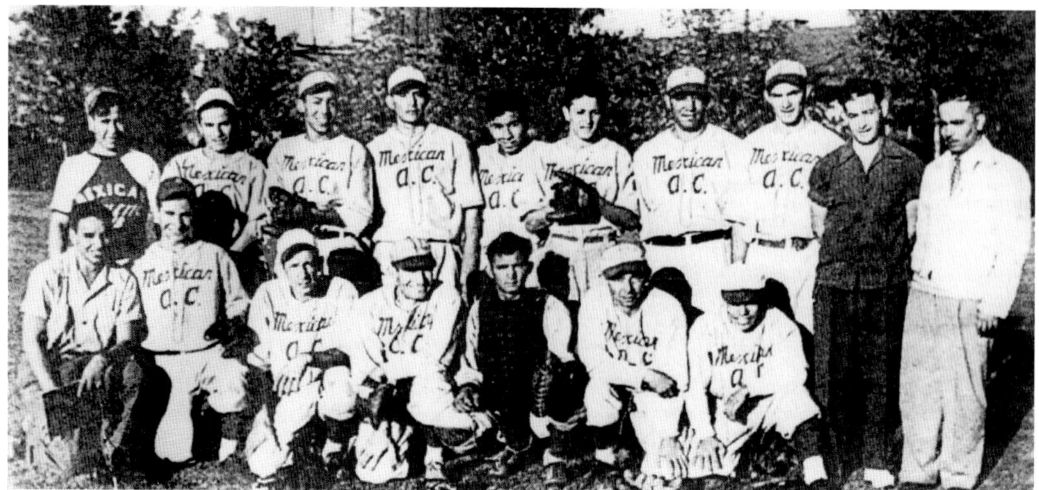

This picture was taken in San Francisco in the 1930s. The Sacramento MAC beat a San Francisco Mexican American team 9-4. The MAC played Mexican American baseball teams from all over Northern California, including Merced, Stockton, Turlock, Tracy, Woodland, and the San Francisco Bay Area. From left to right are (first row) unidentified, Jorge "Corky" Ramírez, unidentified, Jim Herrera, Ernie Cervantes Sr., Clifford Armendáriz, and Jessie González; (second row) Basilio "Buzz" Dávila (manager), unidentified, Larry Gomes, Jess Sánchez, Tubby Ríos, Manual Márquez, Julian Cisneros, Bill Sarillana, Lupe Cisneros, and unidentified. (Courtesy of Mexican American Hall of Fame Sports Association.)

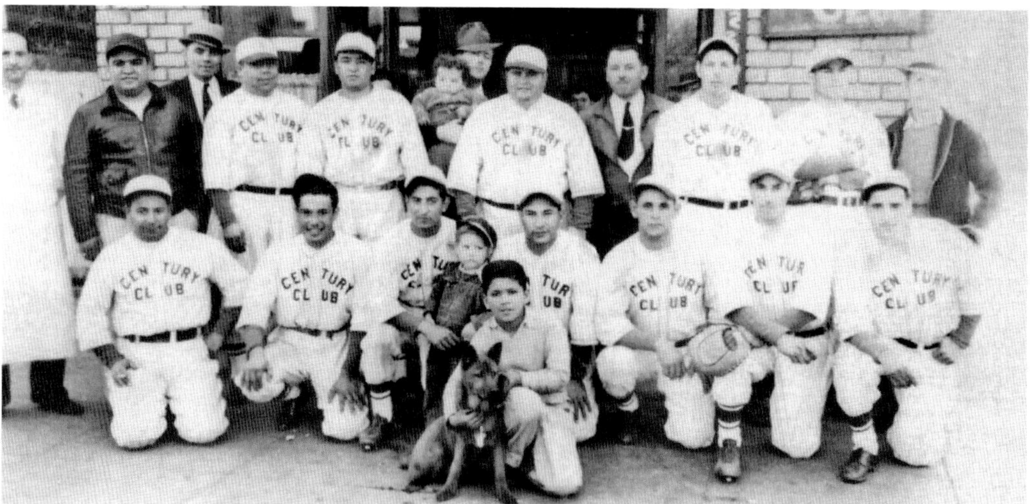

This is the Century Club baseball team that won the pennant in the Federal Division of the Sacramento Winter Baseball League in 1939. From left to right are (first row) Ed Moreno, Frank Sánchez, Jack Trujillo, Henry García (batboy), Richard Moreno (mascot), Ed Trujillo, Trini Campos, Jess Saucedo, and James Pérez; (second row) unidentified, Joe García (manager), unidentified, Pete Urías, Charles García, unidentified man with baby, Mario Moreno, unidentified, Soco Trillo, John Cafarelli, and Julio Reséndez (coach). (Courtesy of Mexican American Hall of Fame Sports Association.)

Pictured here is Corky Ramírez playing Senior American Legion baseball (19 years of age and under) in the late 1930s. American Legion baseball is amateur baseball that provides young men an opportunity to develop their skills, personal fitness, and leadership qualities, and to have fun. Legion baseball started in 1925 in South Dakota; by the 1930s, it had spread to the Sacramento Valley. Manhart Post No. 391 is a local team that has a very competitive history dating to the 1930s. Corky Ramírez had a long career in Sacramento playing with the MAC. (Courtesy of Tom Ramírez.)

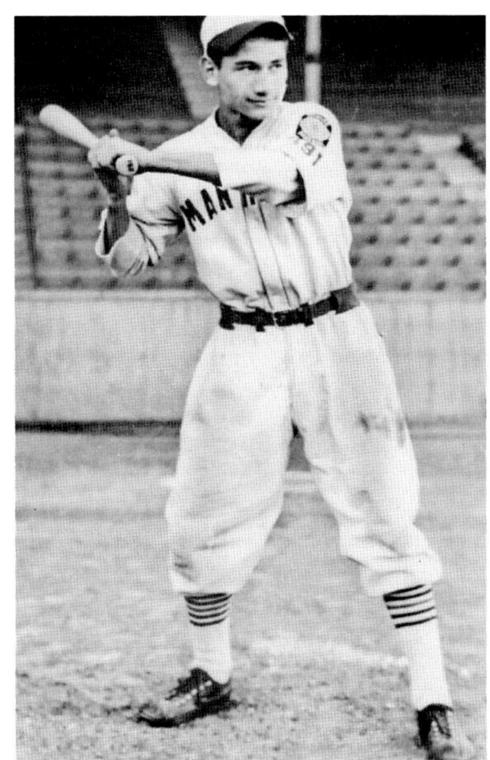

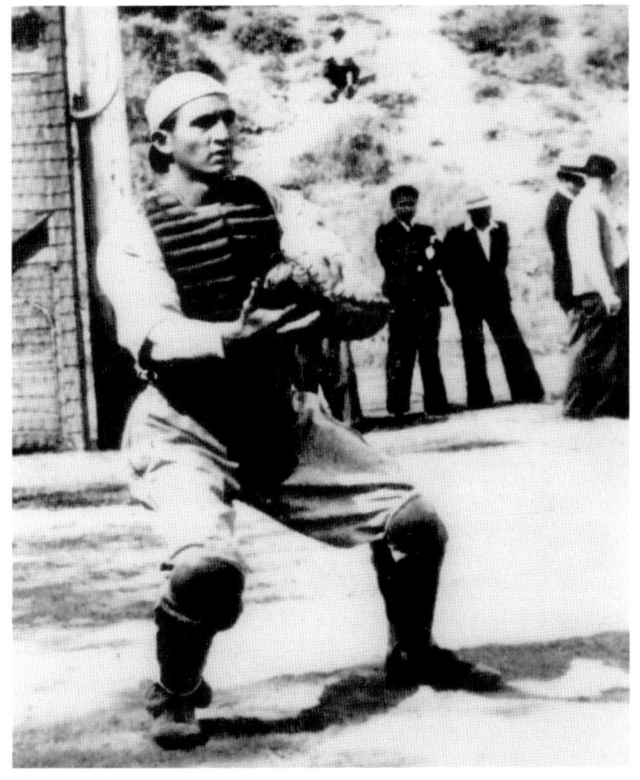

Ernie Cervantes Sr. was good enough to turn down a contract with the St. Louis Browns because he was married and making more money contracting trucks to the City of Sacramento. The Browns' offer was made in the 1930s, when Mexican Americans were uncommon in the major leagues. Instead of playing with the Browns, Cervantes played many years in Sacramento with the MAC. His passion for the game was passed down to his children and grandchildren. Cervantes's four sons and daughter played baseball as well. There have now been four generations of Cervantes family baseball in Sacramento. (Courtesy of Ernie Cervantes Jr.)

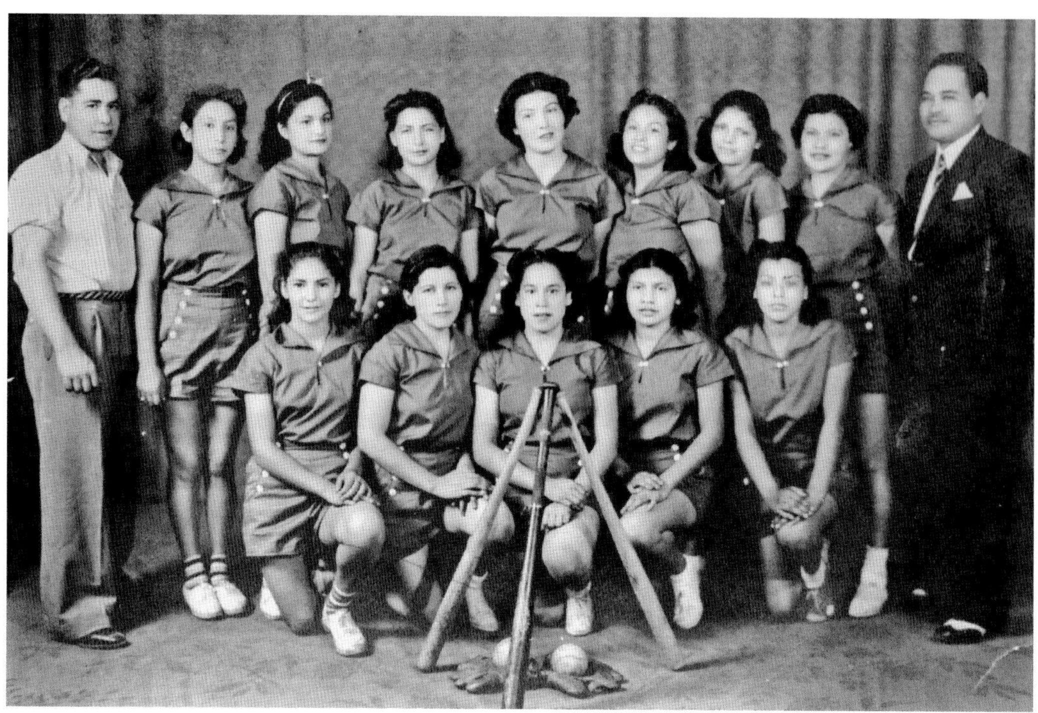

All the young women on this 1930s MAC softball team were from the same Sacramento neighborhood and played together for nearly four years. The team was coached by Basilio "Buzz" Dávila, who was inducted into the Sacramento Mexican American Hall of Fame. Consuelo "Chelo" Sánchez is second from right in the second row. Other team members included Linda Sánchez (bottom left), Jennie Dávila, Mary Dávila, Muzzie Valenzuela, Teresa Rojas, Josephine "Josie" Rojas, Babe Cervantes, Lily López, Margaret Rojas, Adeline Huerta, and García Carrillo. (Courtesy of Mexican American Hall of Fame Sports Association.)

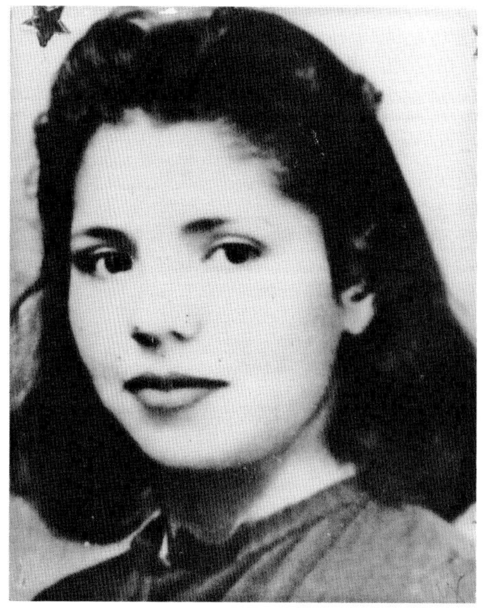

Born in 1923, Consuelo "Chelo" Sánchez played for the MAC women's team during the late 1930s. She grew up in a multiethnic immigrant community in downtown Sacramento near Eighth and O Streets, and the team played at Tenth and P Streets at what is now Roosevelt Park. Sánchez met Manuel Ramírez during the late 1930s at a neighborhood dance at the Ranchero Club near Southside Park off Sixth and X Streets; they would later start a family together. (Courtesy of Juanita Ramírez-Evans.)

Manuel Ramírez is pictured with his mother, Damiana Baro Ramírez, when crossing the US-Mexico border at El Paso, Texas, in 1920. Fleeing the violence and economic turmoil brought about by the Mexican Revolution, Manuel and his mother migrated from Mazatlán, Mexico, to Sacramento and eventually settled in downtown off Sixth and P Streets. Manuel's stepfather worked for the Southern Pacific, and Manuel joined the Civilian Conservation Corps as a teenager during the Great Depression. He went on to have a long career as a baseball player, manager, and umpire. (Courtesy of Juanita Ramírez-Evans.)

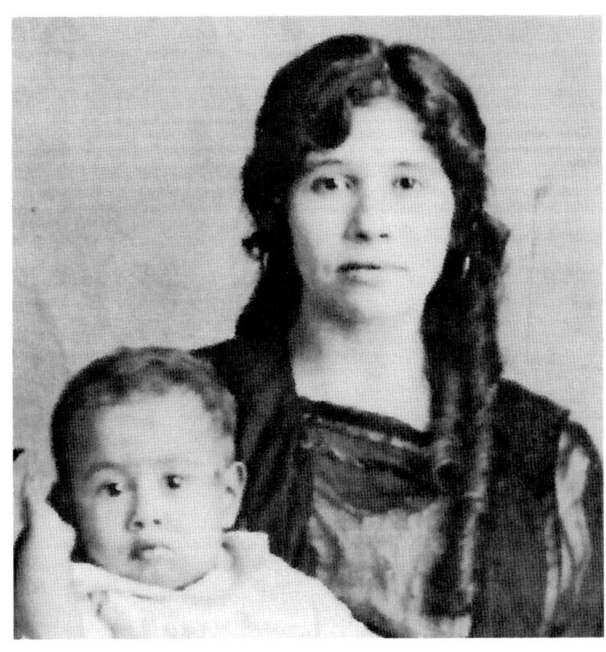

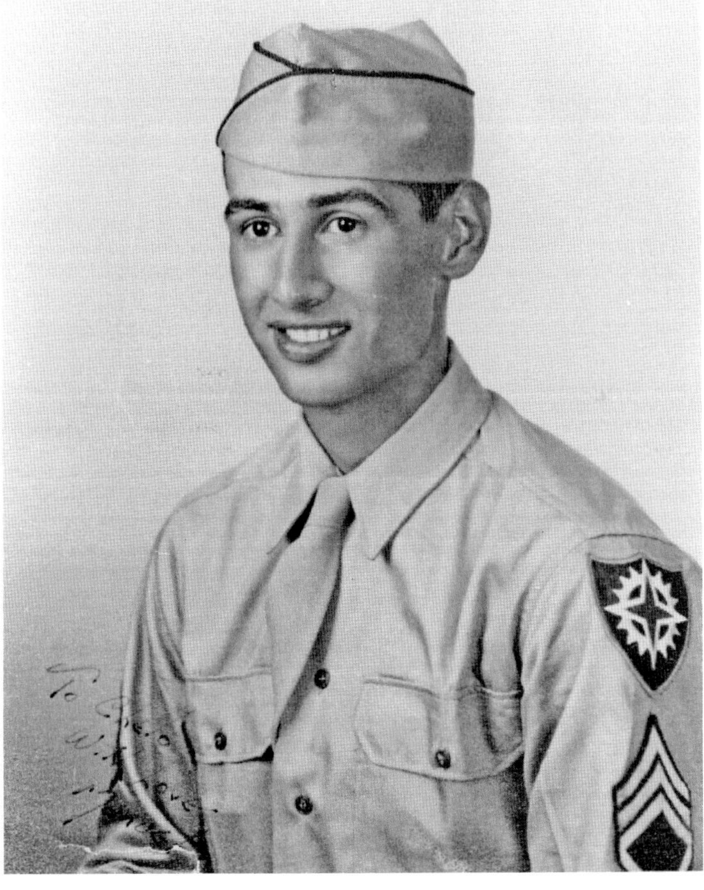

Manuel Ramírez joined the US Army in 1941 and served in World War II; he fought at the Battle of the Bulge. When Ramírez joined the Army, he was not a US citizen, but after five years of service, he decided to become a naturalized citizen before he was discharged in 1946. When he returned home, he played for and managed the MAC baseball team, on which he played alongside his younger brother Jorge "Corky" Ramírez. (Courtesy of Juanita Ramírez-Evans.)

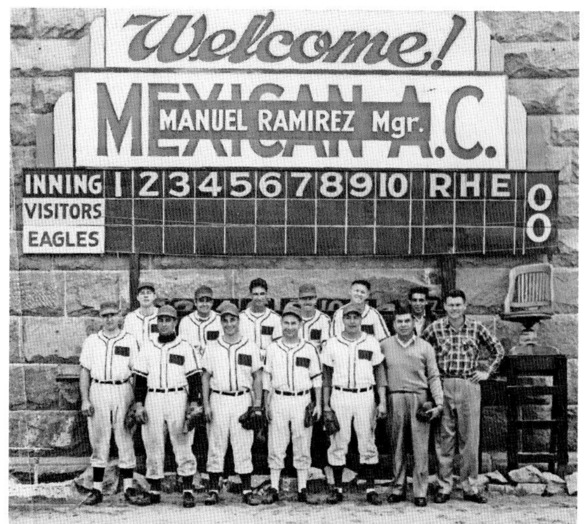

The MAC is pictured at Folsom Prison in the late 1940s. From left to right are (first row) Tony Alvarado, Mike Hernández, unidentified, Jorge "Corky" Ramírez, Ted Sánchez, and Paul Sánchez; (second row) Frank Ríos, Butch Granico, Manuel Ramírez (manager), Pete Benicio, two unidentified, and former Sacramento Solon Curt Schmidt. The MAC and the prison team, the Represa Eagles, played in the Sacramento County League, but the Eagles obviously were not a traveling team. (Courtesy of Gary Ríos.)

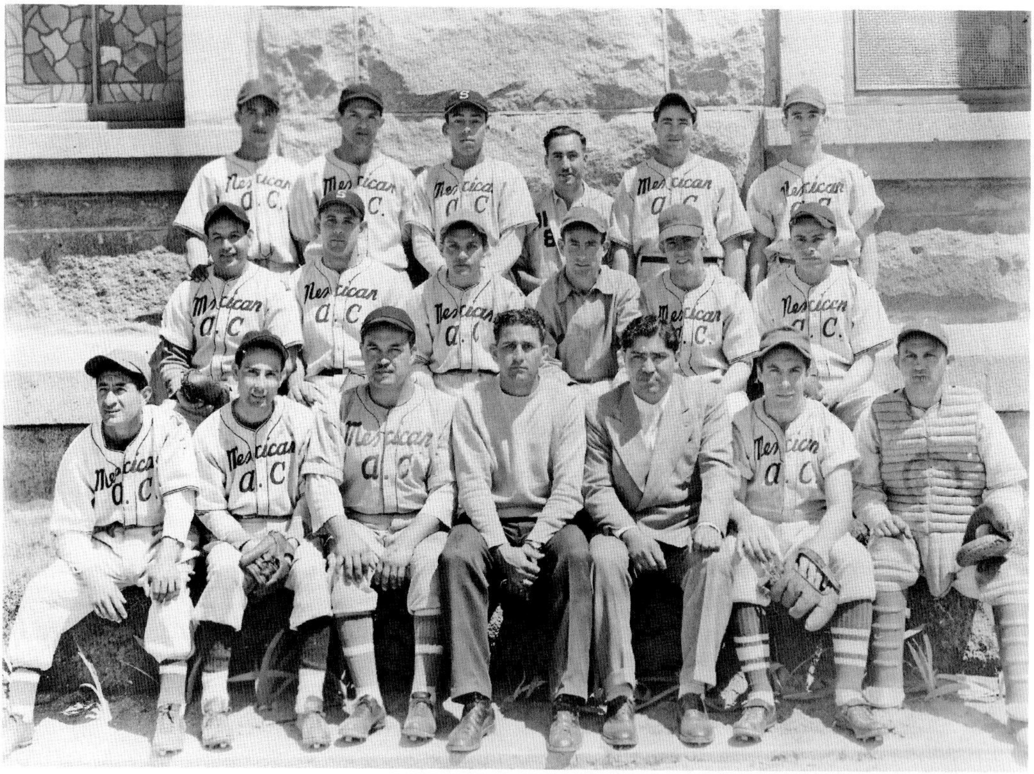

This post–World War II MAC team included some new faces as men returned home from the war. The team is posing in front of the Folsom Prison chapel before a game against the prisoners or an exhibition game. From left to right are (first row) Manuel Ramírez, Ray Lujan, Frank Sánchez, unidentified, Julian Cisneros, unidentified, and Ernie Cervantes Sr.; (second row) Ted Sánchez, Trinidad Campos, three unidentified, and Chon Hernández; (third row) Manual Cisneros, Bill Sarillana, Larry Gomes, Tony Guerra, Tony Alvarado, and unidentified. (Courtesy of Mexican American Hall of Fame Sports Association.)

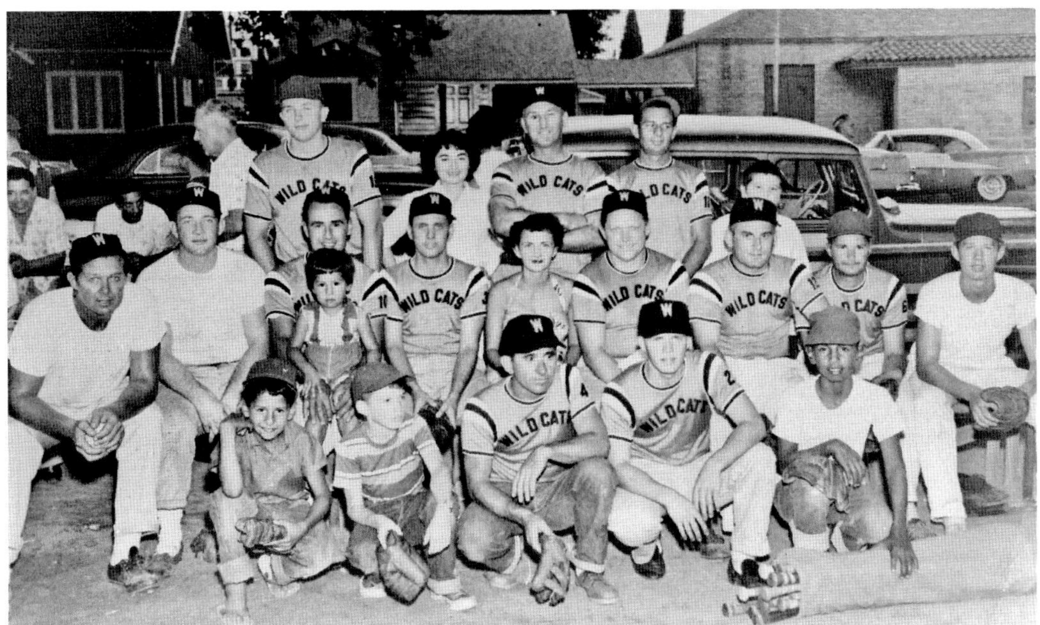

Manuel and Chelo Ramírez eventually started a family, but he continued to play baseball after his children, Tony, Bobby, and Juanita, arrived. Ramírez is seen in 1959 (second row, third from left) holding Juanita with brothers Bobby (first row, far right) and Tony (first row, far left). This team is the Sacramento Wildcats. Manuel eventually worked for the City of Sacramento for 32 years as a mechanic for service vehicles. (Courtesy of Juanita Ramírez -Evans.)

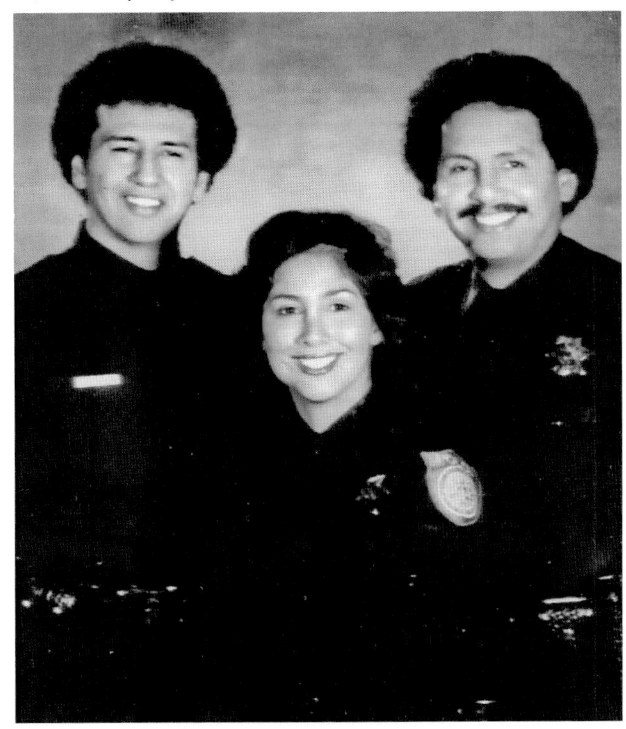

In 1977, Juanita Ramírez became the first Latina to join the Sacramento Police Department. When she joined the police department, she was interviewed by Rosie Gayton for *El Progreso*. Her brothers Tony (left) and Bobby (right) also served on the police department and played sports. All members of Juanita Ramírez's immediate family have been inducted into the Sacramento Mexican American Hall of Fame Sports Association. (Courtesy of Juanita Ramírez-Evans.)

Mexican Tossers Defeat Jackets

The Mexican Athletic Club of American A Division of the Winter Baseball League defeated the Red Jacket Tribe yesterday in a baseball game by a score of 4 to 3.

Julian Cisneros pitched a nine hit game and struck out ten.

Jimmie Herrera starred for the Mexicans, getting four hits out of five times at bat. E. Cervantes and Pete Urias got three hits each.

Downs for the losers got three blows.

The score:	R.	H.	E.
Mexican A. C.	4	15	0
Red Jacket Tribe	3	9	3

The batteries: J. Cisneros and Cervantes; J. Murphy and E. Petrali.

The MAC teams often appeared in the *Sacramento Bee* for their athletic talent and accomplishments. This article from January 29, 1940, describes the MAC baseball team as belonging to the American A Division of the Winter Baseball League. The MAC team defeated a Native American team called the Red Jacket Tribe 4-3, with Julian Cisneros striking out 10 hitters. Jimmie Herrera collected four hits, while Ernie Cervantes Sr. and Pete Urías got three hits each. (Courtesy of the Mexican American Hall of Fame Sports Association.)

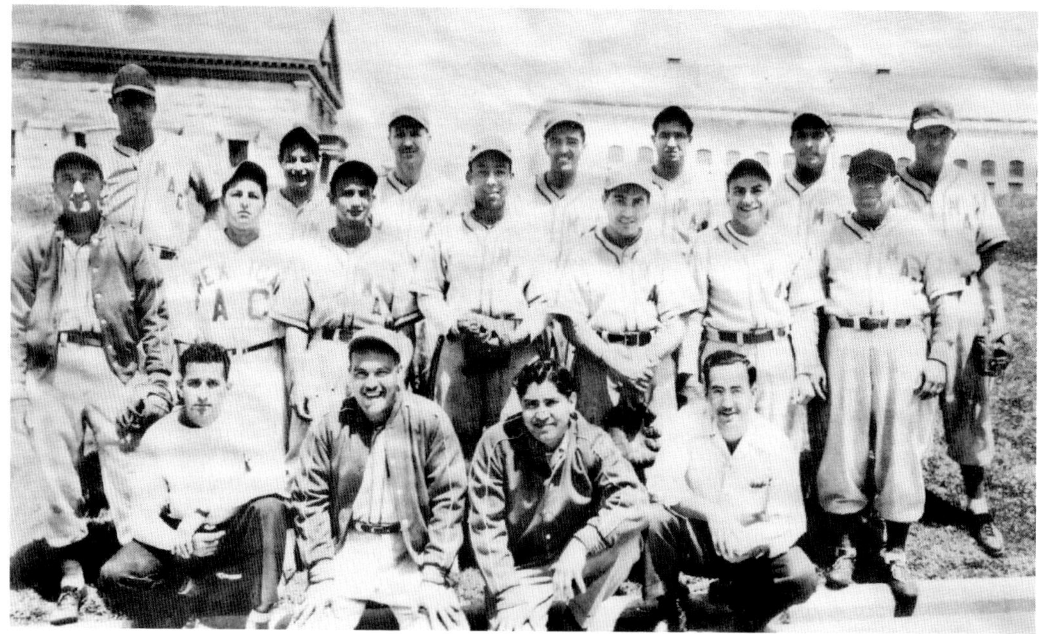

The MAC team visits Folsom Prison in the late 1930s or early 1940s. From left to right are (first row) the Folsom Prison team manager, Frank Sánchez, Mose Cisneros, and Tony Guerra; (second row) John Stanich, Leo Cervantes, Ernie Cervantes Sr., Larry Gomes, Jess Torres, Richard Maldonado, and Pete Urías; (third row) unidentified, Lupe Cisneros, unidentified, Pete Benicio, Tony Alvarado, John Caranza, and Bill Sarillana. (Courtesy of Mexican American Hall of Fame Sports Association.)

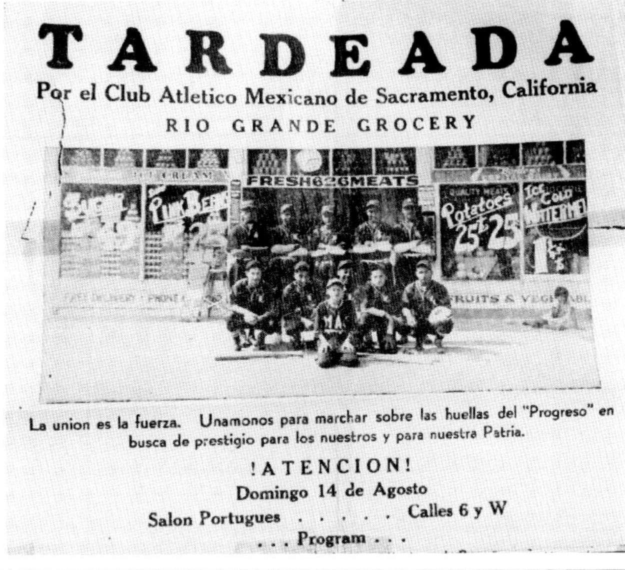

The MAC and the Rio Grande Grocery advertise a *tardeada*—an afternoon fiesta—held on August 14, 1937, at the Salon Portugues off Sixth and W Streets. The fine print roughly translates to "There is strength in unity. We unite to march toward progress and in search of prestige for our Mexican community." This statement reflects the unity within Sacramento's Mexican community during the time. (Courtesy of the Mexican American Hall of Fame Sports Association.)

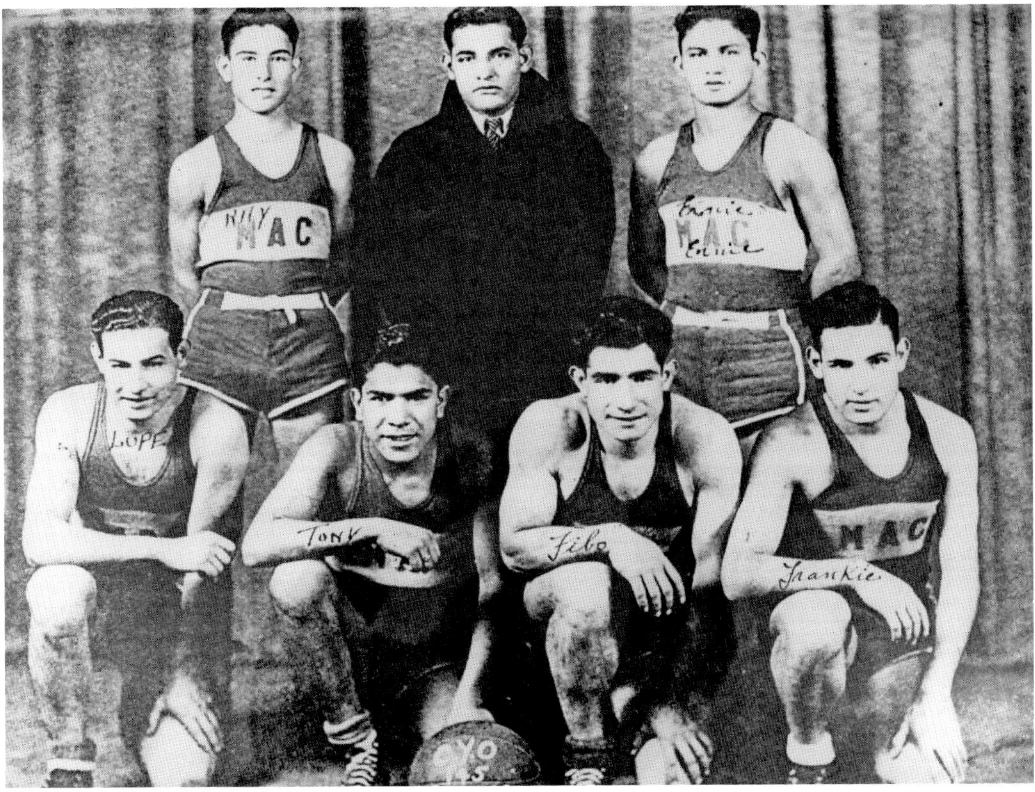

The MAC also sponsored other sports and social activities, including basketball. Pictured here is the MAC basketball team from the late 1930s. From left to right are (first row) Lupe Cisneros, Tony Rojas, Fibo Herrera, and Frank Cisneros; (second row) Ray Lujan, Manuel Cisneros, and Ernie Cervantes Sr. This team won the Catholic Youth Organization (CYO) championship. All of these players also played baseball. (Courtesy of the Mexican American Hall of Fame Sports Association.)

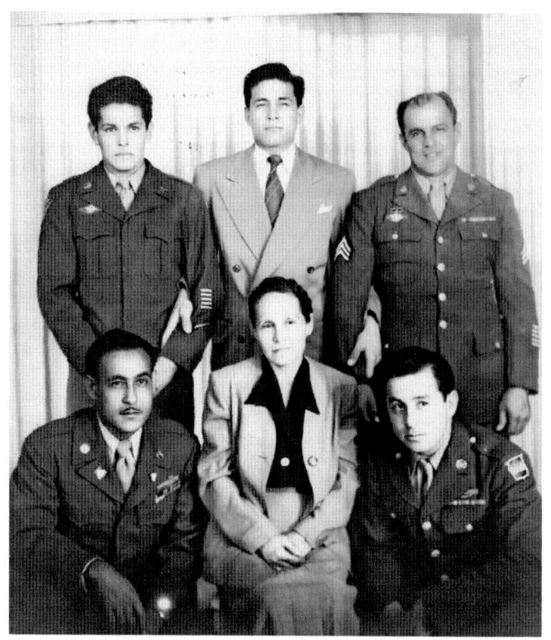

Enriqueta Andazola (seated at center) lived in Sacramento for more than 70 years and played an important role as a leader in the Mexican American community. She founded important Mexican civic organizations, including the first Mexican women's society (Las Amigas del Hogar) in the city during the late 1920s and, more notably, Las Madres Mexicanas de Guerra—Mexican War Mothers—–in 1942. All four of her sons and her son-in-law served during World War II. From left to right are Joe Ramírez (kneeling), Edgardo Ramírez, John Ramírez, Abraham Salgado, and Paul Ramírez. Some of Enriqueta's sons played baseball for the MAC Tigers. (Courtesy of Diana Salgado Zúñiga.)

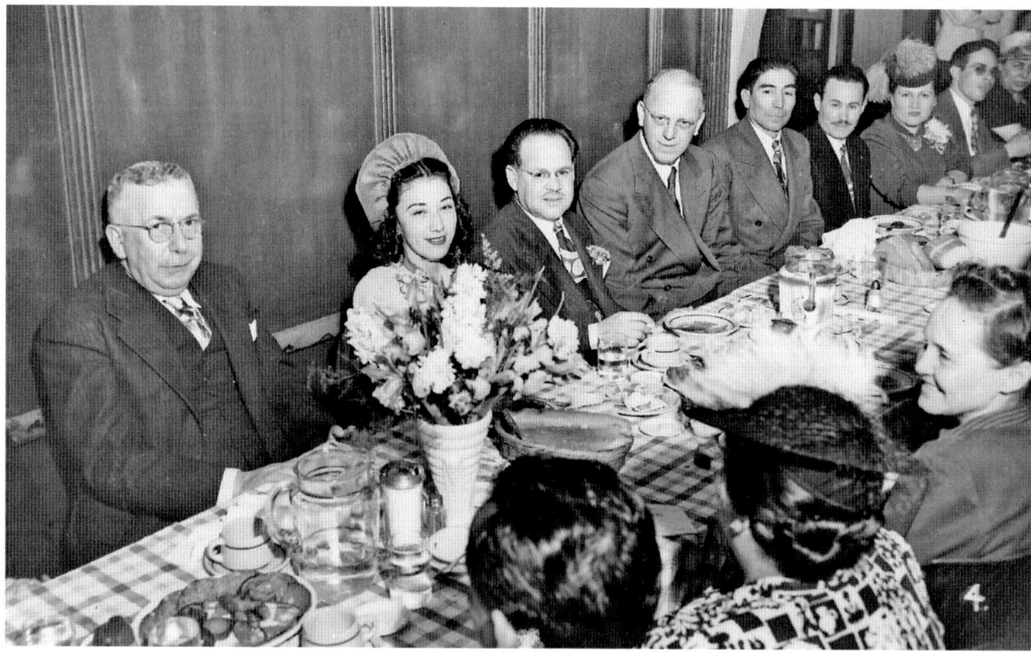

Enriqueta Andazola is pictured at bottom right with her head turned toward the camera at a dinner for Mexican consul Adolfo G. Dominguez at The Español restaurant in 1941. Dominguez is seated third from left on the far side of the table. Earl Warren, a district attorney from Los Angeles at the time, is seated to the right of him. Warren went on to become governor of California and the 14th chief justice of the US Supreme Court. During the course of Enriqueta's leadership within the Sacramento Mexican community, she became acquainted with prominent politicians and several California governors. (Courtesy of Diana Salgado Zúñiga.)

The Mexican War Mothers held dances and cooked meals for Mexican American soldiers stationed in Sacramento or in nearby communities. In addition, they held letter-writing campaigns for soldiers abroad and visited injured soldiers recovering at local military hospitals. This is a pamphlet for a formal dance sponsored by the Mexican War Mothers for World War II veterans. Such events underscore the importance of the Mexican American contribution to the war effort, not only abroad, but on the home front as well. (Courtesy of Diana Salgado Zúñiga.)

Madres Mexicanas

Baile Formal

En Honor de los Veteranos
de la Guerra

Native Sons Hall
Martes Febrero 26 a 7:30 P. M.

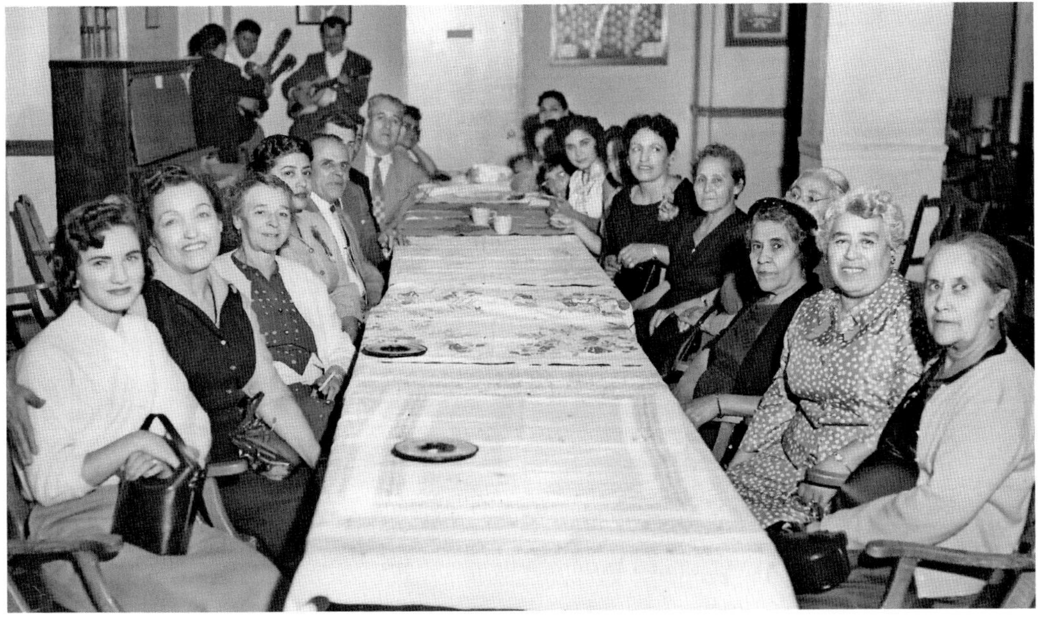

When the war concluded, the Mexican War Mothers continued working as a civic group, and in 1948, they resolved to raise funds to build a statue to honor the Mexican American sacrifice during World War II. It is estimated that over 500,000 Mexican Americans served in the war, and many more contributed on the home front. Between 1948 and 1951, the war mothers fundraised by selling *pan dulce* and tamales at the local Catholic church to help build the statue. Some of the war mothers shown here are (from left to right on the left) "Little" Gracie Esparza, Grace Esparza, Elena Zonala, and Ofelia Campos with husband Angel Campos; Enriqueta Andazola is on the right side, fifth from the front. (Courtesy of Diana Salgado Zúñiga.)

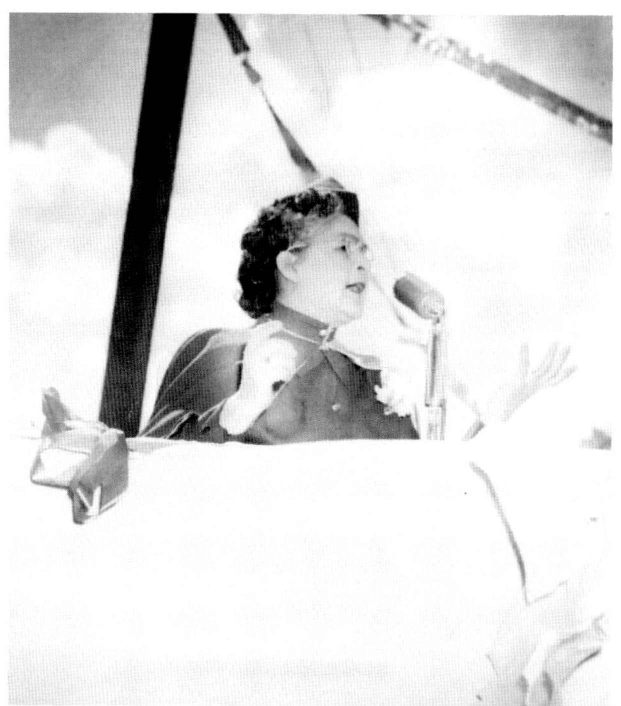

After fundraising for three years, the Mexican War Mothers paid for the statue to be sculpted in Italy and shipped to Sacramento. The statue depicts a Mexican American soldier armed with a rifle. It was dedicated in May 1951 at the Sacramento Mexican Center at Sixth and W Streets near Southside Park. This image shows Angelina Cervantes, member of the Mexican War Mothers, speaking at the event. Her son, Ernie Cervantes Sr., served in World War II and is known as "Mr. Baseball" in the Sacramento Mexican community. (Courtesy of Eddie Cervantes.)

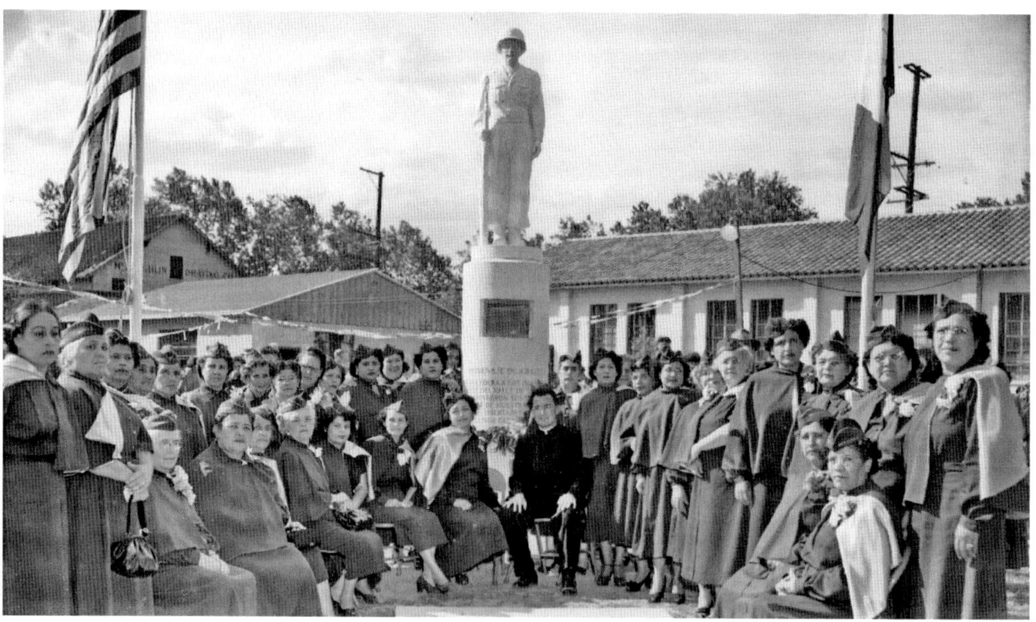

This is the statue of the Mexican American soldier, now commonly referred to as "El Soldado Latino," at the dedication ceremony in 1951. The Sacramento Mexican community rallied behind the Mexican War Mothers to help accomplish their goal of honoring the Mexican American sacrifice during World War II. This unique and special public monument showcases the unity and grassroots strength within Sacramento's Mexican community. Members of the Mexican War Mothers proudly pose in front of the statue. (Courtesy of Diana Salgado Zúñiga.)

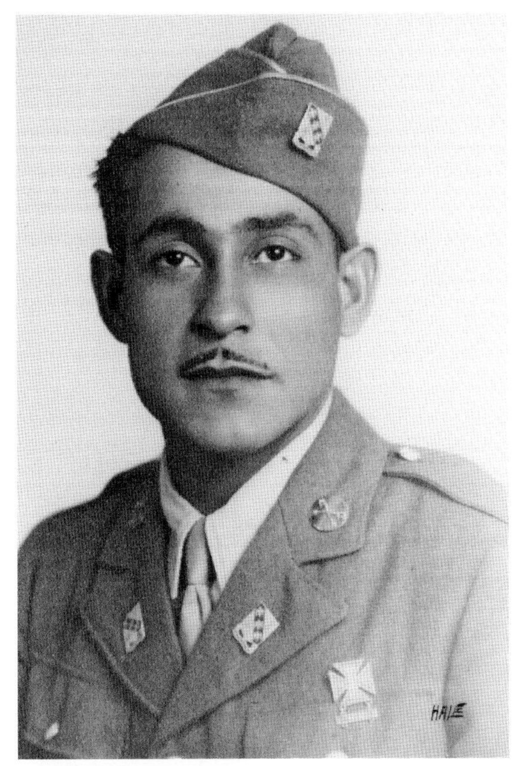

Joe Ramírez served in World War II and was one of Enriqueta Andazola's sons. A photograph of him was the reference the Italian sculptor used to design the statue. When the Mexican Center closed its doors in 1975, Joe Ramírez, Enriqueta Andazola, and various Mexican organizations successfully lobbied California governor Jerry Brown to have the statue relocated in front of the California State Capitol. (Courtesy of Diana Salgado Zúñiga and Lydia Ramírez Lofton.)

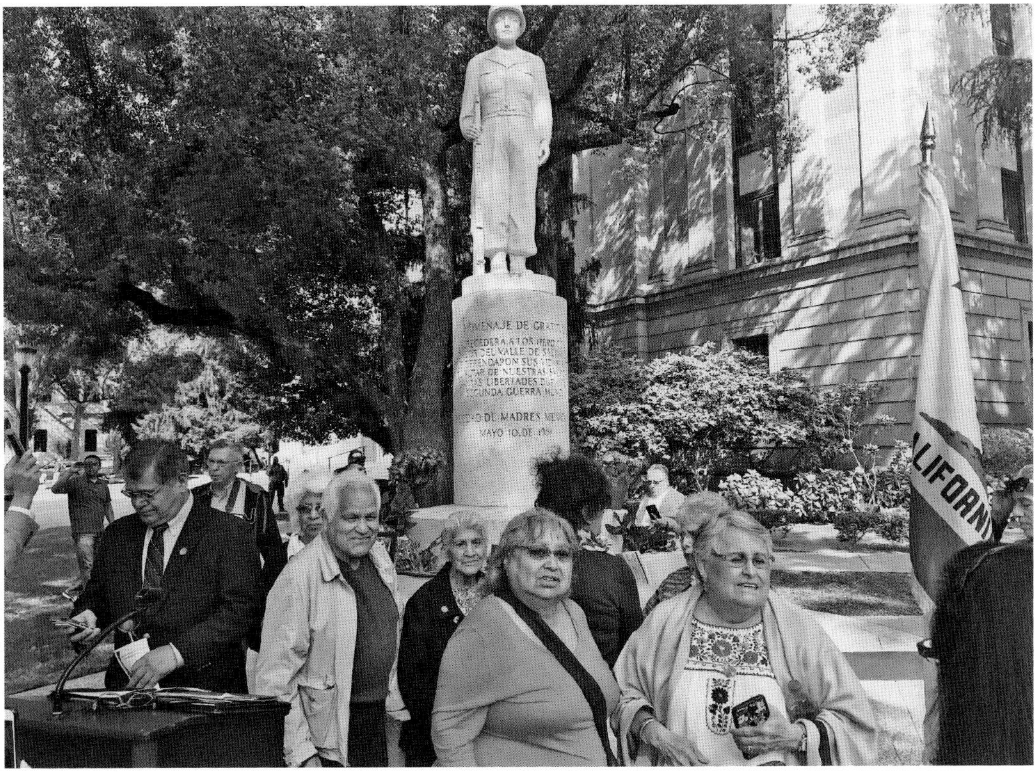

In 2015, the statue was vandalized, and an effort to repair and restore the monument soon followed. This photograph was taken in October 2017, when "El Soldado Latino" was rededicated. Family members of the Mexican War Mothers and community residents celebrated the rich history of the statue and the legacy that it continues to carry on. (Courtesy of Mark Ocegueda.)

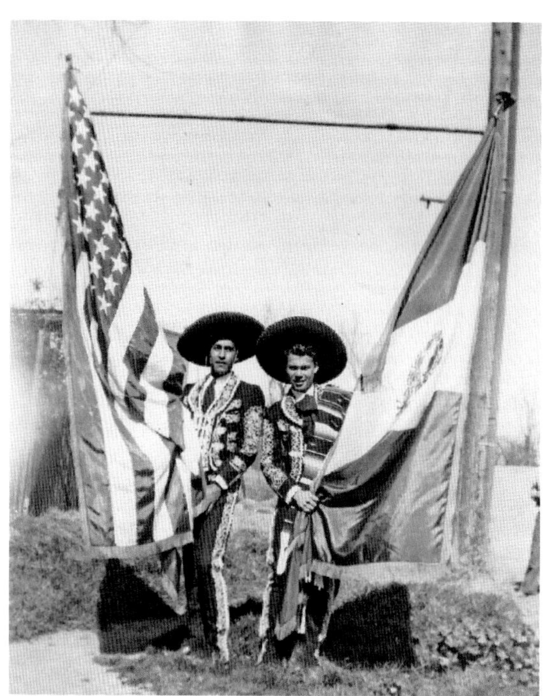

Another popular sport within the Mexican community was *charrería*. These rodeos were popular in Mexico during the 19th and early 20th centuries and promoted national identity. The pastime eventually developed a following in Mexican communities in the United States when film stars like Jorge Negrete popularized the image of gallant Mexican horsemen. Joe Ramírez (left) and another Sacramento *charro* proudly hold the Mexican and US flags as symbols of their Mexican American identities. (Courtesy of Diana Salgado Zúñiga.)

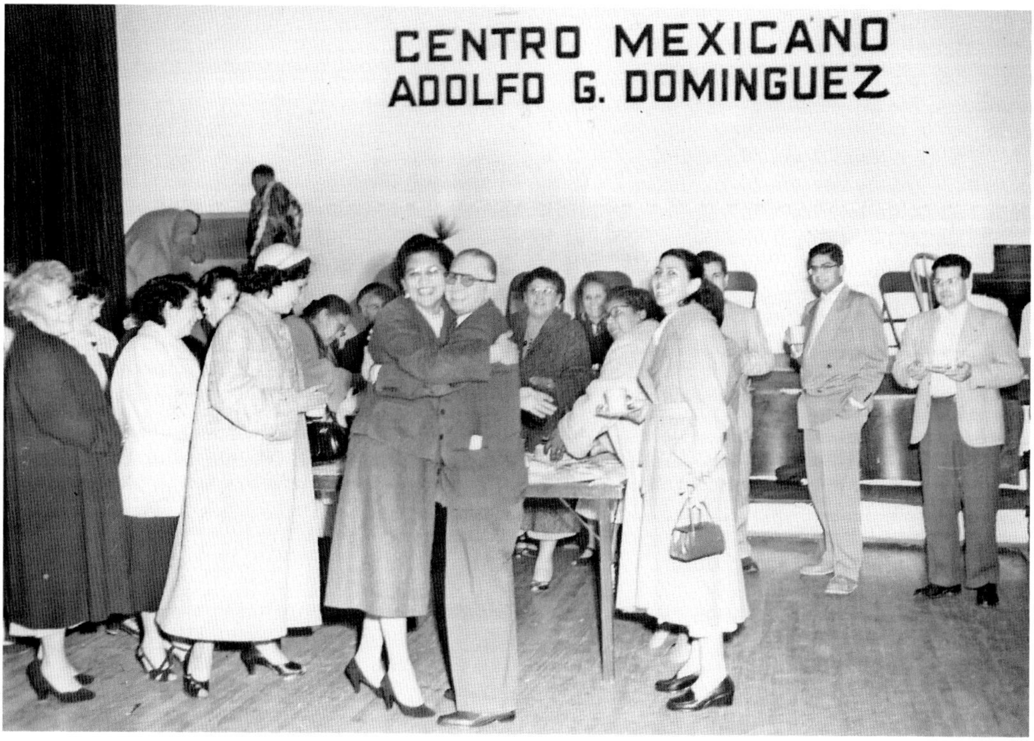

The Sacramento Mexican Center served as the heart of the Mexican community for many years. This image shows founding members Enriqueta Andazola and Phil Zúñiga as the Mexican community celebrates the opening of the center in 1948. (Courtesy of Diana Salgado Zúñiga.)

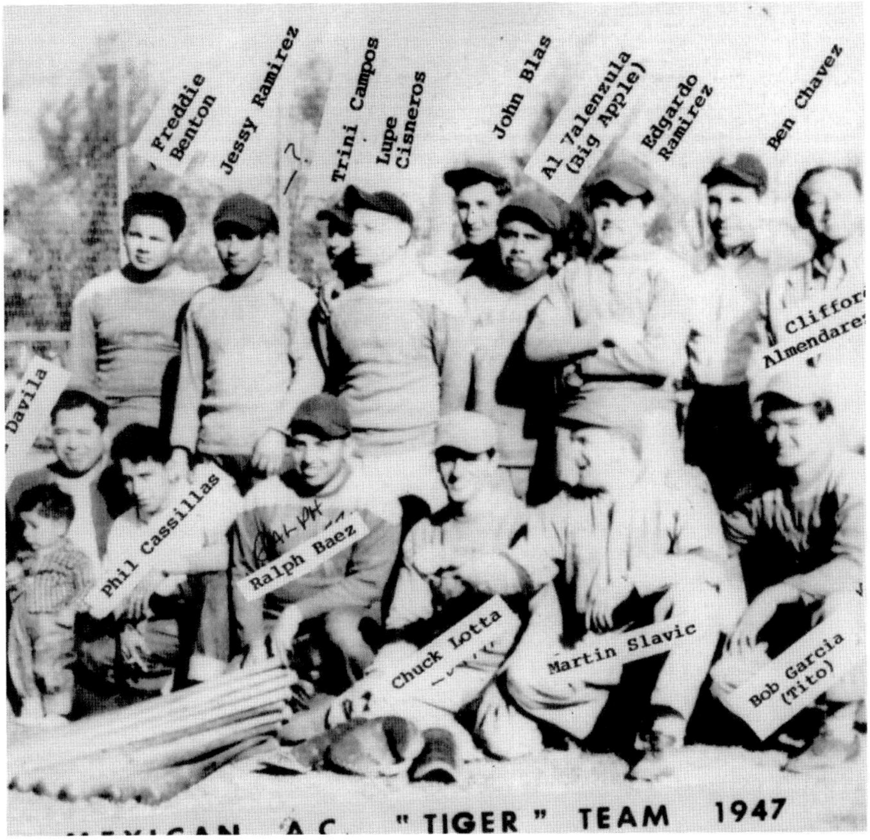

Freddie Benton
Jessy Ramirez
Trini Campos
Lupe Cisneros
John Blas
Al Valenzula (Big Apple)
Edgardo Ramirez
Ben Chavez
Clifford Almendarez
Davila
Phil Cassillas
Ralph Baez
Chuck Lotta
Martin Slavic
Bob Garcia (Tito)

"TIGER" TEAM 1947

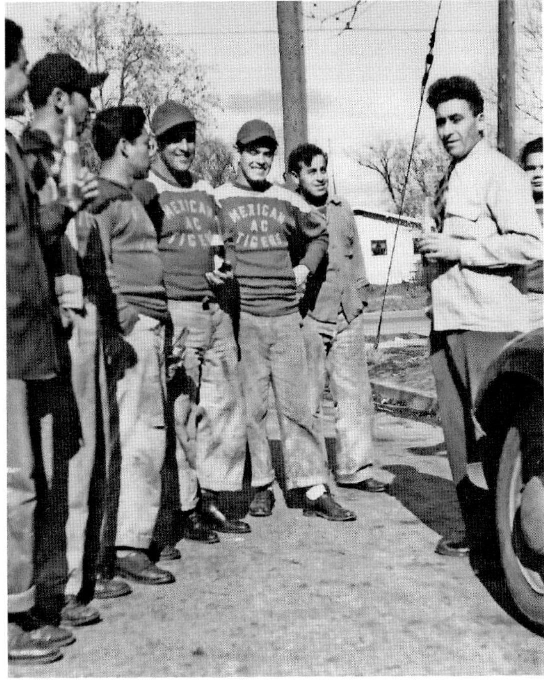

This is the post–World War II MAC Tigers, the club's B team. The names are clearly visible, and players like Chuck Lota, Lupe Cisneros, and Trini Campos were later promoted to the MAC A team. The picture was taken at the ballpark at Twenty-First and C Streets (now Ulysses S. Grant Park) in Sacramento in 1947. With returning war veterans and an economic upswing beginning, the MAC rosters swelled, and so did all County and Winter League rosters. The image at left shows the MAC Tigers enjoying some beverages after a game. Manager Abe Salgado is fourth from left, Edgardo Ramírez is fifth from left, and Paul Ramírez is sixth from left. (Above, courtesy of Mexican American Hall of Fame Sports Association; left, courtesy of Diana Salgado Zúñiga.)

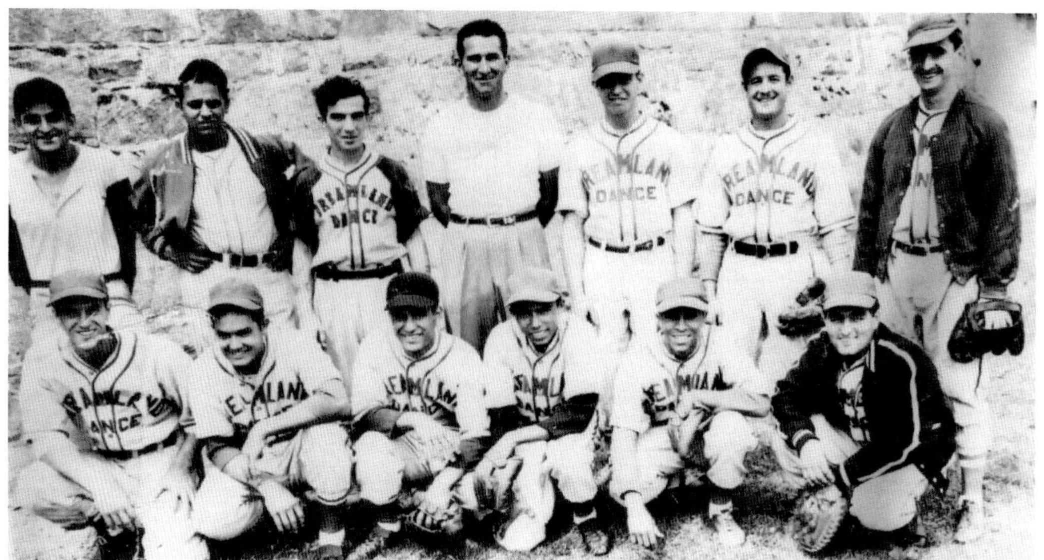

The Dreamland Dance sponsored a baseball team in the 1940s comprised mainly of Mexican Americans. They pose in front of a wall of Folsom Prison prior to playing an exhibition game. Dreamland Dance was originally owned by Ed Kripp, a baseball player in Sacramento in the 1890s and manager of the 1898 California League champion Sacramento Gilt Edge. Kripp owned and built the original professional baseball park at Riverside Boulevard and Broadway, called Buffalo Park at first and later Edmonds Field in the 1940s and 1950s. (Courtesy of Mexican American Hall of Fame Sports Association.)

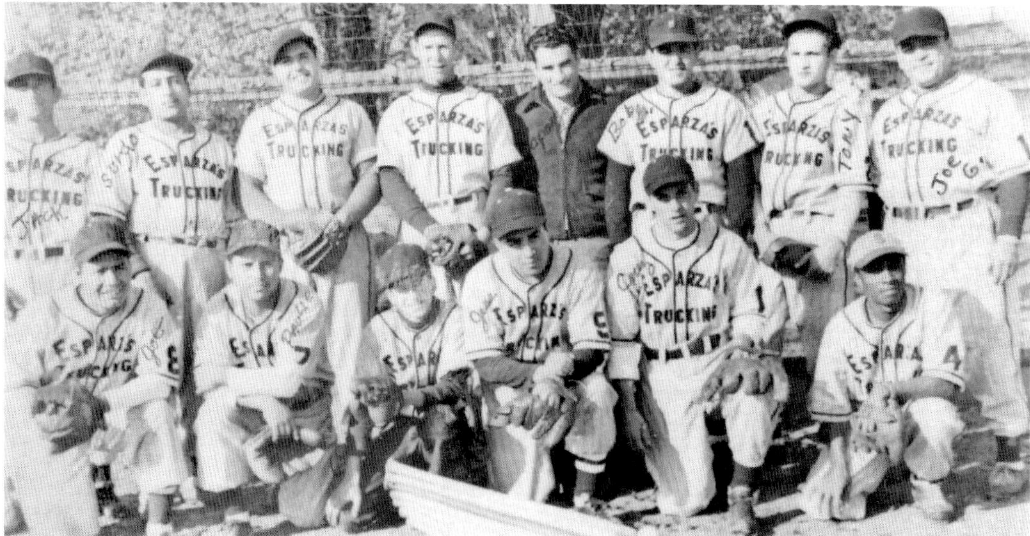

Esparza Trucking was a lower-division team in the Sacramento area that played on Sunday afternoons at local ballparks. The team, pictured in the late 1940s or early 1950s, was sponsored by Jack Esparza (second row, center), who owned the trucking company. Jack was no ball player, but he had a love of the game and stayed connected to the Mexican American community with his sponsorships. (Courtesy of Mexican American Hall of Fame Sports Association.)

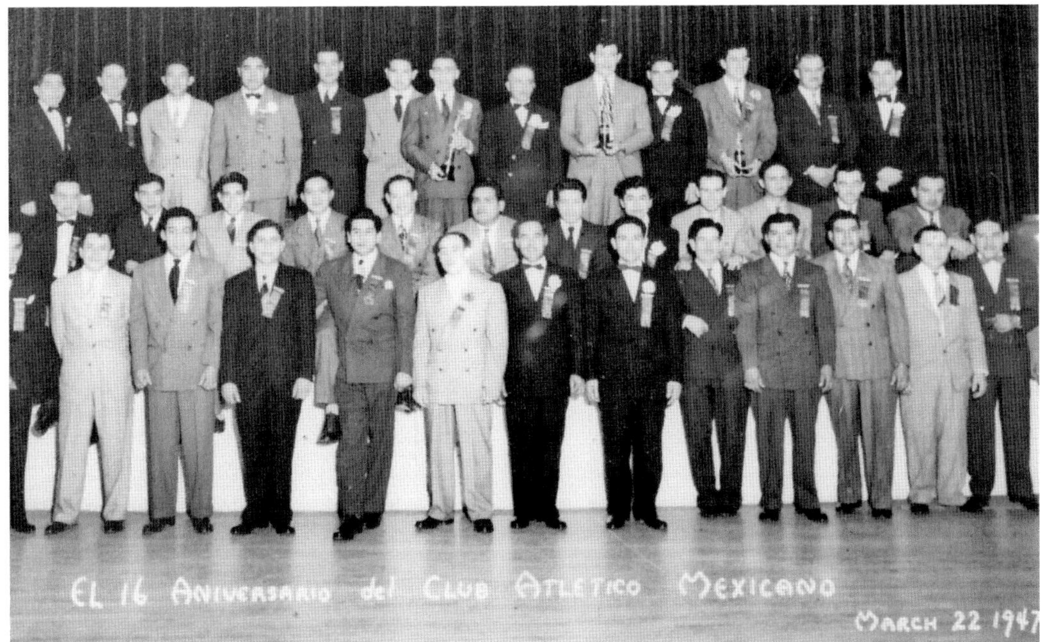

This picture was taken on March 22, 1947, at a dinner celebrating the 16th anniversary of the MAC, or Club Atlético Mexicano. The MAC was formed in March 1931 to support a baseball team, but it soon became a cultural force for Mexican Americans in the area. In the 1930s and 1940s, the MAC supported softball and basketball teams and social activities. MAC teams competed at the highest level of the Sacramento County and Winter Leagues. Local sports writer Bill Conlin stated that the MAC had a "splendid record for its charity work." (Courtesy of Mexican American Hall of Fame Sports Association.)

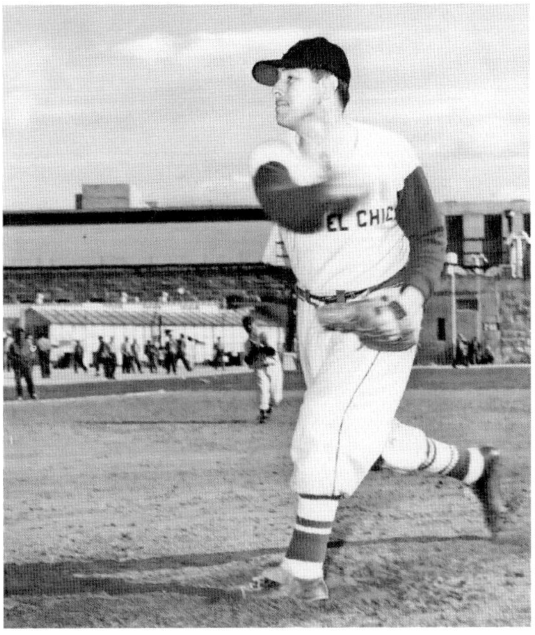

Frank Ríos warms up his arm prior to pitching a game at Folsom Prison. He played for El Chico's restaurant, located in Joe Marty's bar at Fifteenth Street and Broadway, a block down the street from Edmonds Field, the home of the old Pacific Coast League (PCL) Sacramento Solons. (Joe Marty had played for the Chicago Cubs and Sacramento Solons.) Ríos played in the Sacramento County and Winter Leagues, often for the MAC, in the 1940s and 1950s. El Chico and the prison team, the Represa Eagles, played in the Sacramento County League. Both of Frank's sons, Ed and Gary, excelled on local sandlots and went on to play professional baseball. (Courtesy of Gary Ríos.)

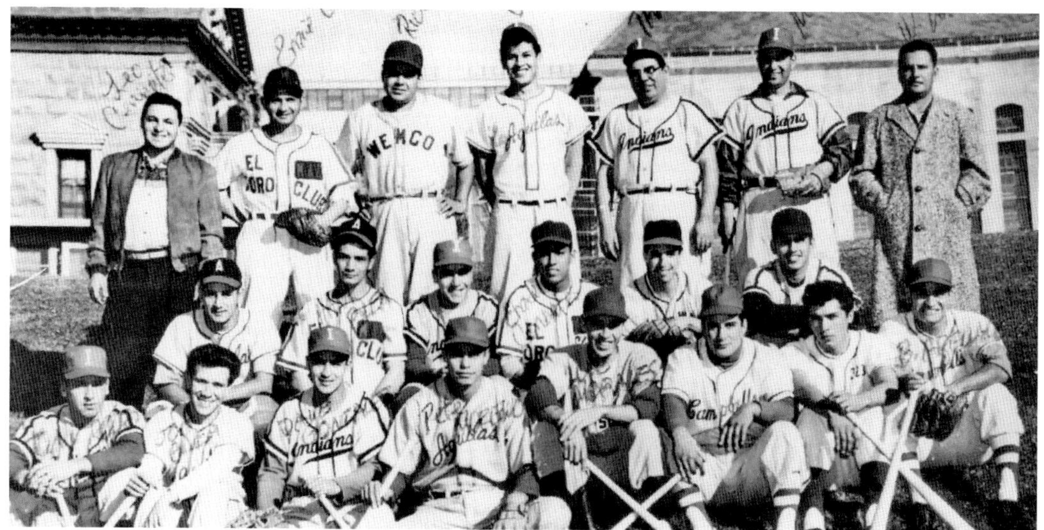

The Mexican American All Star team is pictured in 1958 at Folsom Prison before playing the Represa Eagles. The Eagles had many former minor- and major-league players. From left to right are (first row) Tony Rojo, Joe Blea, Dave González, Lupe Moreno, three unidentified, and Ben Arellano; (second row) unidentified, Hank Blea, unidentified, Ernie Cervantes Jr., and two unidentified; (third row) Leo Cervantes, Ernie Cervantes Sr., Richard García, Bobby Saenz, T.M. López, Mike Hernández, and W. López. (Courtesy of Mexican American Hall of Fame Sports Association.)

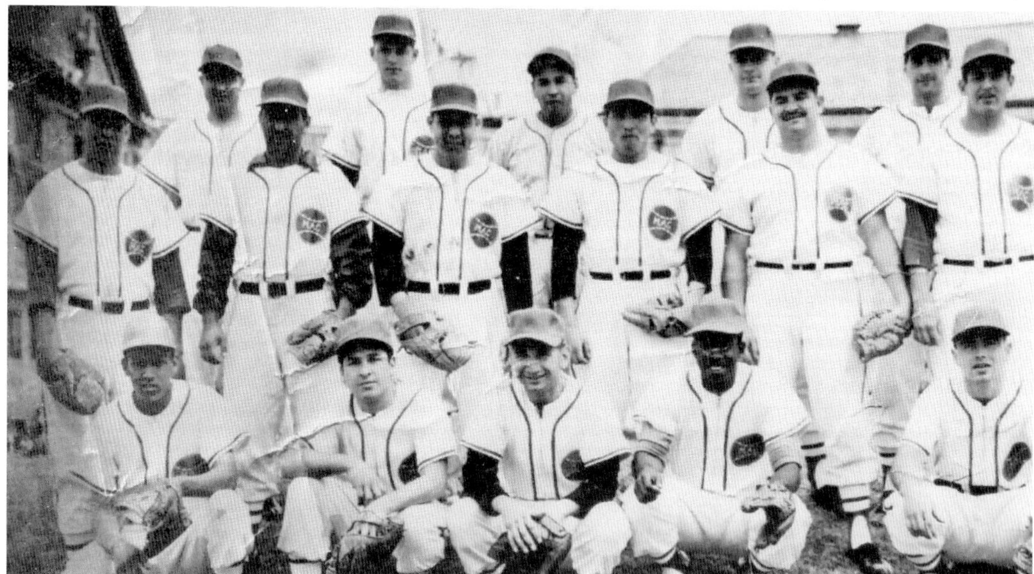

The MAC baseball team is at Folsom Prison ready to play the Represa Eagles around 1958. All these A team players were graduates of the MAC B team and other local and college teams. From left to right are (first row) Ernie Cervantes Jr. (the first MAC batboy), Tony Rojo, Corky Ramírez, unidentified, and Dick Alejo; (second row) Andy Campos, Mike Hernández, Pete Campos, Louie Contreras, Rudy Saenz, and Al Zúñiga; (third row) Tony Alvarado, Bob Shoemaker, Joe Moreno, Jim Fellos, and Joe Viega. (Courtesy of Mexican American Hall of Fame Sports Association.)

Ernie Cervantes Sr. and son Ernie Jr. also played baseball while serving in the military. It is very rare to find a father and son who both played ball while in the military. Ernie Sr. (pictured) was stationed in Guam during World War II between 1943 and 1945. While there, he was a truck driver, athletic director, and coach for the baseball team. His team featured major league stars Phil Rizutto of the New York Yankees and Pee Wee Reese of the Brooklyn Dodgers. (Courtesy of Ernie Cervantes Jr.)

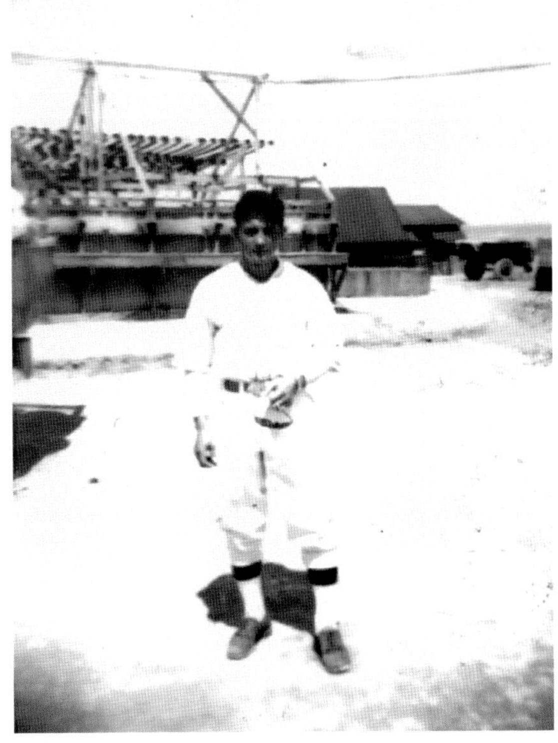

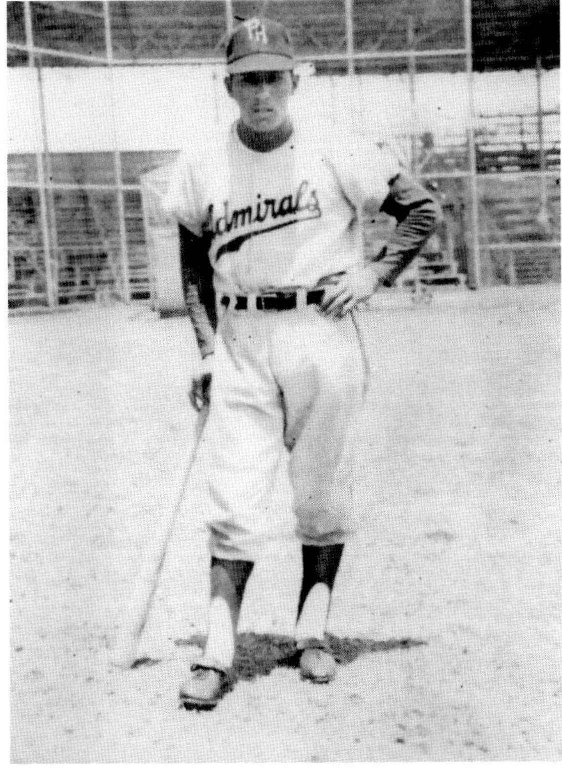

In 1960, Ernie Cervantes Jr. received his basic training at the Naval Training Center in San Diego. He was assigned to Pearl Harbor, Hawaii, and played for the Admirals baseball team, which belonged to the Hawaii All Service Military League. (Courtesy of Ernie Cervantes Jr.)

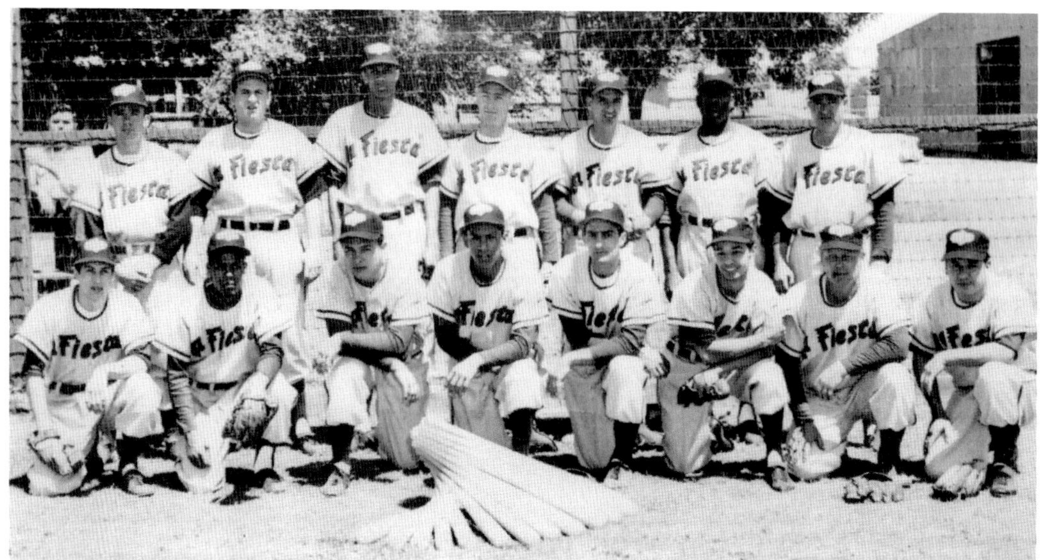

The La Fiesta team played in the Sacramento County League at Leiva Park at Front and W Streets in 1966. The players are from previous MAC rosters and include B team graduates, local college players, and a couple of MAC old-timers. From left to right are (first row) Ray Márquez, Norman Blackwell, unidentified, Ernie Cervantes Jr., Joe Viegas, Bobby Gonzalvez, unidentified, and Tony Rojo; (second row) Tom Higgins, Don Nanini, John Blackwell, unidentified, Chuck Lota, unidentified, and Tony Alverado. (Courtesy of Mexican American Hall of Fame Sports Association.)

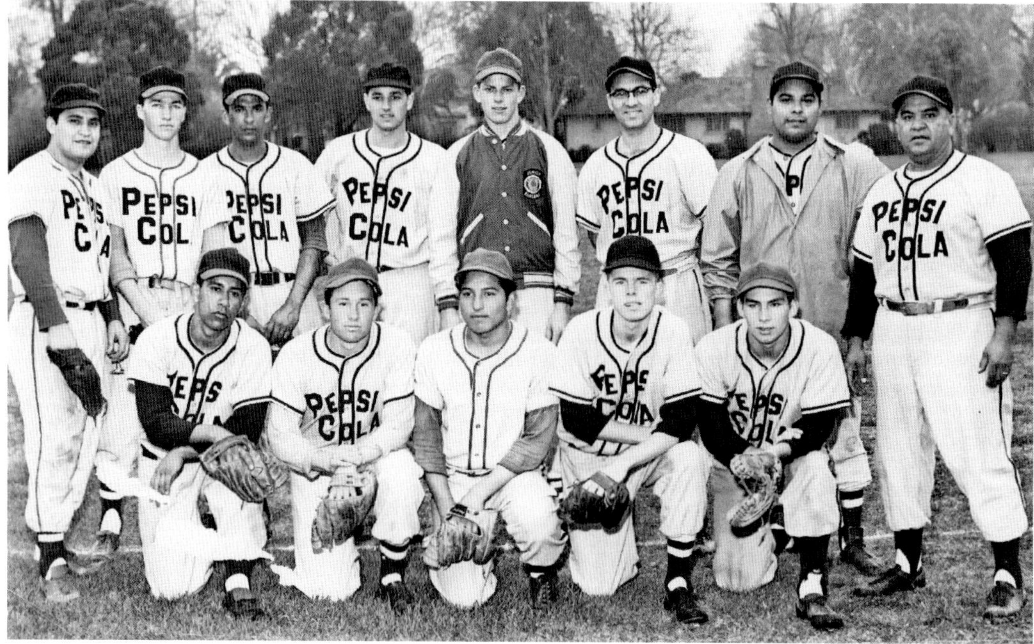

This is a 1960s Sacramento team that featured many Mexican American players and was sponsored by Pepsi Cola. (Courtesy of the Mexican American Hall of Fame Sports Association.)

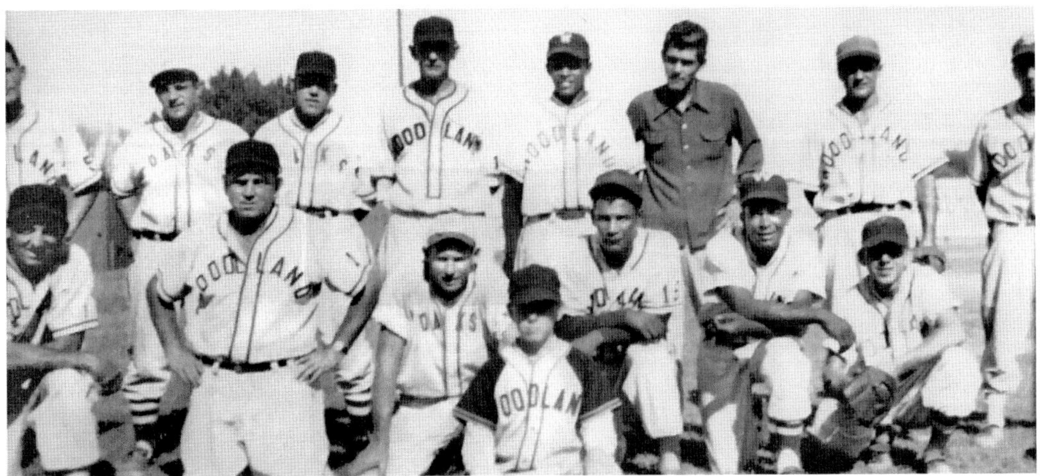

Jose "Mousey" Zaragoza stands in the second row, third from right, in this 1950 Woodland, California, team picture. Woodland, an agricultural community west of Sacramento, often played other Mexican teams from the region. At 16, Zaragoza enlisted in the US Navy, and served in the Pacific during World War II. He served in the military again during the Korean War. Zaragoza worked at Fibreboard in Stockton for many years and was active as union shop steward. He coached his children's Little League teams for years and was instrumental in starting girls' softball in the Stockton area with Angelo Galindo. He helped tutor his daughter Suzie while she played softball at Stagg High School. In his later years, he umpired various baseball and softball games. (Courtesy of Randy Zaragoza.)

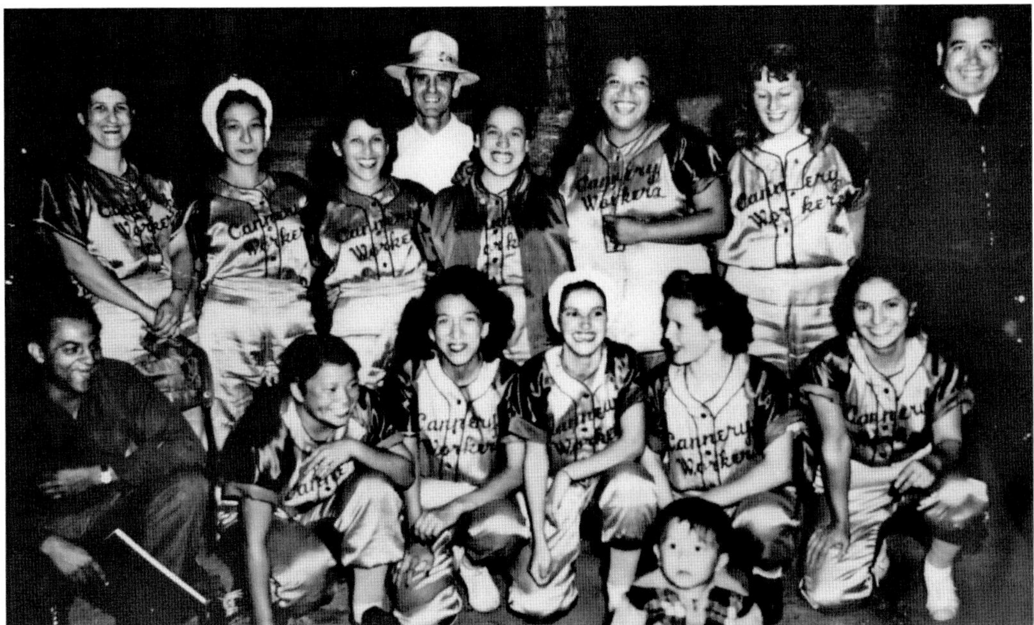

The Cannery Union Aguilas won the 1962–1963 American Division title in the Sacramento Winter Baseball League. The team beat the MAC Aguilas in a 12-inning thriller that ended 12-11. (Courtesy of Mexican American Hall of Fame Sports Association.)

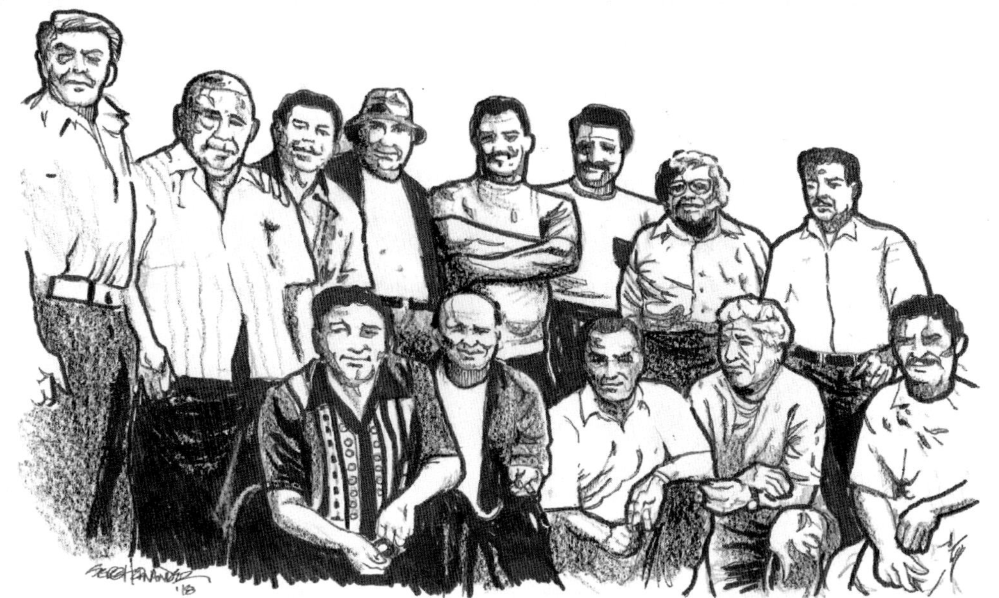

In 1973, Rudy Saenz founded the Mexican American Hall of Fame Sports Association. Original members depicted here are, from left to right, (kneeling) Luís Contreras, Ernie Cervantes Sr., Hank Sánchez, Ray García, and Rudy Saenz; (standing) Richard García, Pete Benton, Eddie Vásquez, Star Venezuela, Julian Solís, Felipe González, Joe Castillo, and Rodrigo Perredia. (Courtesy of Sergio Hernández.)

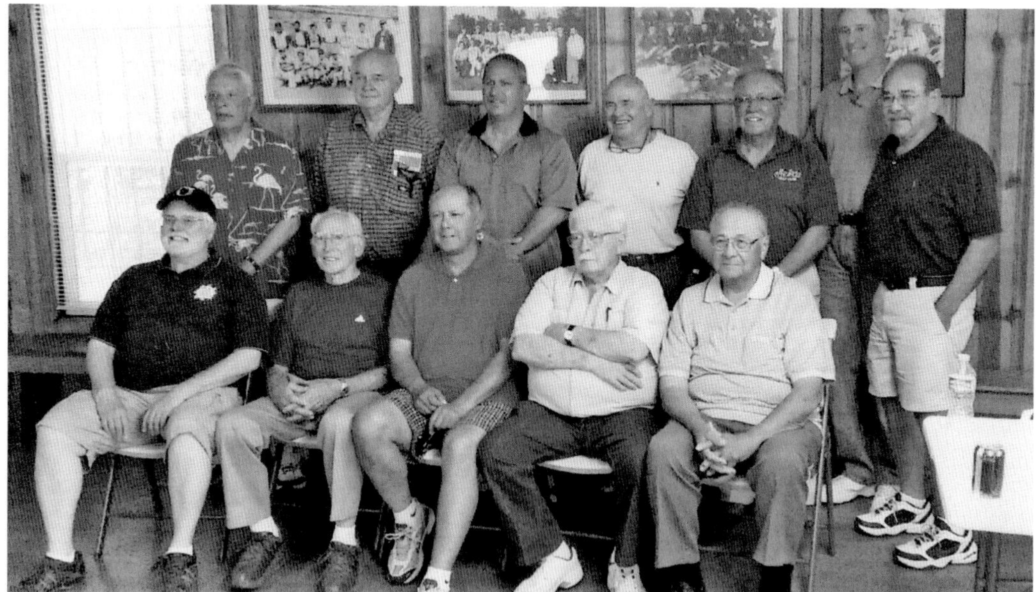

On July 15, 2012, former players and families brought photographs and other memorabilia dating to the 1930s to the Mexican American Hall of Fame Sports Association. From left to right are (first row) Alan O'Conner, Cuno Barragán, Eddie Cervantes, Joe Duarte, and Hank López; (second row) Julius Reséndez, Jim Fellos, Eric Cervantes, Dick Alejo, Ernie Cervantes Jr., Tom Crisp, and Pete Campos. (Courtesy of Richard A. Santillán.)

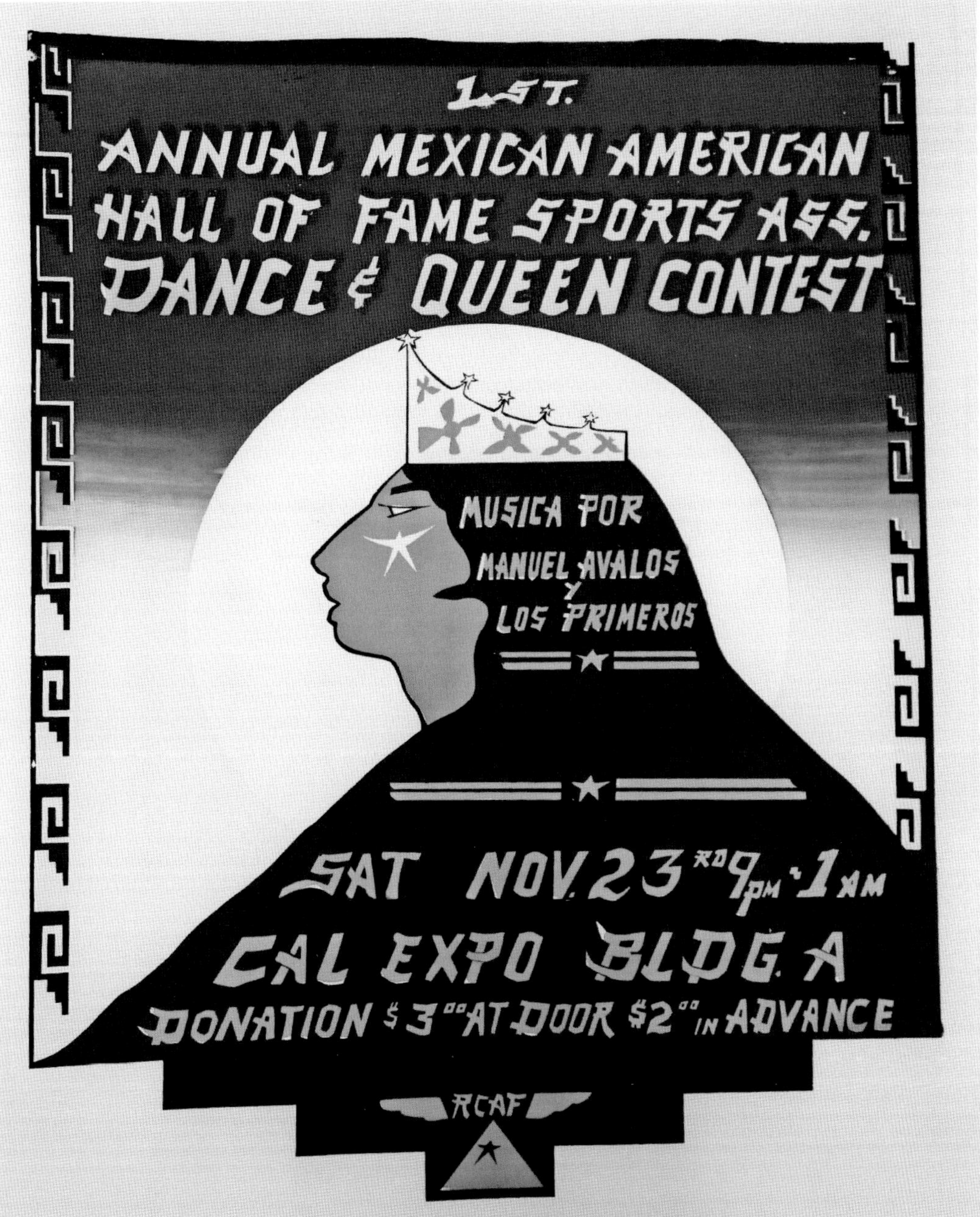

This poster was done by Royal Chicano Air Force (RCAF) artist Juanishi Orosco in 1974. The poster promotes the first annual Mexican American Hall of Fame Sports Association Dance and Queen Contest held at the Cal Expo. The Royal Chicano Air Force is a Sacramento-based Chicano art collective founded in 1970 to foster arts in the community and promote political awareness. The RCAF is one of the most significant Chicano/Latino art collectives of the 20th century and continues to be active today. (Courtesy of Juanishi Orosco and the Department of Special Collections and University Archives at California State University, Sacramento.)

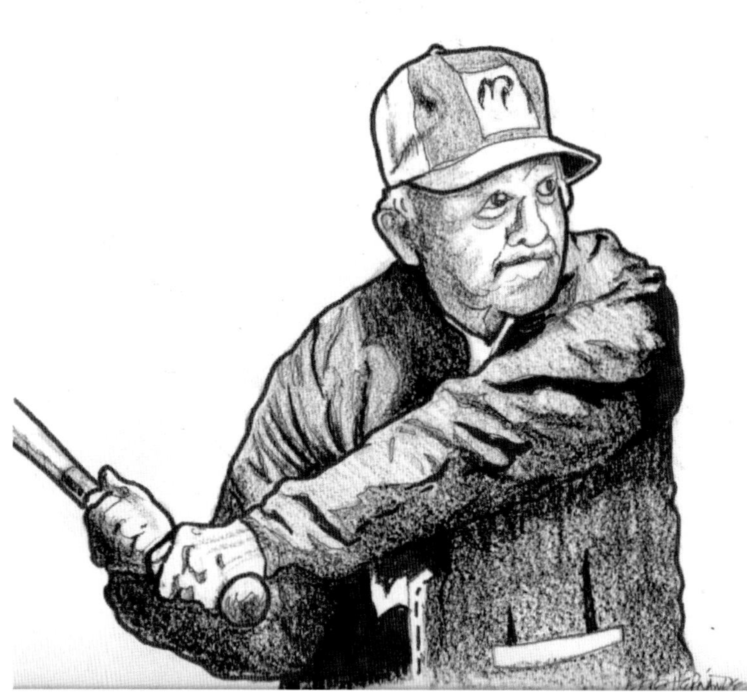

Ernie Cervantes Sr. will forever be regarded as "Mr. Baseball" in the Sacramento Mexican community. He is shown here at age 74 taking a swing during a picnic at McKinley Park. Over 500 people attended the picnic held by the Mexican American Hall of Fame Sports Association, which raised money for youth athletic programs. (Courtesy of Sergio Hernández.)

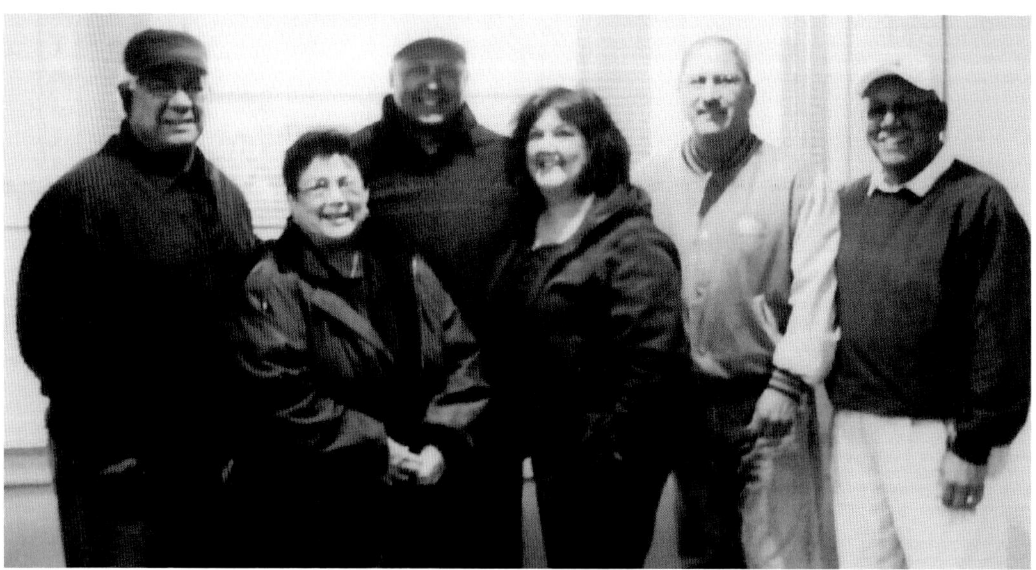

The Cervantes family from Sacramento has produced four generations of athletes including baseball and softball players dating to the 1930s. Pictured here are, from left to right, siblings Eugene, Rachel, Edward, Cecilia, Eric, and Ernie Cervantes. Among them, they have played on Little League, Babe Ruth, American Legion, high school, college and university, and church teams. They have also played semiprofessional and professional baseball in the United States and Mexico, as well as military ball. Their occupations include parole agent, counselor, teacher, vice principal, principal, and high school coach. (Courtesy of the Cervantes family.)

Youth Baseball from Sandlots to University Diamonds

It has been said that baseball is at its heart a kid's game. Indeed, the game is played by youth and will always be a joyful youthful experience for those who grow into adulthood playing it. Many of Sacramento's Mexican American residents learned baseball by going to their local diamonds and swinging the bat with their siblings, parents, friends, and coaches. Others served as batboys for the adult teams and quickly fell in love with *béisbol*. Those who had the opportunity played on Little League, Pony League, or Babe Ruth teams. Others played for neighborhood sponsored teams or on CYO clubs. Prior to the era of state-of-the-art pitching machines, batting cages, batting helmets, aluminum bats, and well-maintained fields, thrifty neighborhood coaches dipped into their own pockets to subsidize equipment and uniforms. They taped together old bats and balls that could be used over and over again so that the youth might get a chance to play.

As others continued to play the game into their early adolescent and teenage years, they often played for their local middle school and high school teams. The Cervantes brothers all played for Sacramento's Bishop Armstrong High School Falcons (now called Christian Brothers). Gene was a key player as a catcher and second baseman on Sacramento's Bishop Armstrong team that posted a 22-2 record in 1962. The team beat four conference champions that year, and local baseball buffs consider it to be one of the best high school teams to ever play in the Sacramento area. Players like Chado Vasquez played for the same school on the Gaels baseball team during the early 1950s. Many went on to play for Sacramento City College, including George Mojica, Cuno Barragán, and even major-league Hispanic Hall of Famer and Elk Grove native Buck Martínez. This chapter chronicles the youthful sport from sandlots to college diamonds.

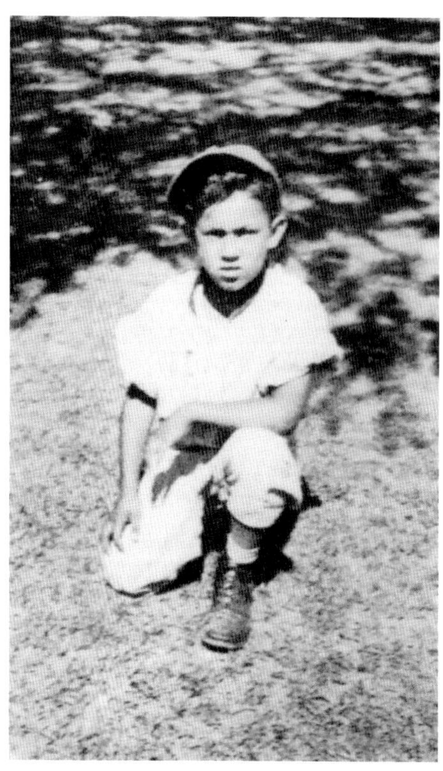

Ernie Cervantes Jr. was the first and only batboy of the MAC. This was the start of a successful baseball career. He went on to play with the MAC A team as well as other local, county, college, and military teams. This picture was taken at the McKinley Park ball field in Sacramento. (Courtesy of Ernie Cervantes Jr.)

The 1940s Monks softball team finished second in the Girls' Division of the Sacramento City Municipal Night Softball League, playing under the lights at Roosevelt Park at Tenth and P Streets. Josephine Barragán was one of the team's top players. From left to right are (first row) Mary Albrica, Teresa Rajas, Ann Stanich, Jean Bath, and Arleen Matson; (second row) Margaret Sousa, Hazel McKerros, Rosalie Hackett, Virginia Queirola, Josephine Barragán, Dolores Yenick, and Dorothy Rakestraw. The team's star pitcher, Ann Stanich, was the first woman elected to the Softball Hall of Fame. (Courtesy of Cuno Barragán.)

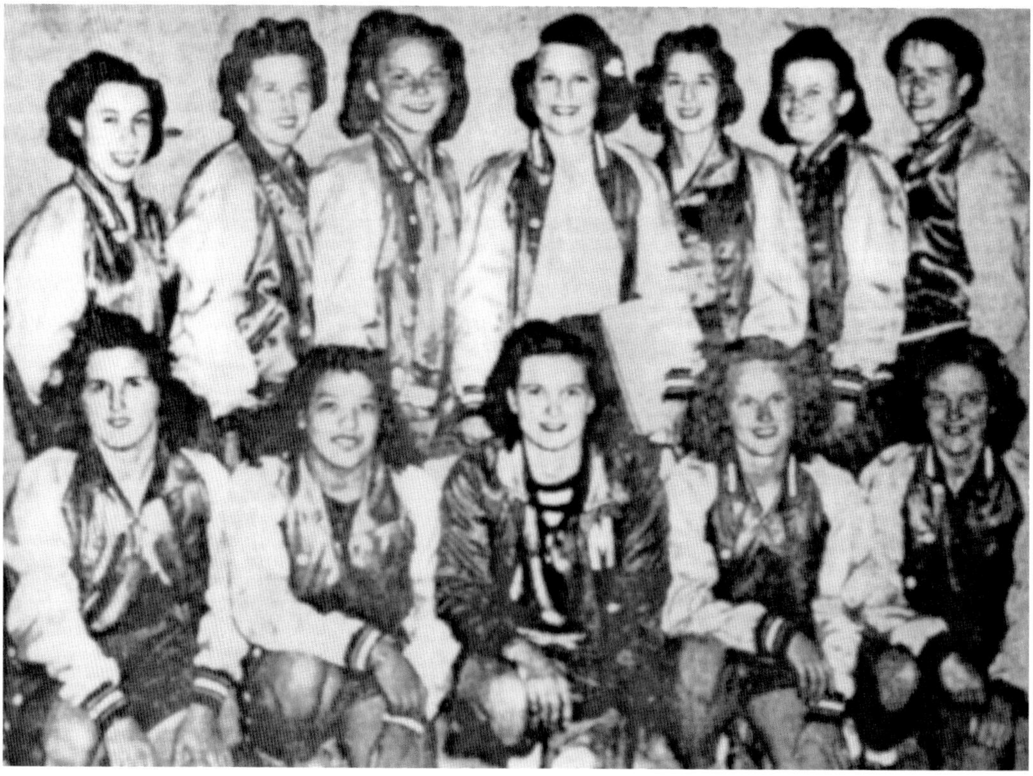

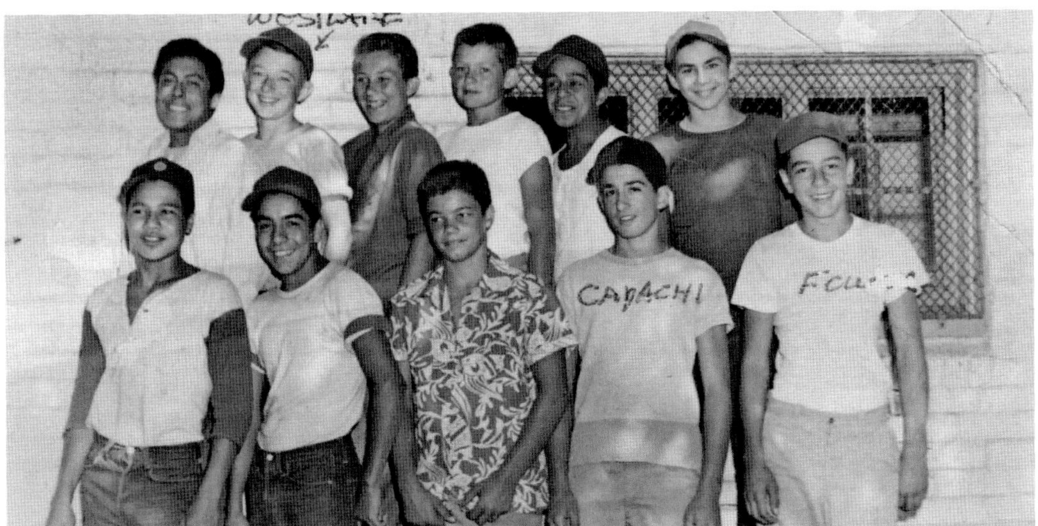

The 1949 California Upholstery baseball team won the championship of the Sacramento City Boys Summer League 150 Pound Division. The picture was taken on September 3, 1949, at McKinley Park. From left to right are (first row) Louis Armendáriz, Ruben Placencia, Gil Laidlaw, Nick Capachi, and Ed Fowler; (second row) Everet Meléndez, Jim Westlake, Frank Eakes, Jim Feenstra, Alfonso Arroyo, and Manuel López. The old city leagues promoted baseball for all Sacramento kids, including the Mexican American community. (Courtesy of Nick Capachi.)

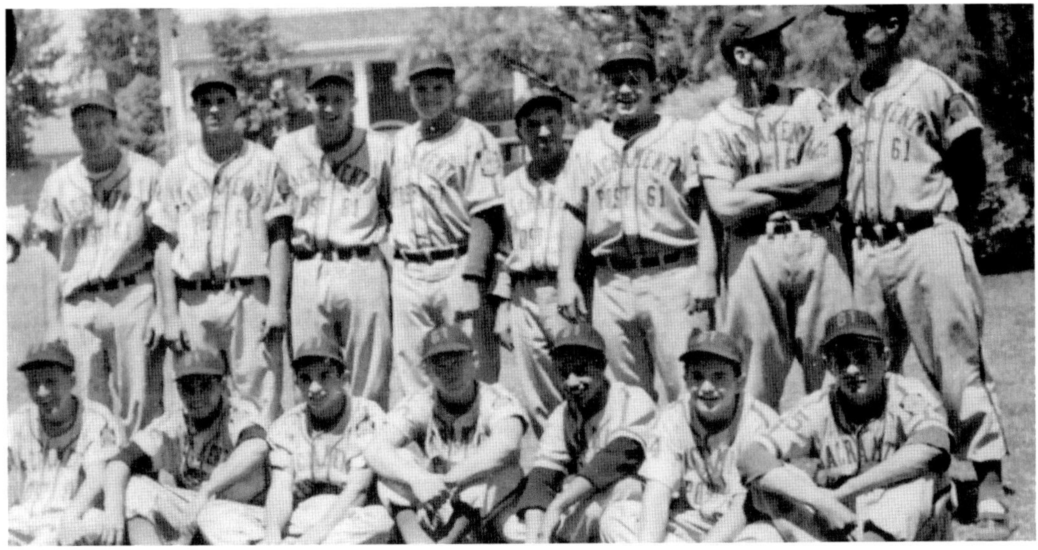

This is the 1951 Post 61 American Legion baseball team. Legion baseball was very popular in the 1950s, with World War II vets coaching, encouraging, and cheering for their sons. Immediately after World War II through the 1970s, Post 61 was one of the top Legion teams in California and featured the best local talent in the area. From left to right are (first row) Bill Werry, Dick Alejo, Pete Stathos, Bob Ayers, Bob Gonsalves, Ray Lesdesma, and Bruce Parsons; (second row) Jim Fellos, Jan Aitken, Roger Herkowitz, Mike Toomey, George Lial, Don Deary, Dick Traversi, and Gene Hurych. (Courtesy of Jim Fellos.)

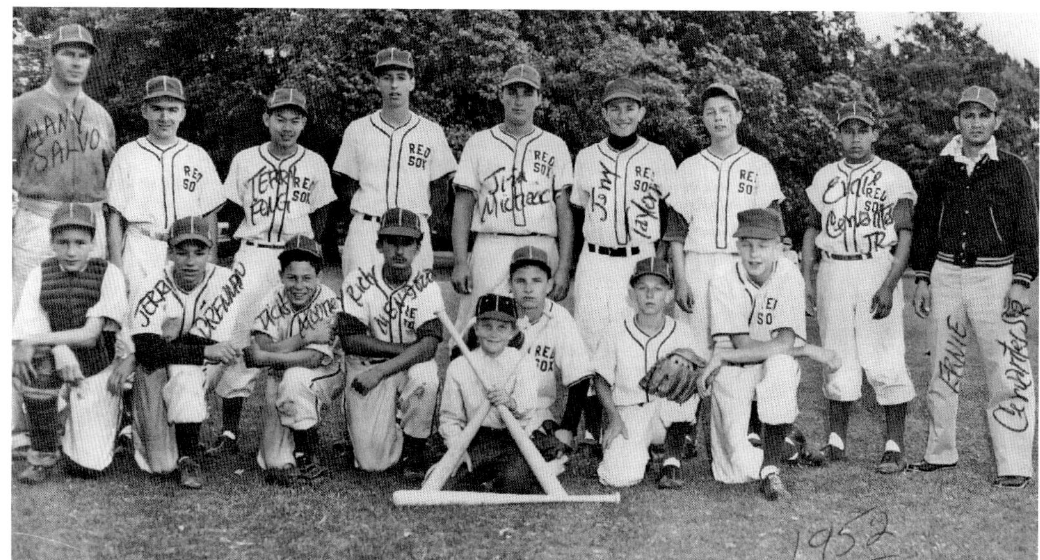

This picture was taken in 1952 at McKinley Park in Sacramento. The Red Sox were the winners of the Babe Ruth championship that year. From left to right are (first row) unidentified, Jerry Brennan (deputy sheriff), Dick Mooney (University of Idaho cattle appraiser), Richard Mendoza (restaurant and bar business), and four unidentified; (second row) Manny Salvo (former major-leaguer and Sacramento Solon), unidentified, Terry Fong, unidentified, Jim Mickacich (University of Notre Dame football player and local attorney), Jerry Taylor, unidentified, Ernie Cervantes Jr. (Youth Authority School administrator), and Ernie Cervantes Sr., "Mr. Baseball." (Courtesy of Ernie Cervantes Jr.)

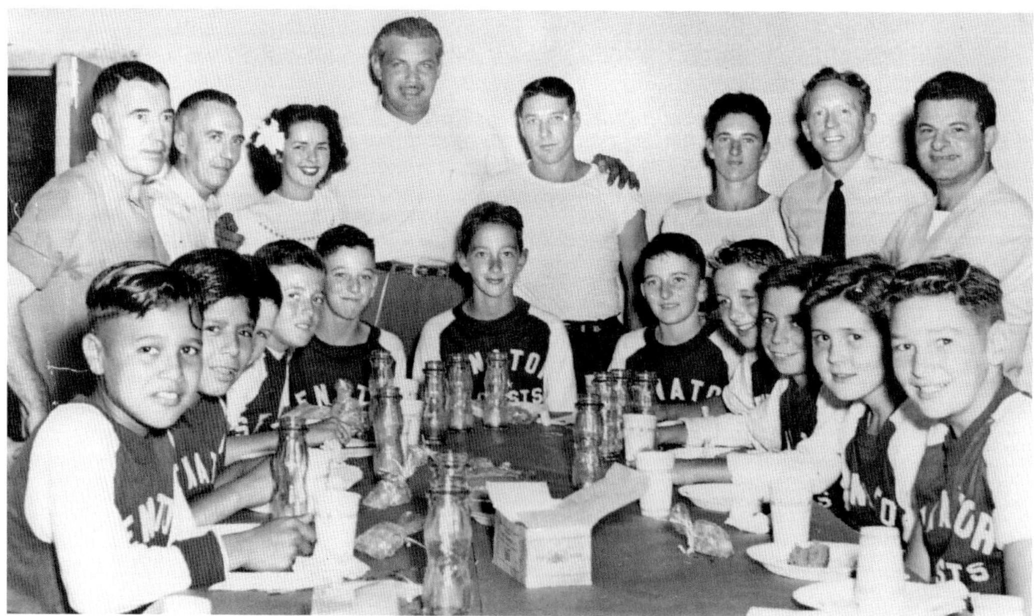

This is a youth baseball team that featured Mexican children from Sacramento. (Courtesy of the Mexican American Hall of Fame Sports Association.)

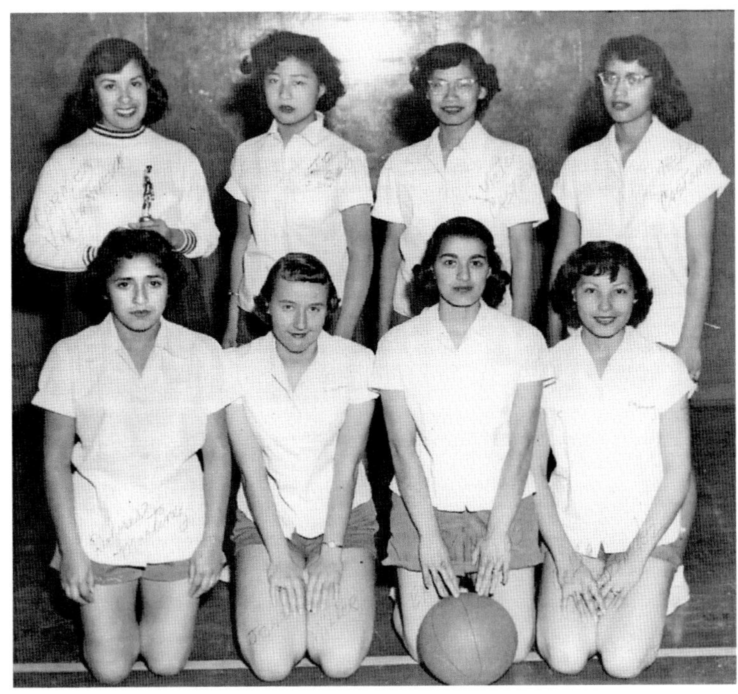

Other sports that Mexican youth enjoyed included basketball. This is a girl's CYO basketball team. From left to right are (first row) Dolores Martínez, Jean Miller, Ernestine Salas, and Celia Hernández; (second row) Carmen Villanueva, Jo Sah, Victoria Castanon, and Helen Castanon. (Courtesy of the Mexican American Hall of Fame Sports Association.)

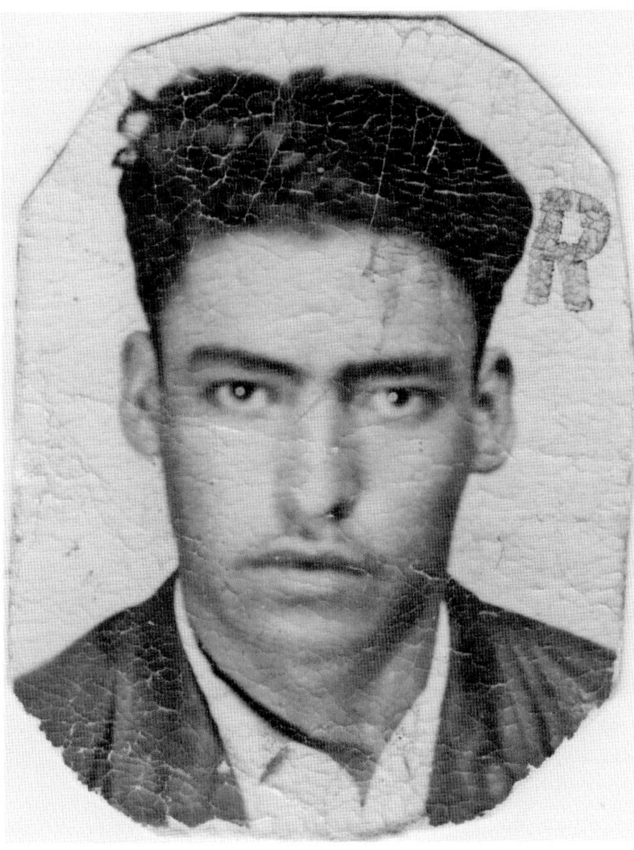

Pedro López Ortiz participated in the *bracero* program during the 1950s and early 1960s. The bracero program was a labor agreement between the United States and Mexico that started during World War II and ended in 1963. López, a former baseball player in Zacatecas, Mexico, worked as a bracero in New Mexico, Arkansas, and eventually California. He recalled the indignity of being sprayed with DDT, a harmful pesticide, when crossing the border. Border agents used the spray to fumigate braceros due to the era's racist stereotypes that cast Mexicans as threats to public health. While working in Northern California, López picked lettuce, apples, pears, and grapes. (Courtesy of Gerardo López.)

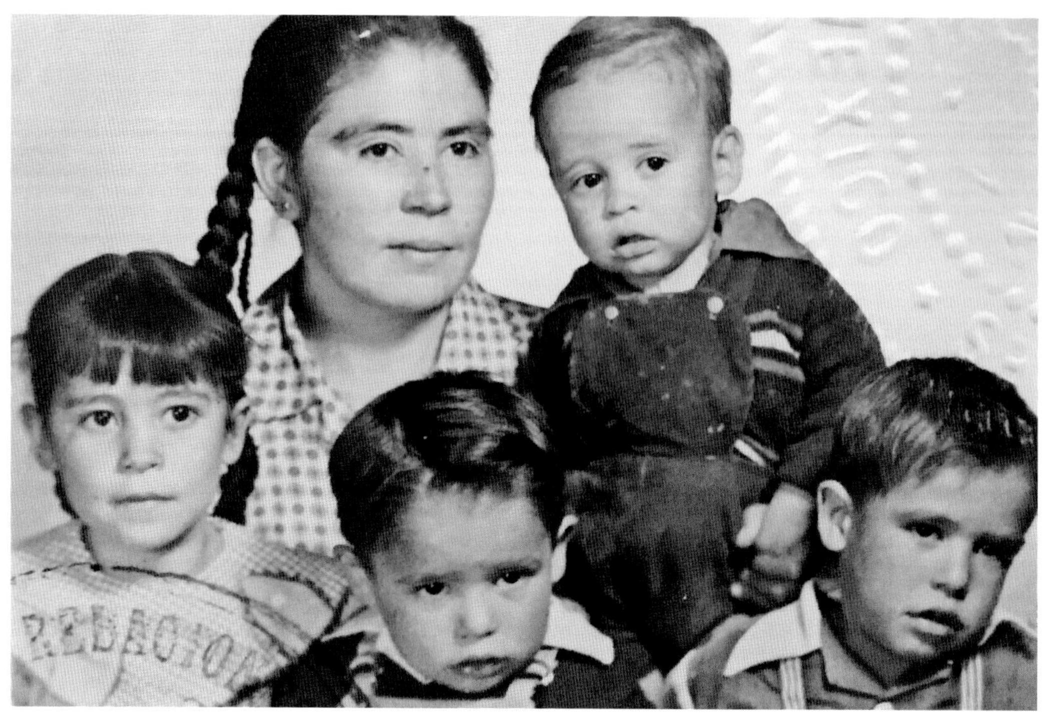

As the bracero program concluded, Mercedes López took a train from Zacatecas to the Mexicali-Calexico border to reunite with husband Pedro López in 1963. Accompanied by their children, (from left to right) AnaMaria, Gerardo, Hugo (in Mercedes's arms), and Antonio, Mercedes met Pedro at the border, and they trekked to Northern California, where the family settled in Ukiah. Many families involved in the bracero program often had to maintain long-distance relationships and marriages. Frequently, the only form of communication for months, and even years, was letters. Since reuniting the family in 1963, Mercedes and Pedro have continued to live in Ukiah. They have been married since April 28, 1950. (Courtesy of Gerardo López.)

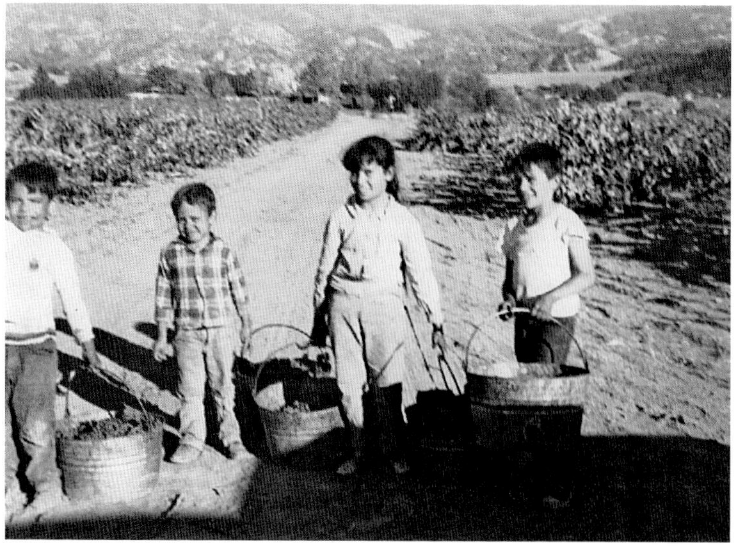

From left to right, Gerardo, Hugo, AnaMaria, and Antonio López are pictured in 1967 assisting with the grape harvest at Parducci Winery in Ukiah. Mexican children commonly helped their parents work in the fields. Ukiah is in the heart of California's famous wine country. (Courtesy of Gerardo López.)

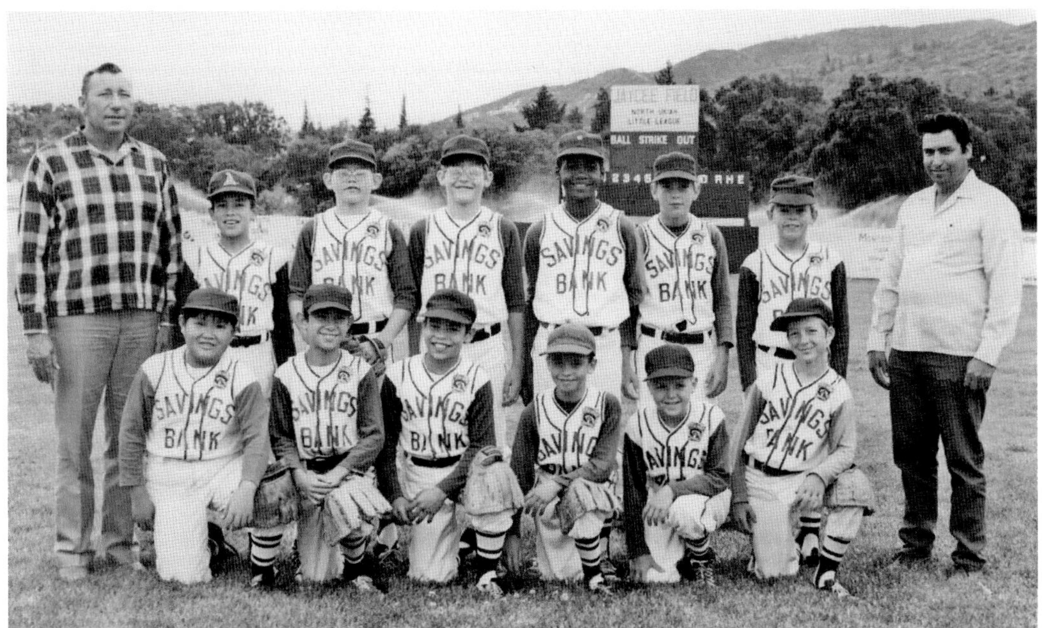

Pedro López (far right) eventually passed on the love of the game to his children by coaching the Ukiah Little League team in the 1970s. His sons Gerardo (kneeling, third from left), Hugo (kneeling, fourth from left), and Antonio (standing, second from left with "A" on hat) are pictured here. Pedro's daughter AnaMaria (not pictured) was the official score book keeper for the team. (Courtesy of Gerardo López.)

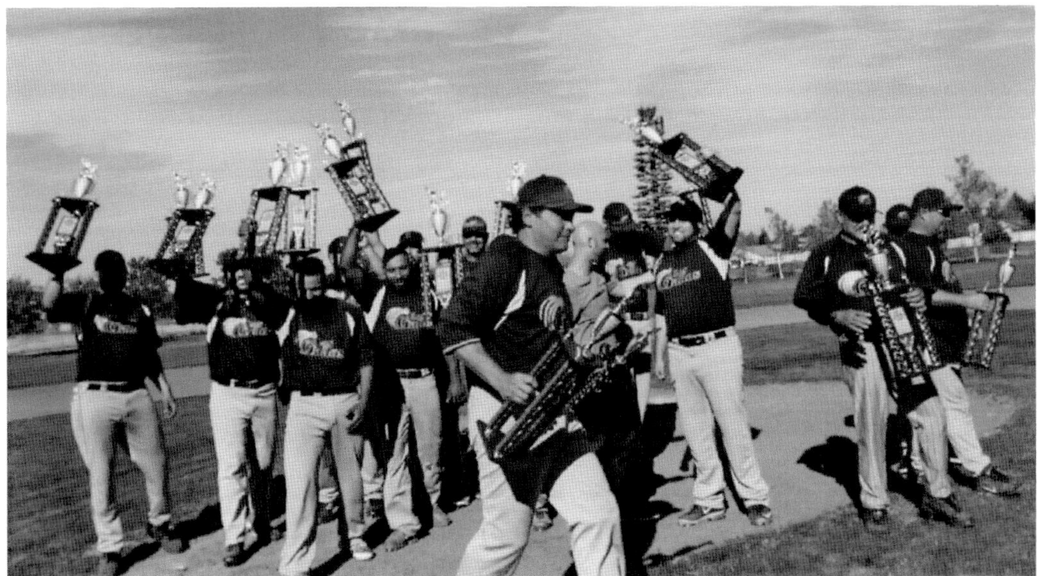

Los Gallos de Sacramento celebrate winning the championship in the Liga Latina de Béisbol de Sacramento in 2016. Gerardo López (center with trophy), who managed the team, lives in Elk Grove and is a member of and inductee into the Mexican American Hall of Fame. (Courtesy of Gerardo López.)

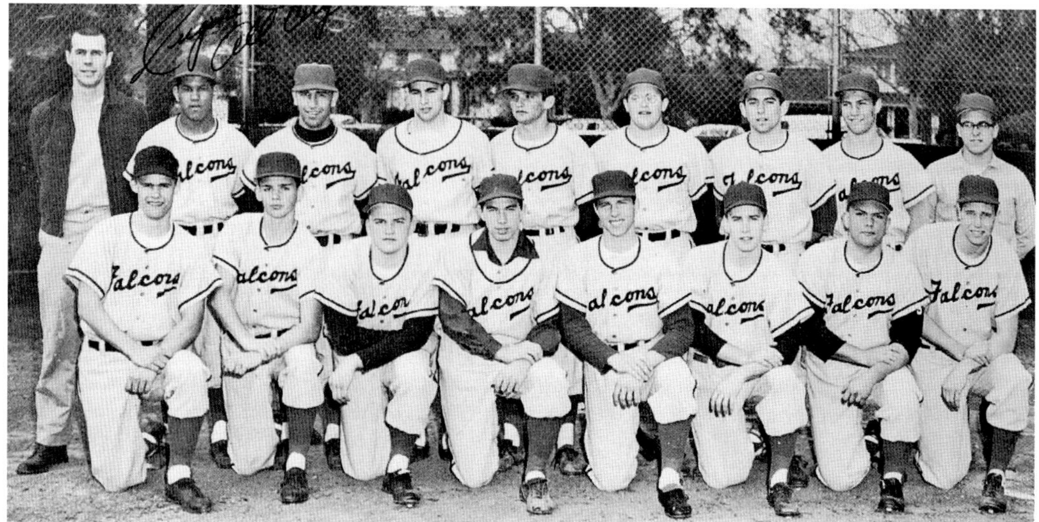

Gene Cervantes is one of the four baseball sons of Ernie Cervantes Sr., along with Ernie Jr., Eddie, and Eric. Gene was a key player as a catcher and second baseman on Sacramento's Bishop Armstrong (now Christian Brothers) High School Falcons, who posted a 22-2 record in 1962. The Falcons boasted six All-City selections (a feat that has not been duplicated since), including Gene, who hit a whopping .367 that year. Coach Dick Sperbeck is at far left in the second row; Gene is next to him. (Courtesy of Christian Brothers High School.)

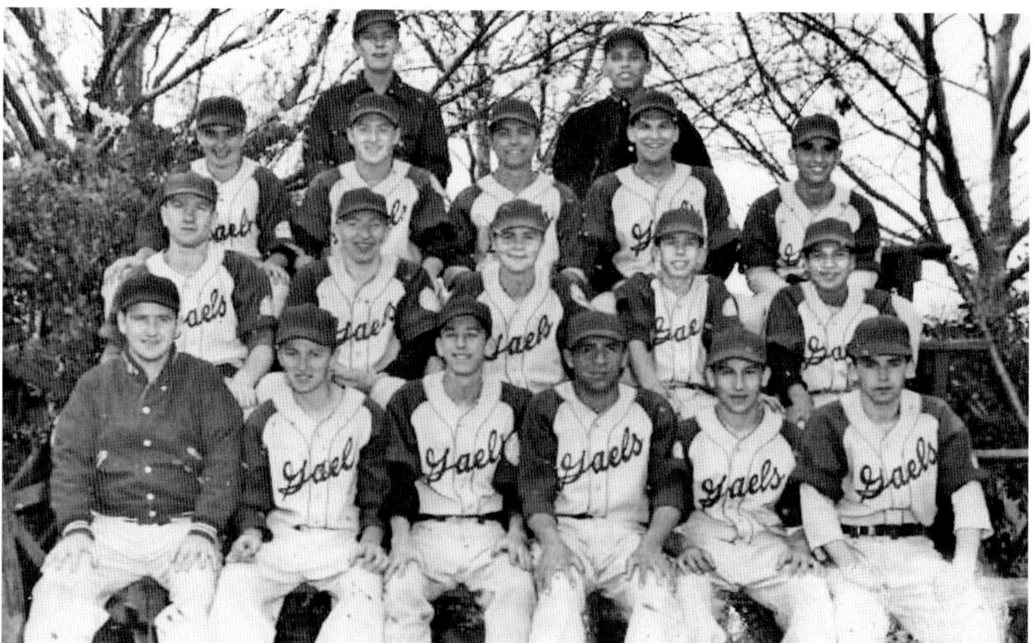

This is the 1951 Christian Brothers Gaels, who went on to win the city championship. Al "Chado" Vasquez is second from right in the second row. Vasquez became president of the high school's La Salle Club and served in this capacity for 14 years—the longest tenure of any La Calle Club president. (Courtesy of the Mexican American Hall of Fame Sports Association.)

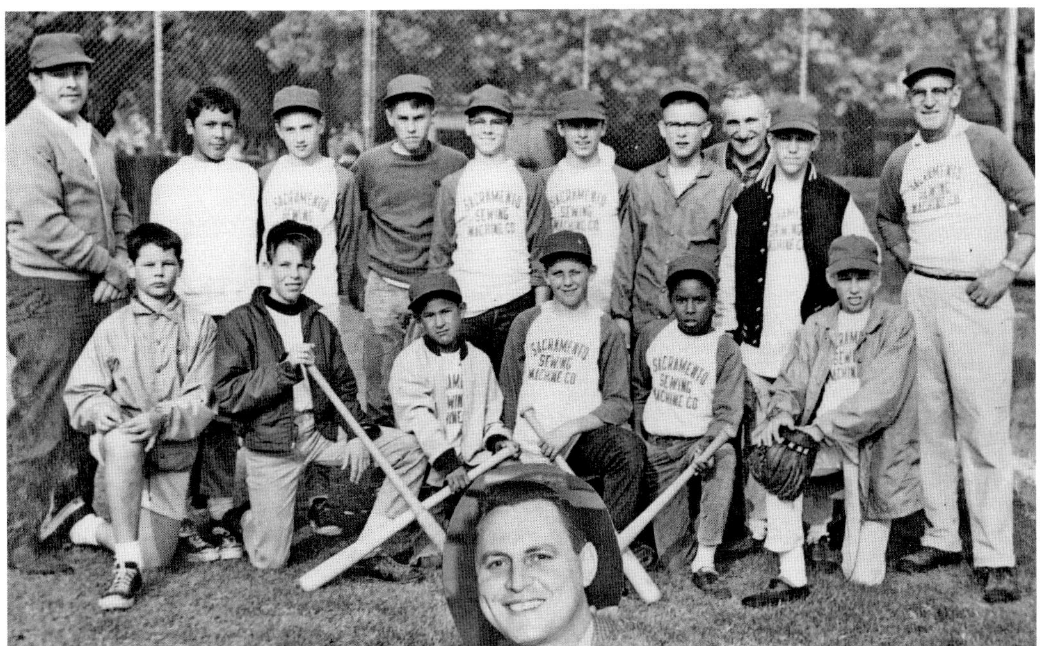

Eddie Cervantes (second row, second from left) played on this 1965 youth baseball team sponsored by the Sacramento Sewing Machine Company. Frank Ríos (far left) coached this team and was later inducted into the Mexican American Hall of Fame Sports Association. Eddie Cervantes eventually played professional baseball. Eric Cervantes (first row, third from left) served as the batboy and also went on to play professional baseball. Randy Brown (first row, fourth from left) played professional baseball with the Montreal Expos. (Courtesy of Eddie Cervantes.)

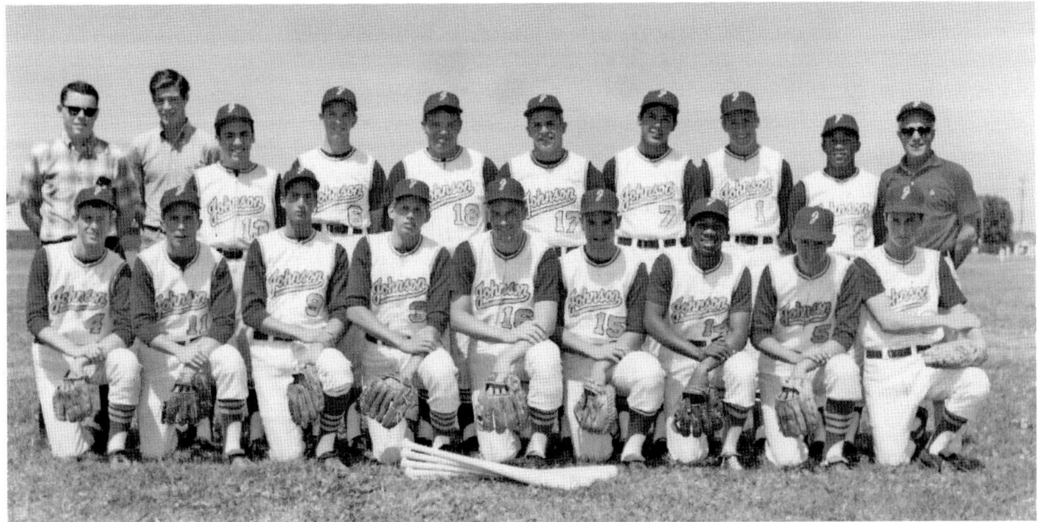

Eddie Cervantes (second row, fourth from right) went on to play baseball at Hiram W. Johnson High School in Sacramento. He wore number seven and played shortstop during his senior year in 1969. After graduating, he continued playing the game at Sacramento City College. (Courtesy of Eddie Cervantes.)

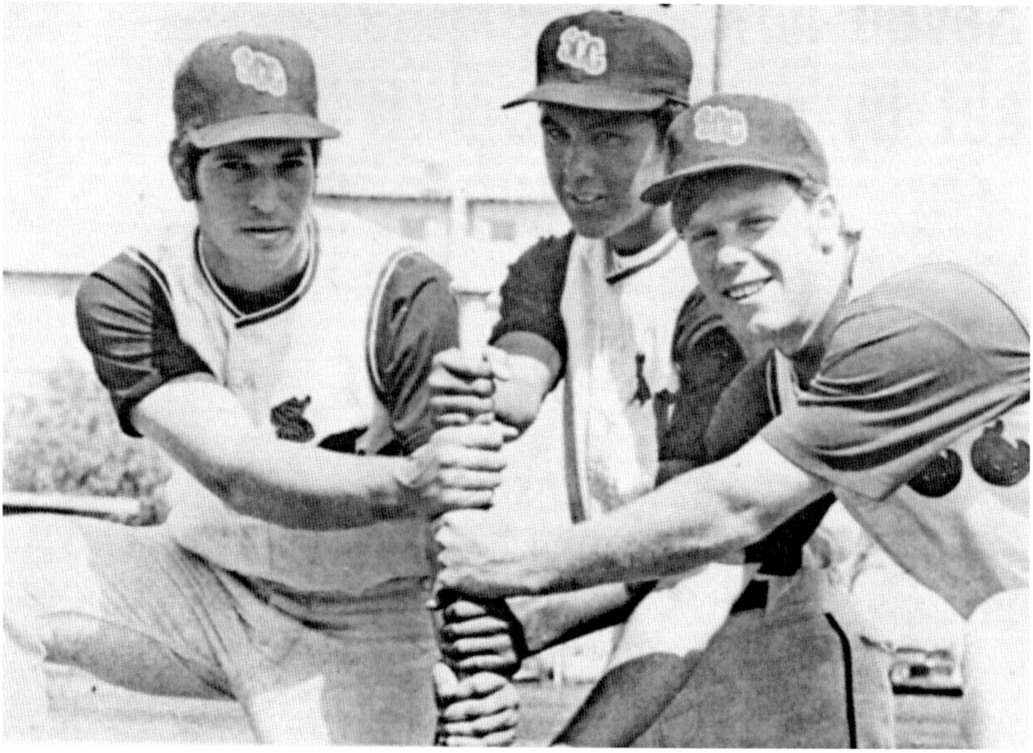

Eddie Cervantes (center) is shown playing for Sacramento City College in 1971. He served as co-captain of the team with Mike Willet (left) and John Hughes (right). The team won the Valley Conference championship that season. Cervantes (starting shortstop) and Hughes (starting pitcher) were named co-MVPs that year. (Courtesy of Eddie Cervantes.)

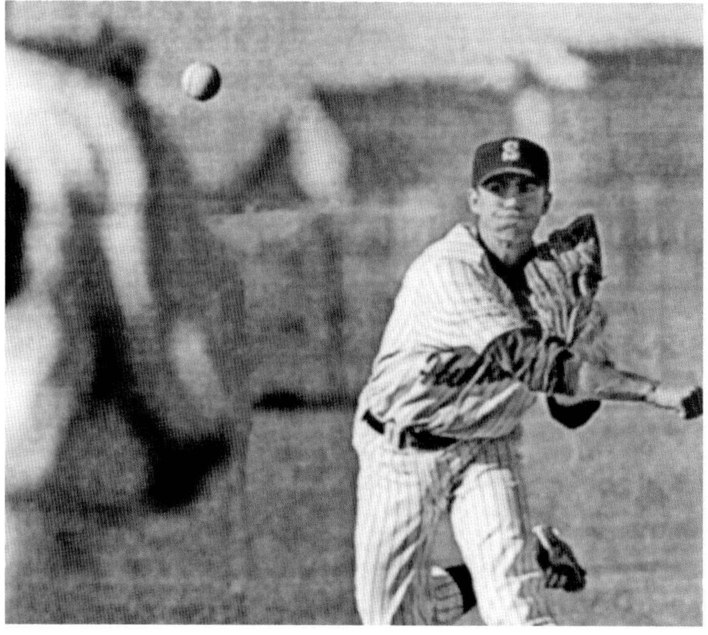

Edward Cervantes is the oldest son of Eddie Cervantes. Edward is shown throwing to first base to complete a double play for Sheldon High School in 1999. He suffered a torn ACL from football and later a broken navicular bone in his hand. These injuries kept him from continuing his baseball career. He is currently a culinary instructor for the Salvation Army at its main facility in Sacramento. (Courtesy of Eddie Cervantes.)

Alex Cervantes is the son of Eddie Cervantes. Alex is shown in 2010 completing a double play for the Lodi Baseball Club, a summer baseball team made up of college players from around the country. After completing his studies at Yuba College, Alex worked with various bank institutions before starting his current position as an administrative assistant to the dean of financial aid at Sacramento City College. He continues to play for Sacramento's Los Gallos baseball club. (Courtesy of Eddie Cervantes.)

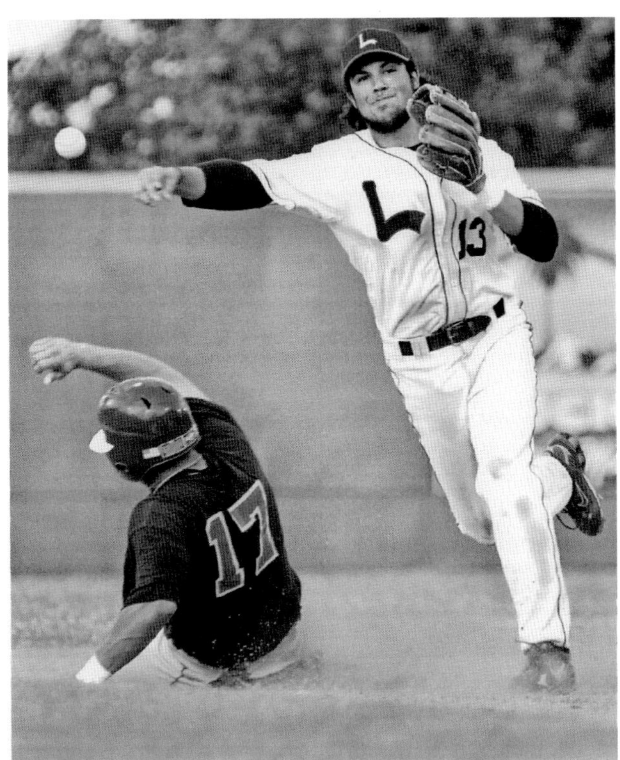

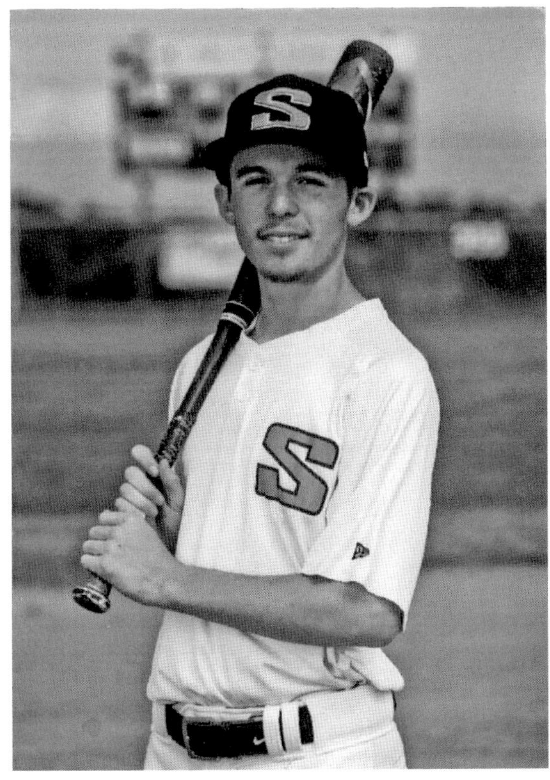

Edward Cervantes's son Edward Jr. is a student-athlete at Sheldon High School in Sacramento and carries a 3.0 GPA. In 2018, Edward Jr. started playing for the junior varsity baseball team, where he played every position except first base. Edward makes four generations––and almost a century––of Cervantes family baseball players in Sacramento. He hopes to continue playing baseball in college. (Courtesy of Eddie Cervantes.)

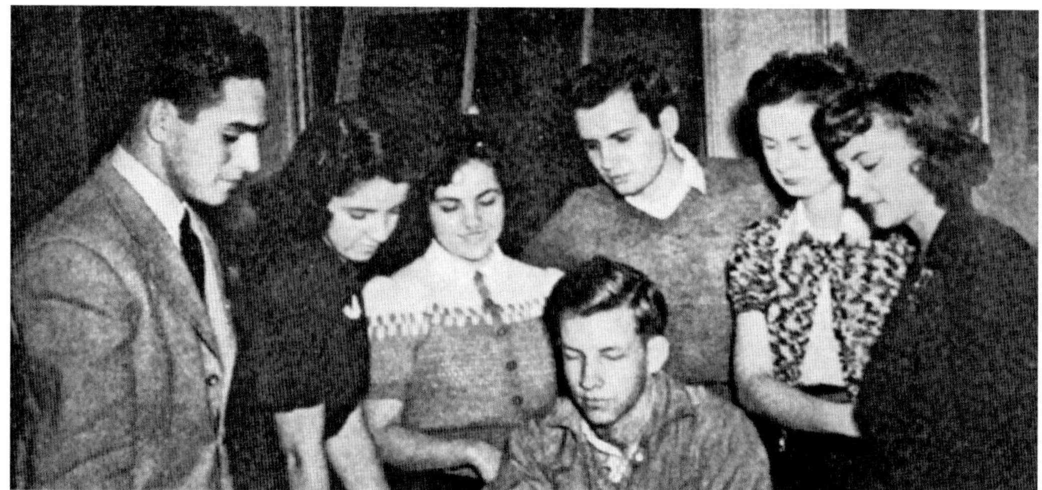

George Mojica (far left) was a stellar player for Sacramento City College in 1942. Mojica also excelled in his studies and is shown here when serving as president of Los Gauchos student Spanish club. The club organized events like Mexican dinners, where some of the white students were introduced to Mexican food for the first time. Sacramento City College's student newspaper, the *Express*, described Mojica on February 2, 1942: "One fellow who would gladden the heart of any college coach is George Mojica, the Mexican Fireball, who throws a baseball so fast that it takes on the appearance of small-size pea to a batter." (Courtesy of Mark Ocegueda.)

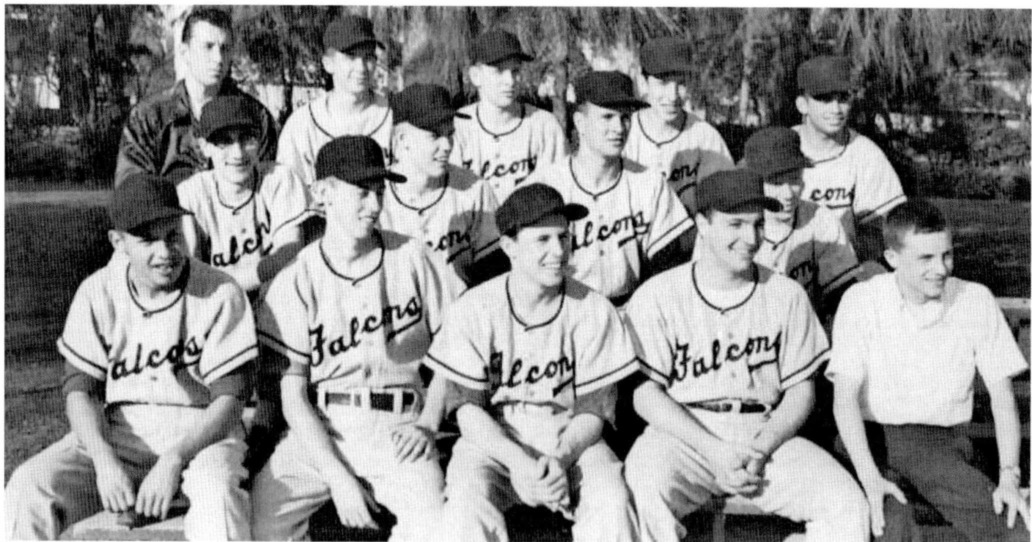

In 1959, the Bishop Armstrong Falcons won the Northern Interstate Conference championship with the help of players like Julius Reséndez (first row, far left). Other players included Pete Mooney, Freddit Thomas, Bob Separovich, Mike Elorduy, and Tom Zanze. When the team reported to Chico for the Northern Interstate Conference Baseball Festival, it had just enough players to fill out the lineup card, as one of the cars carrying several players was involved in a minor accident. The rest of the team showed up 45 minutes late and went on to win the game 4-3. (Courtesy of the Mexican American Hall of Fame Sports Association.)

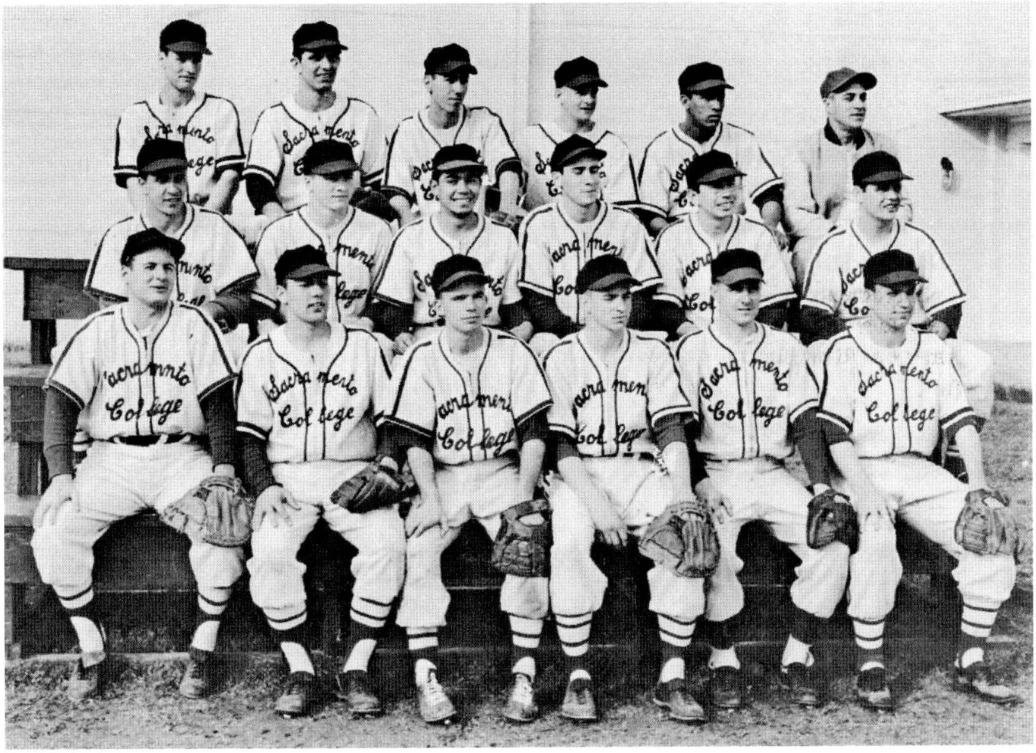

Pictured here is the 1958 Sacramento City College baseball team. From left to right are (first row) Don Nannini, Jerry Silva, Tom Higgins, Bill Ehorn, Richard Cushing, and Bob Gatiss; (second row) Bill Enos, Jim Burroughs, Bob Solorio, John Virga, Salvador "Chado" Vasquez, and Jerry Conway; (third row) Rich Schafer, Jim Gianulias, Rich Gennette, Curt Redhan, Ernie Cervantes Jr., and coach Cliff Perry. (Courtesy of the Mexican American Hall of Fame Sports Association.)

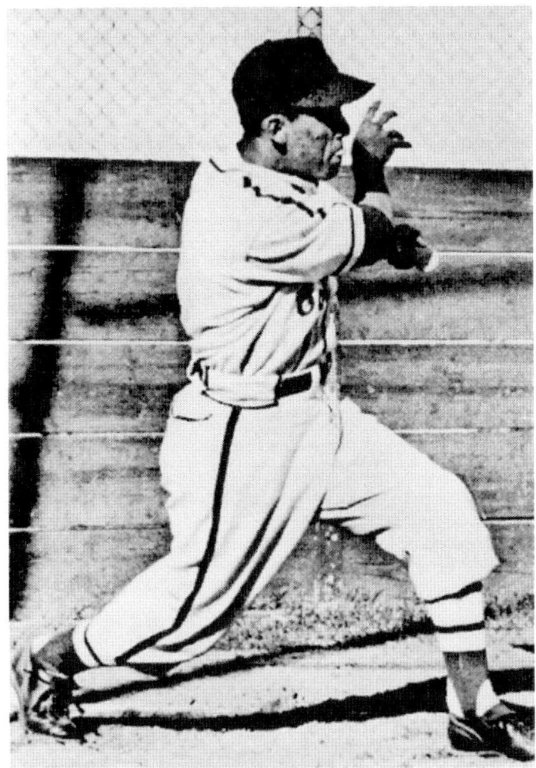

Ernie Cervantes Jr. hits a ball into play for the Sacramento City College Panthers in the late 1950s. (Courtesy of the Mexican American Hall of Fame Sports Association.)

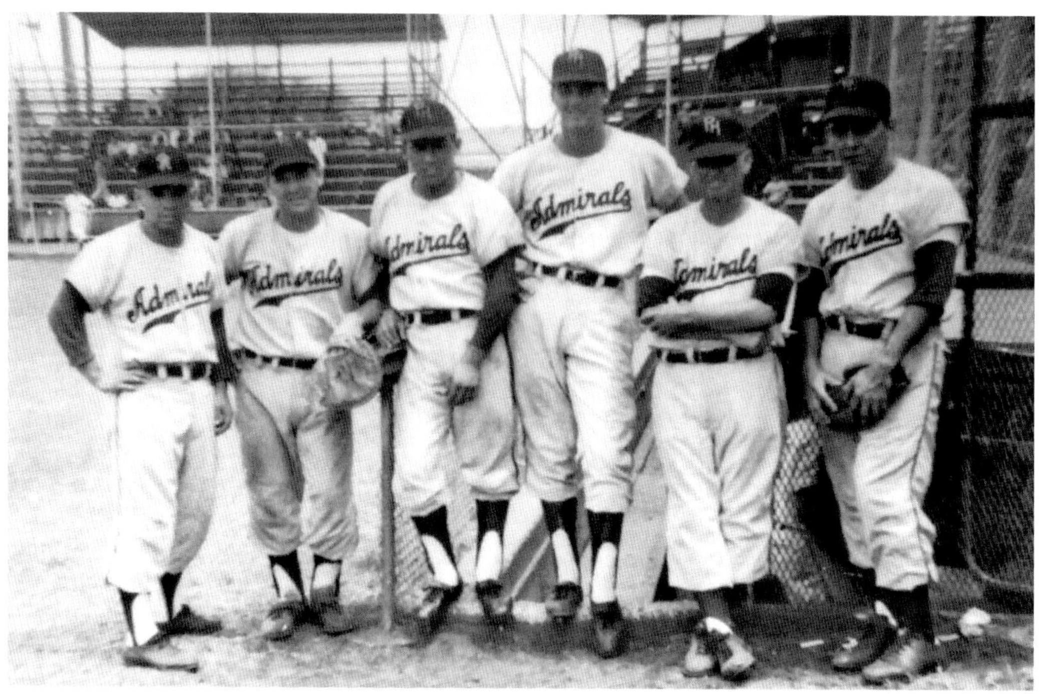

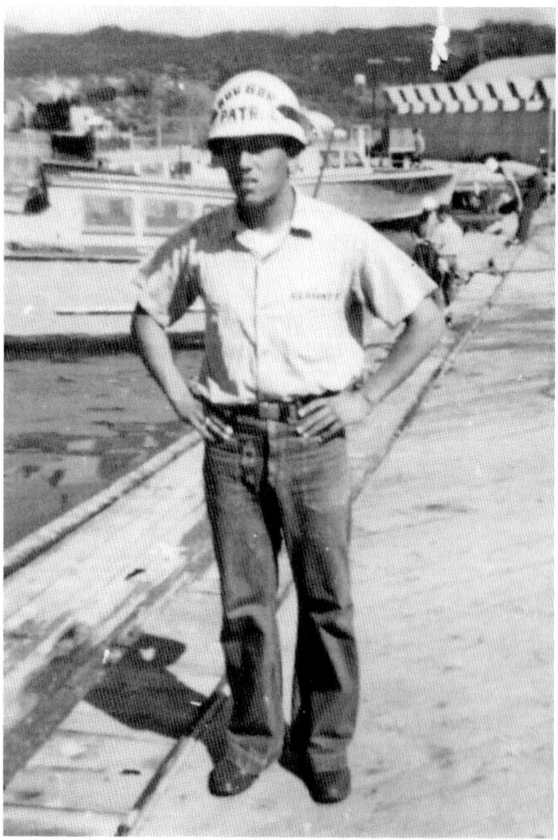

Ernie Cervantes Jr. is shown here in the 1960s (third from left) with the Pearl Harbor Admirals navy team. His father also played baseball while serving in the military during World War II. (Courtesy of Ernie Cervantes Jr.)

In 1960, Ernie Cervantes Jr. entered the Navy. He was assigned to Pearl Harbor and played for the Admirals in the Hawaii All Service Military League. He is shown as he performs one of his duties as harbor patrol. His other various duties included raising and lowering the colors on the USS *Arizona*. Ernie was later assigned to the USS *Forster* and cruised the Bering Strait monitoring the Russian fleet. (Courtesy of Ernie Cervantes Jr.)

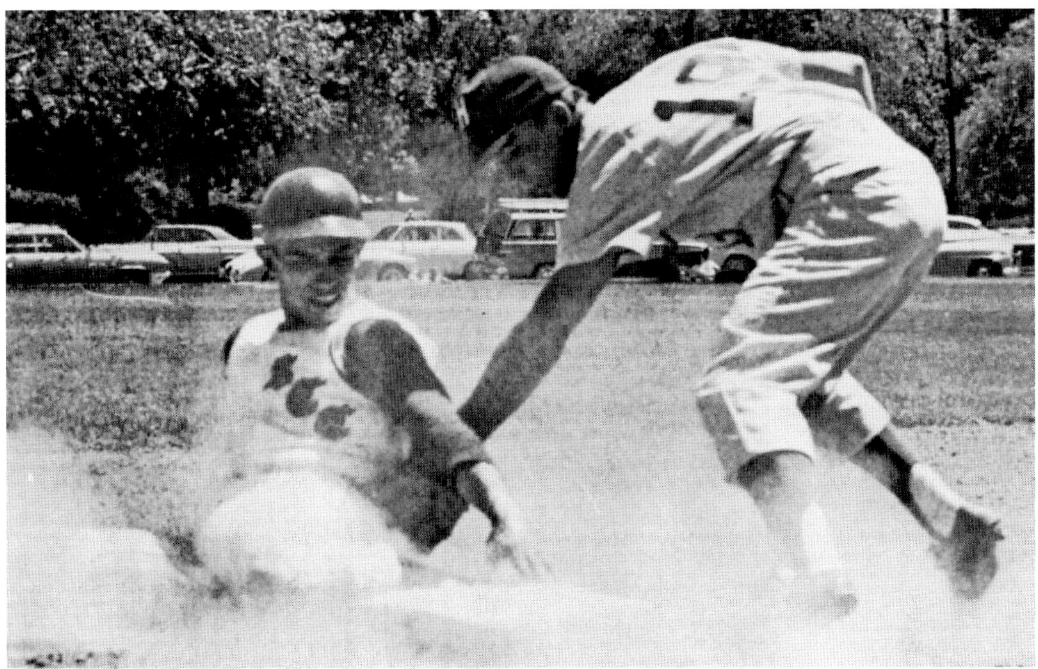

In 1967, John "Buck" Martínez of Elk Grove caught for the Sacramento City College Panthers. Martínez was a gifted player and helped lead the Panthers to a playoff victory over Allencock College. Martínez is shown sliding safely into third after belting a triple into right center field. (Courtesy of Mark Ocegueda.)

In May 1967, Buck Martínez was drafted by the Philadelphia Phillies out of Sacramento City College. Though the Panthers celebrated Martínez's accomplishment, they also lamented the fact that he could not play in the state college championship game, since the Phillies owned his rights as a player. Unfortunately, the Panthers lost the title game against Pasadena City College. Martínez, a .417 hitter that season, could have helped propel the Panthers if only eligible to play. (Courtesy of Mark Ocegueda.)

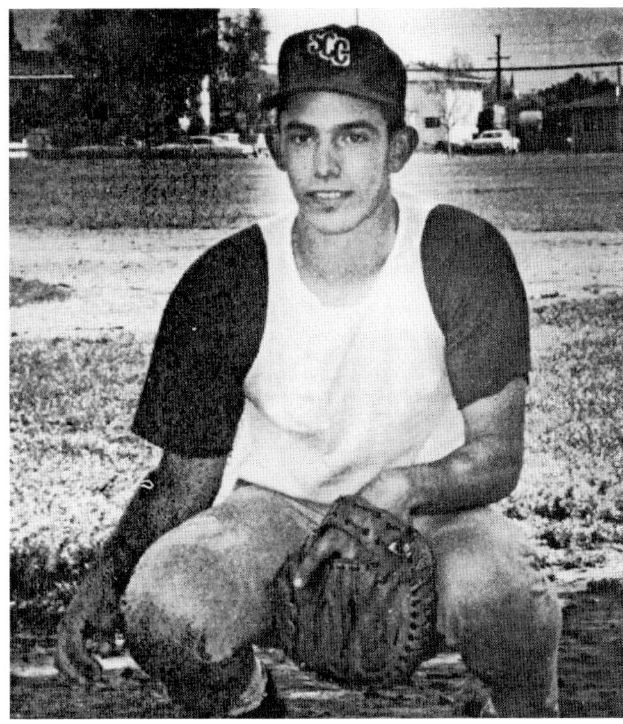

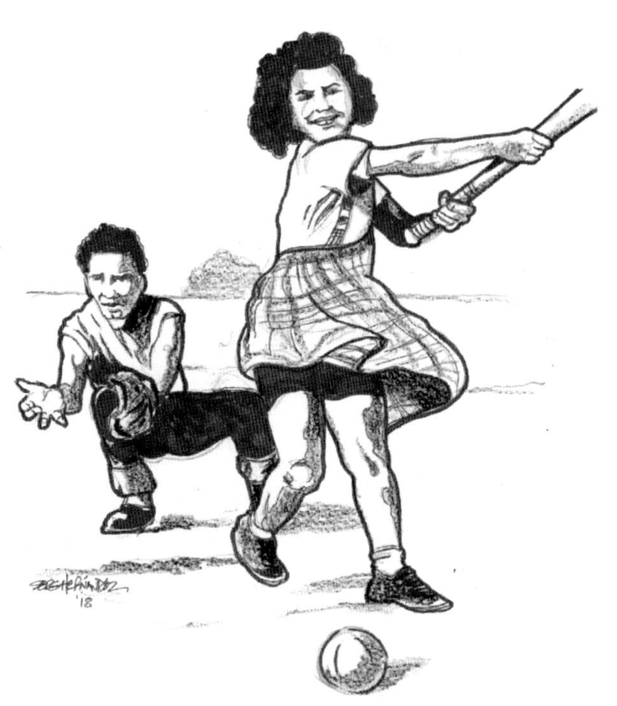

Pictured is Rachel "Beebee" Cervantes at age six taking a swing and learning the fundamentals of softball at the 16th and C Streets park. Tony Delgado, age 15, is playing catcher. This image appeared in the *Sacramento Bee* on March 6, 1947. (Courtesy of Sergio Hernández.)

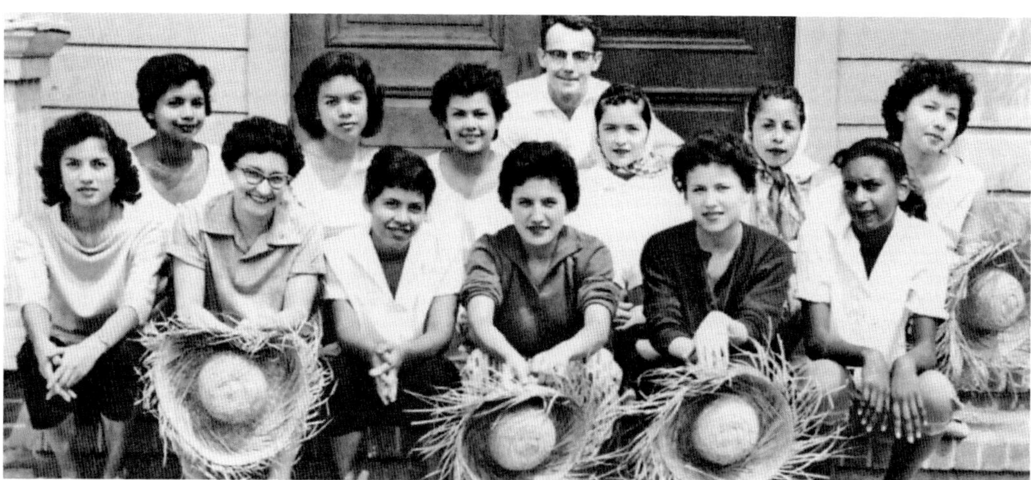

The Cervantes were a talented athletic family. Rachel Cervantes-Wallin (second row, third from left) played for the CYO team in Sacramento around 1956. She played basketball, softball, and volleyball for St. Joseph Grammar School and Bishop Armstrong High School. At the age of 12, she played for the Sacramento Women's Night Softball League. At Sacramento City College, she played basketball, softball, and field hockey and was the top player on the tennis team. She has coached several sports for years. She was a teacher, counselor, and principal in the Sacramento Unified School District. (Courtesy of Rachel Cervantes-Wallin.)

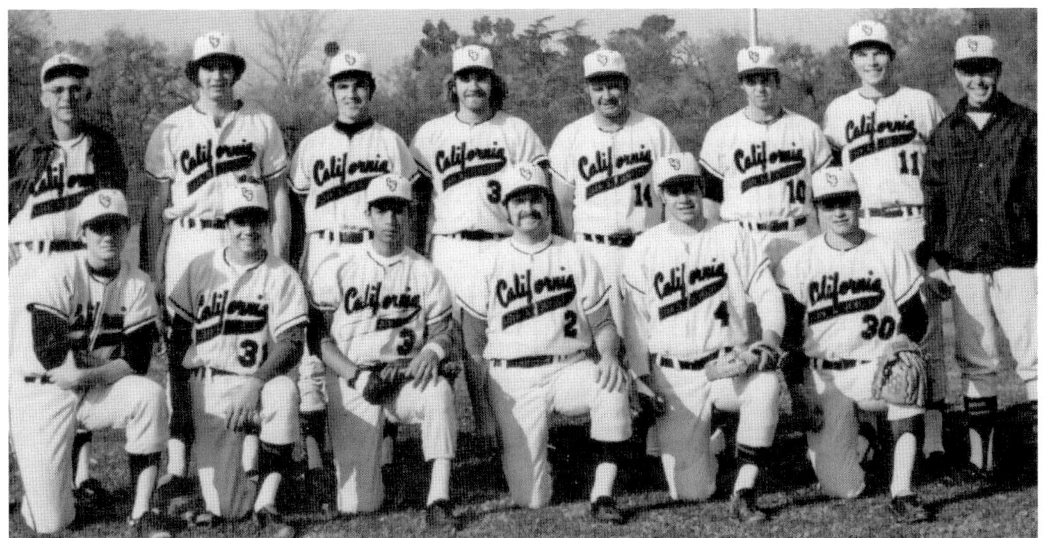

Ramón "Junior" Gonzáles starred at Sacramento City College and won the Valley Conference championship in 1971. He starred at Oregon State and played a couple of seasons in the Northwest League for the Seattle Rainiers, an independent pro team. California Loan and Jewelry sponsored teams in the Sacramento Winter League showcasing local professional players home for the off season. Gonzáles is fourth from left in the first row. Also in the photograph are Dennis Myers (Oakland A's), Fred Luzzi (New York Yankees), Don Murphy (Detroit Tigers), and Bob Forsch, who pitched two no-hitters for the St. Louis Cardinals. (Mexican American Hall of Fame Sports Association.)

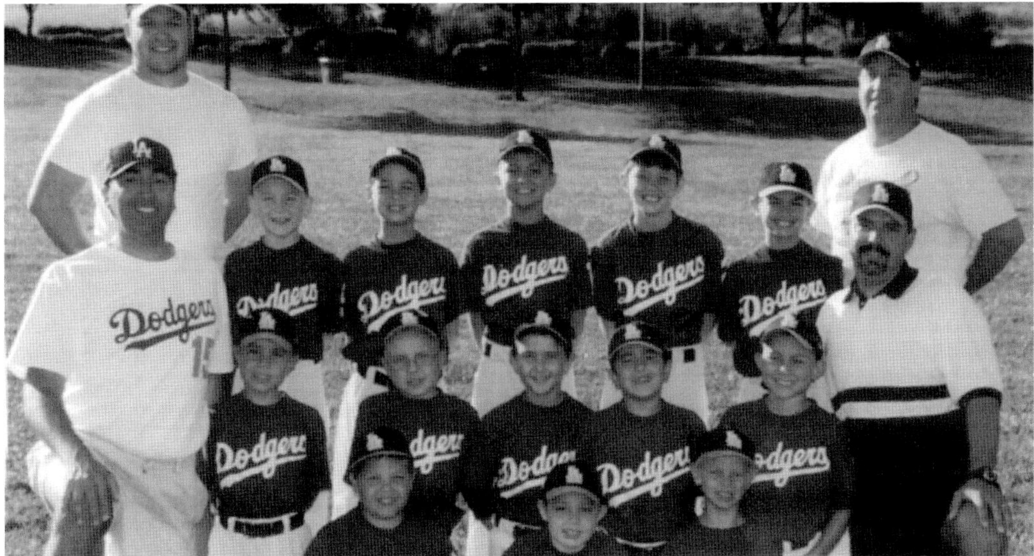

Alec Luna (second row, second player from right) played two years of T-ball with the Rocklin Little League. His father, Anthony (far left, kneeling), coached Alec on several teams. Alec played Pony Fast Pitch League for two years. Besides baseball, he played several years on local and travel soccer teams, usually as goalie or mid-fielder. Alec's sports interests changed in middle school as he joined the wrestling and track teams. (Courtesy of Anthony Luna.)

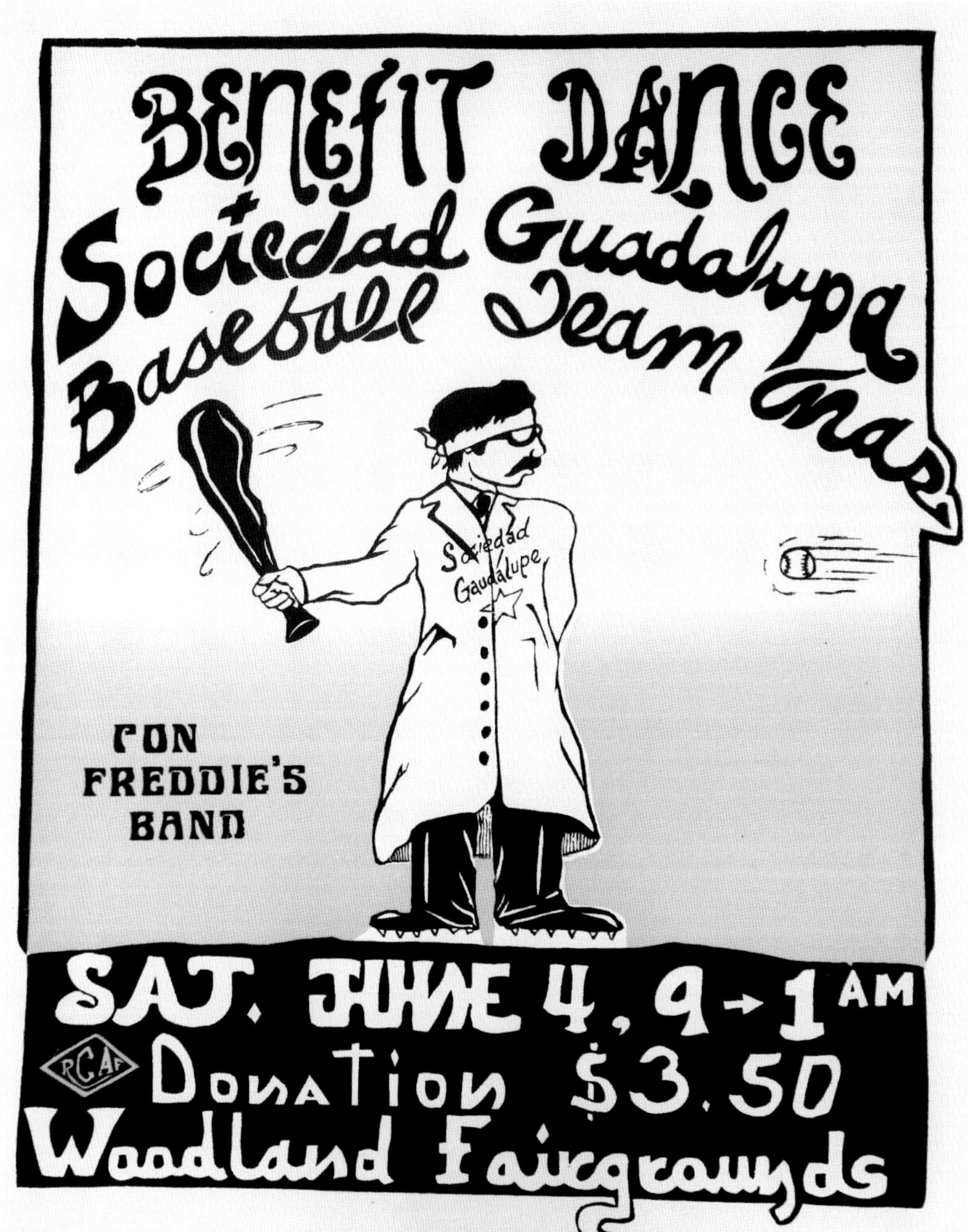

The Royal Chicano Air Force originated with the Mexican American Education Project at Sacramento State in 1968. Over the years, it also produced community posters. This is a poster made by Rudy Cuellar for the Sociedad Guadalupanas baseball team in Woodland. The event was a benefit dance to raise money for the Chicano baseball team. (Courtesy of Rudy Cuellar and the Department of Special Collections and University Archives at California State University, Sacramento.)

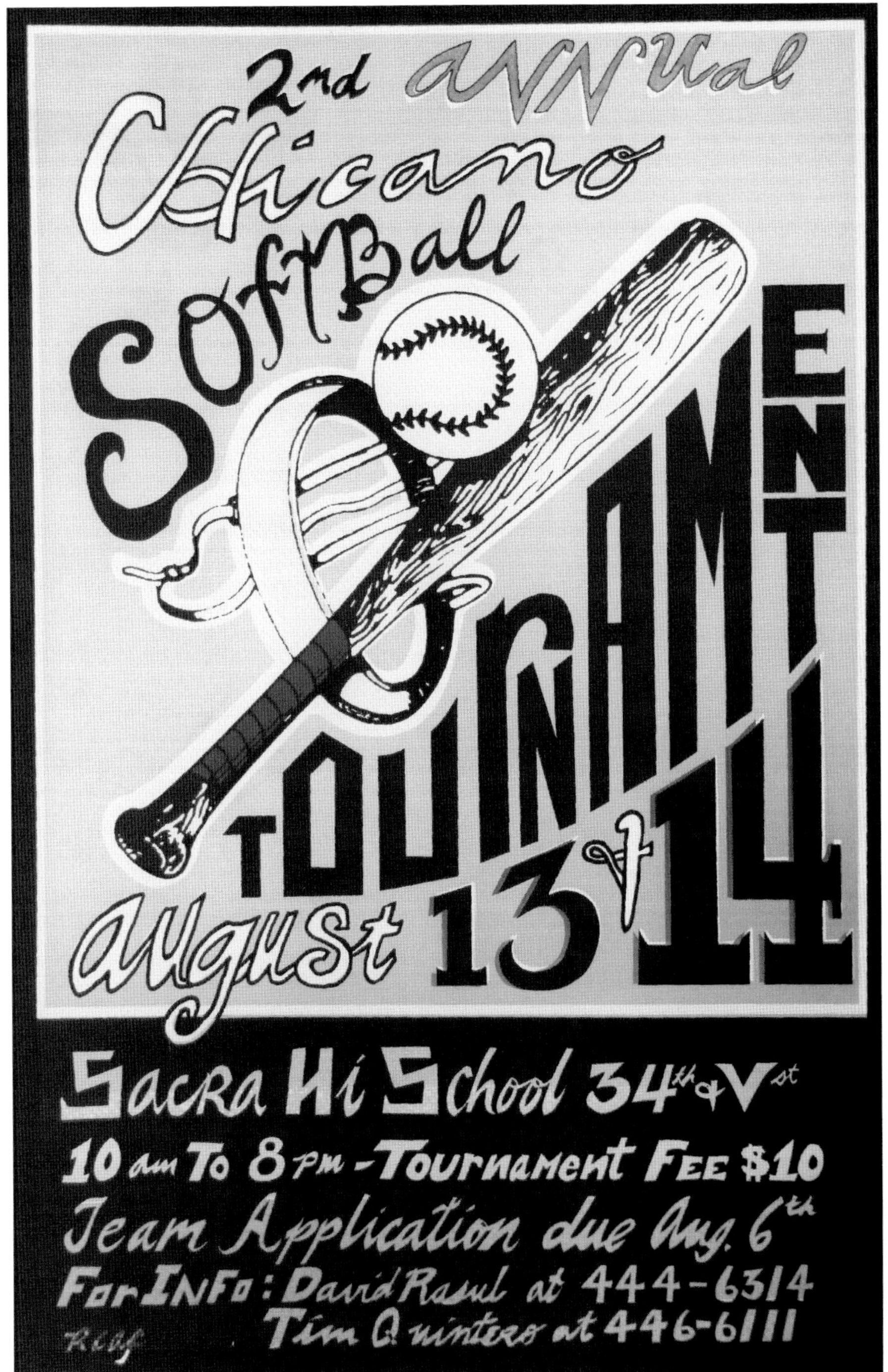

Louie "the Foot" González of the Royal Chicano Air Force designed this poster for the 1977 Chicano Softball Tournament, held at Sacramento High School. (Courtesy of Louie "the Foot" González and the Department of Special Collections and University Archives at California State University, Sacramento.)

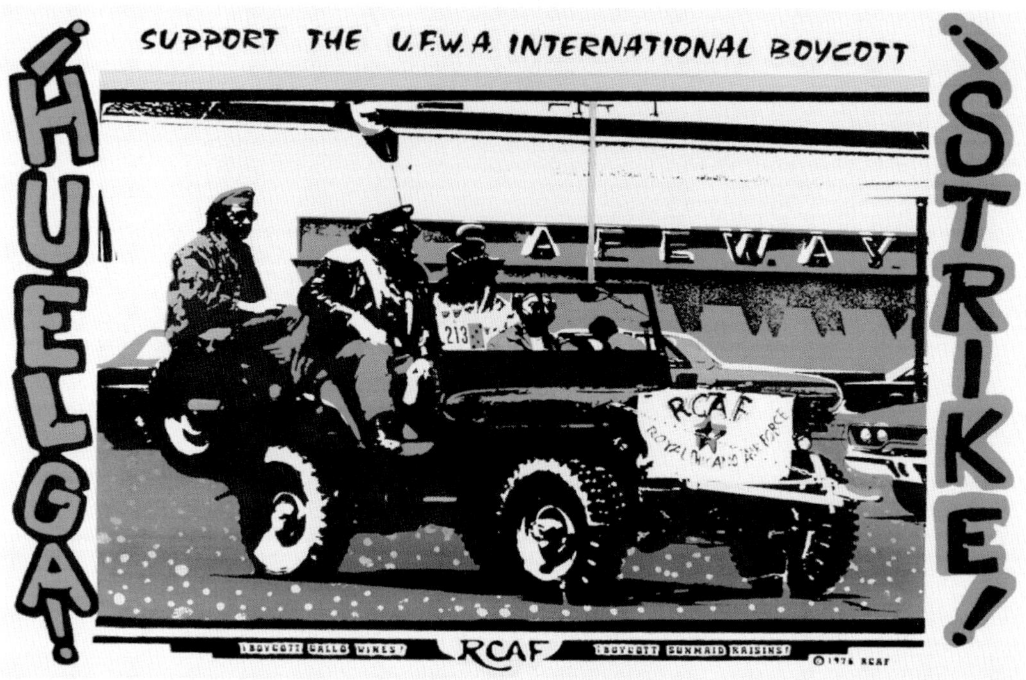

The RCAF utilized art for political purposes and became an important component of the National Farm Workers Association, led by civil rights leaders and labor organizers César Chávez and Dolores Huerta. This image was made by Juanishi Orosco to support the boycott of Sun-Maid Raisins and Gallo Wines. (Courtesy of Juanishi Orosco and the Department of Special Collections and University Archives at California State University, Sacramento.)

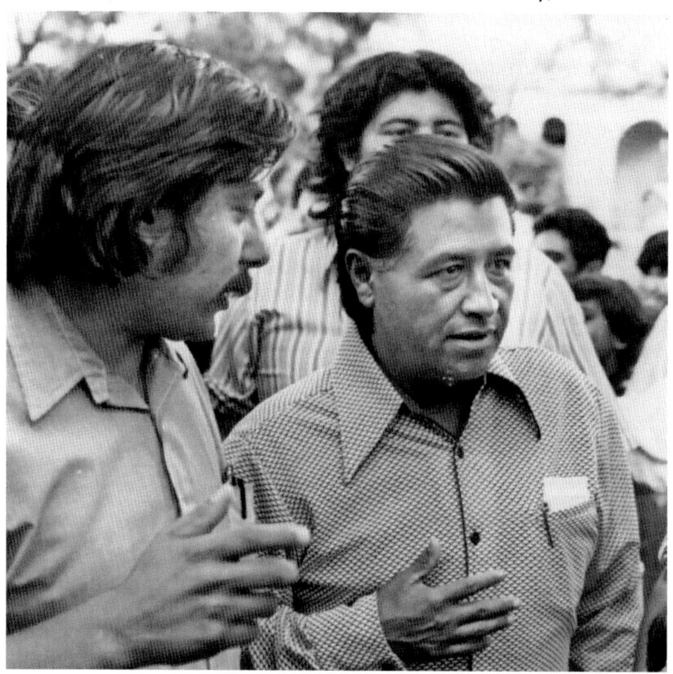

Joe Serna Jr. (left) is pictured with labor organizer César Chávez. Serna and Chávez were migrant farm workers and closely collaborated to further the goals of the National Farm Workers Association and United Farm Workers. Serna was a professor at Sacramento State for many years and eventually became the first Latino mayor of Sacramento in 1992. He was also a member of the RCAF. (Courtesy of the Department of Special Collections and University Archives at California State University, Sacramento.)

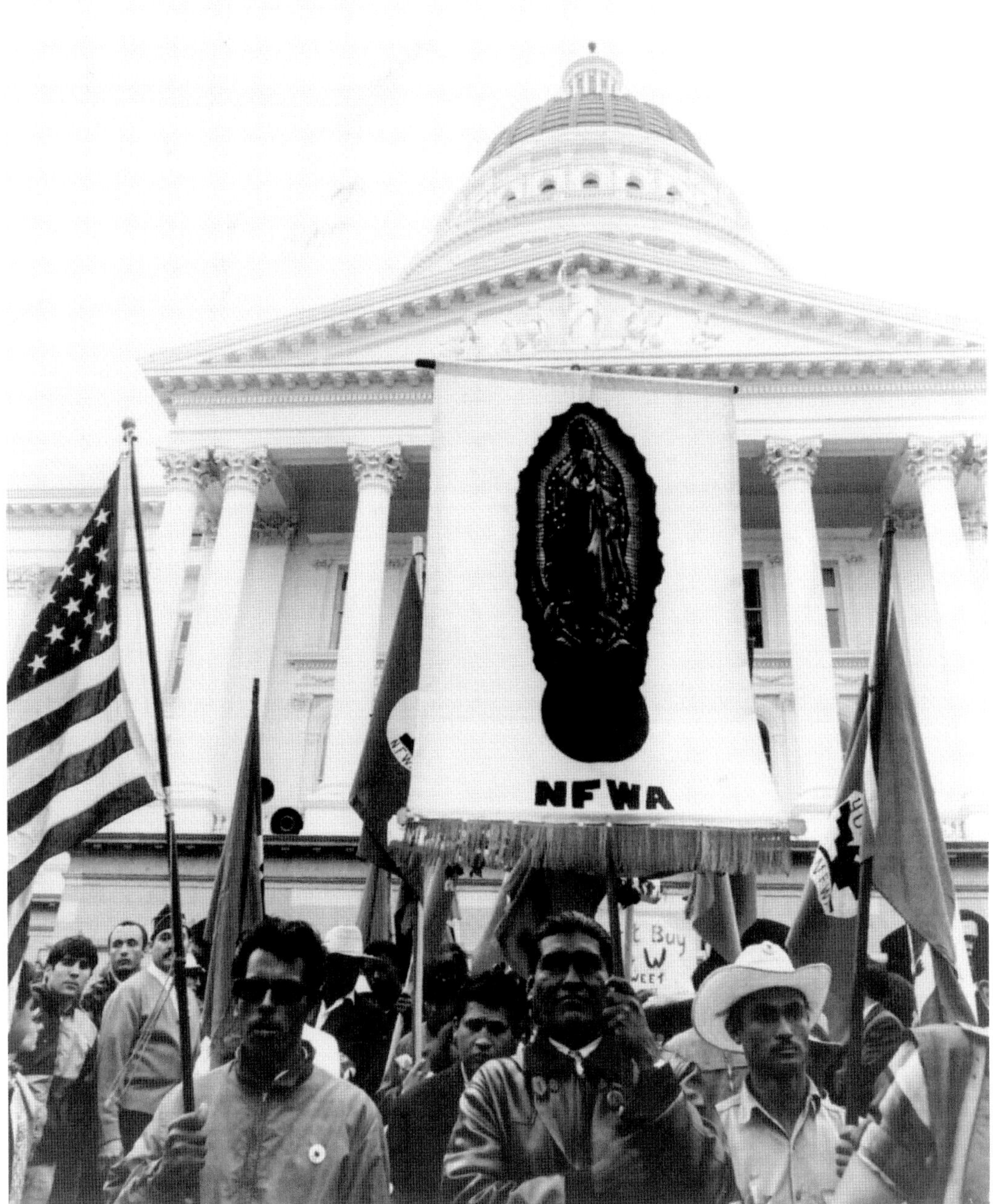

In 1966, César Chávez drew national attention to the struggle against unfair and exploitative labor conditions that Mexican and Mexican American farm workers faced in California's Central Valley by walking from Delano to Sacramento. This 340-mile *peregrinación*, or pilgrimage, took 25 days. Farm workers and their supporters gathered at the steps of the state capitol in Sacramento in April 1966. Members of Sacramento's Mexican community vividly remember this occasion and have cited this event as inspiration for future activism. (Courtesy of Walter P. Reuther Library, Archives of Labor and Urban Affairs, Wayne State University.)

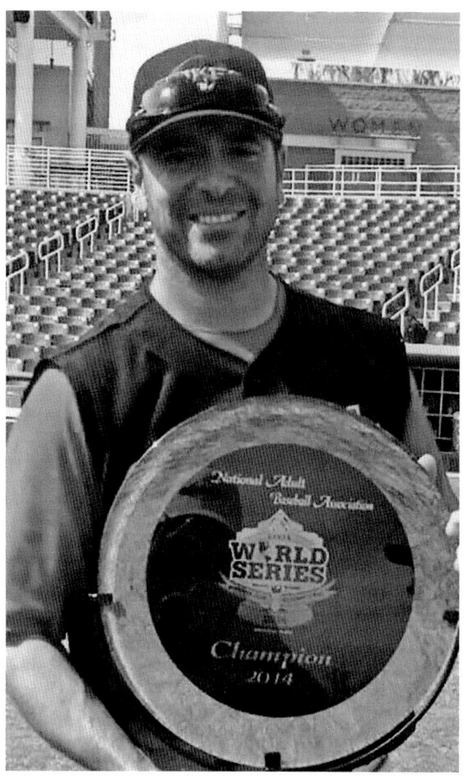

Mike de Necochea was born in Calexico in 1966 and his family moved to Sacramento in 1979. He graduated from C.K. McClatchy High School in 1985. He played football, basketball, and baseball, and was named All-Metro in baseball. He served in the Army and completed his bachelor's degree from the University of San Francisco. He has been the head varsity baseball coach at McClatchy since 2005, where he has won six Metro championships and is the winningest baseball coach in the school's history (244-146-1.) He was inducted into the McClatchy Athletic Hall of Fame in 2016 and is currently an all-star shortstop in the Sacramento Men's Senior Baseball League. He has won three National World Series championships in Arizona as a player. Mike and his wife, Gloria, have been married for 25 years. They have seven kids who are McClatchy alumni (Jeanie, 2001; Tara, 2002; Michelle, 2004; Heather, 2005; Lauren, 2007; Desiree, 2014; and Michael, 2018) and six grandchildren. (Courtesy of Mike de Necochea.)

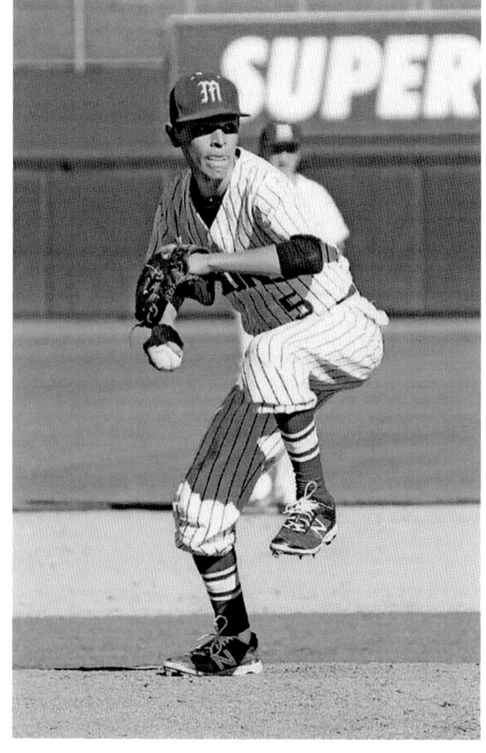

Michael de Necochea Jr. was born in Sacramento in 1999. He was a two-time all-star baseball player for Land Park Pacific Little League and graduated from C.K. McClatchy High School in 2018. Like his father, Michael Jr. played football, basketball, and baseball at McClatchy and made First Team All-Metro Conference in baseball during his senior year. He was an Honorable Mention for the *Sacramento Bee*'s 2018 All-Metro baseball team after finishing with a .361 batting average, 22 hits, and 14 RBIs. He also played stellar defense at second base as evidenced by a .923 fielding percentage. He is currently studying communications at San Francisco State University and is interested in sports broadcasting. (Courtesy of Mike de Necochea.)

Alec Luna (at bat) was born in San Francisco in 1996. His father, Anthony (watching Alec), was born in El Sereno in East Los Angeles and graduated from Wilson High School. Anthony played youth and high school sports, including baseball, football, and tennis. Alec's mom, Julie, was born in Glendale, California, and graduated from Nevada Union High School in Northern California. Anthony and Julie met at Pasadena Community College and both graduated from California State University, Los Angeles. Alec was raised in Rocklin, about 21 miles east of Sacramento, and played Little League from 2001 to 2004. (Courtesy of Anthony Luna.)

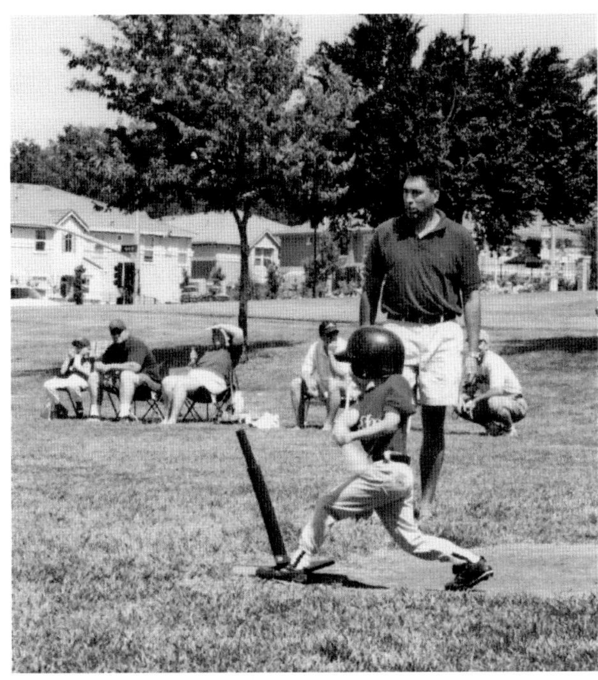

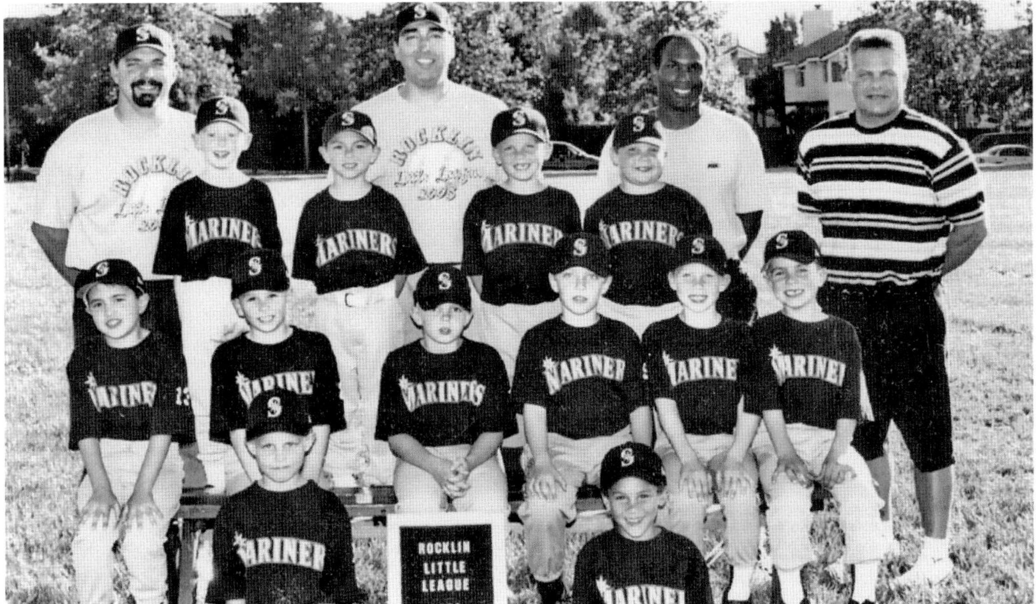

Alec Luna (second row, far left) wanted to be a better tennis player and took private lessons after playing recreational tennis with his father, Anthony (fourth row, second from left), in the summer of 2010. Anthony had been a tennis star at Wilson High School in East Los Angeles. Alec joined the Rocklin High School tennis team and made varsity as a junior. He played both singles and doubles. During his high school days, his interests in computers became stronger. He currently attends California State University, Sacramento as a computer science major. He aspires to be a software engineer and is a diehard Dodger fan. (Courtesy of Anthony Luna.)

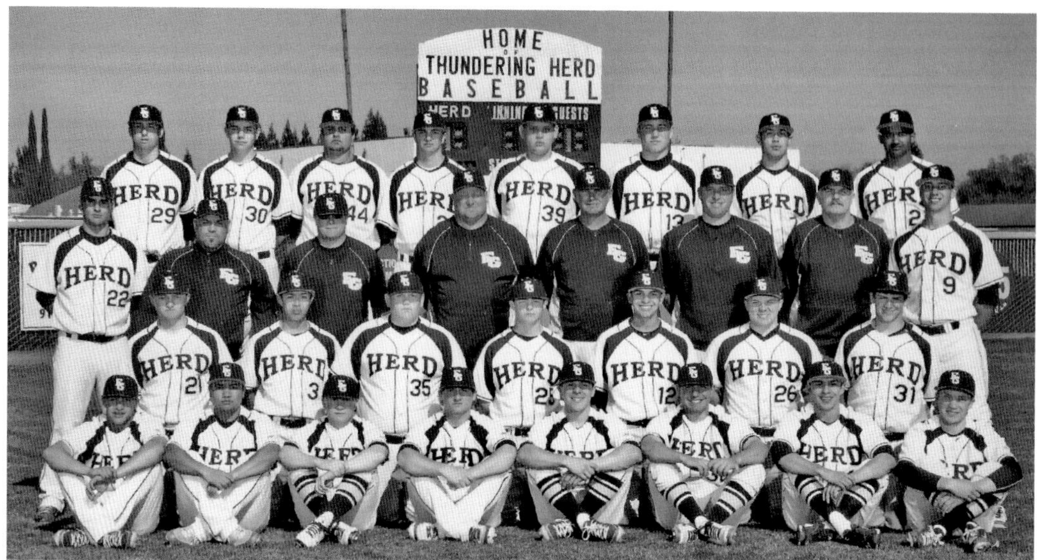

The 2013 Elk Grove High School Thundering Herd were Northern California Division-1 champions. Five players were drafted by major-league organizations. Ryan "Rowdy" Tellez (Fourth row, third from left) won Player of the Year, was named an All-American high school player, and was drafted by the Toronto Blue Jays. Tellez also played for Sacramento's Los Gallos baseball club. Dylan Carson (fourth row, second from right) was a first-round pick by the St. Louis Cardinals. Derek Hill (fourth row, far right) was a first-round pick by the Detroit Tigers and played for Los Gallos. Don Núñez (third row, far right) was drafted by the Colorado Rockies and played for Los Gallos. Nick Madrigal (first row, second from right) was selected fourth overall by the Chicago White Sox in the 2018 draft after winning the College World Series with Oregon State. Madrigal is the highest major-league draft pick ever out of the Sacramento area. (Courtesy of Greg and Lori Tellez.)

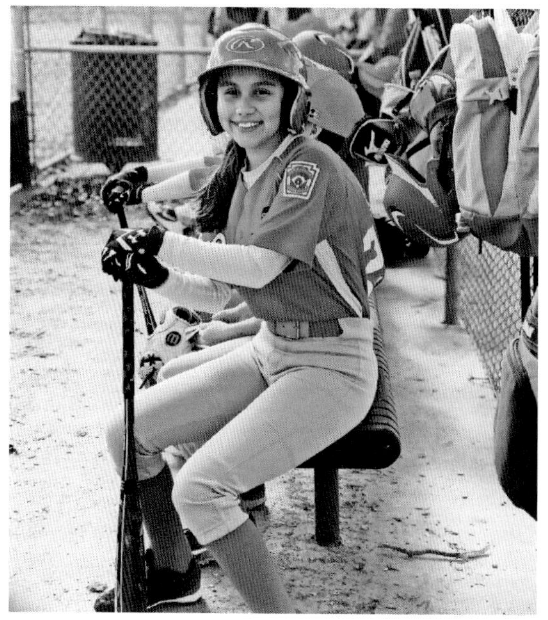

Sophia Delgado helps to carry on the legacy of Mexican American baseball in Sacramento. In 2018, Delgado began playing for the Angels of the Pocket Little League in South Sacramento. Delgado is the only female player for the Angels and pitches for the baseball team. As a first-year player on the team, she struck out eight batters in one game, hit the ball well, and made the all-star team. (Courtesy of Rosie Gayton.)

Mexican Americans and Professional Baseball

Mexican Americans have been scouted and evaluated by major-league teams since the early 20th century. It is believed that in 1908, Frank Arrellanes became the first Mexican American to play in the major leagues when he pitched for the Boston Red Sox. Late in the 1910 season, Arrellanes joined the Sacramento Senators in the PCL. In the interwar years from the 1920s into the early 1940s, more Mexican Americans joined semiprofessional teams, and the more talented players even made it into "the show." After World War II, major-league teams scouted for more Mexican American players, and they entered the professional leagues with greater frequency. Cuno Barragán is perhaps the most renowned Mexican American player from Sacramento who went on to the major leagues when he joined the Chicago Cubs in 1961. Prior to playing for the Cubs, Cuno played for Sacramento High School, Sacramento City College, and the PCL Sacramento Solons. After retiring from the game in 1963, Cuno returned to Sacramento and mentored a new generation of baseball players. Some of them, like pitcher Fred Arroyo, continued in Cuno's footsteps as they also entered the major leagues.

Sacramento's "Mr. Baseball," Ernie Cervantes Sr., even had some of his sons go on to play professional ball. In 1971, Eddie Cervantes starred on the Sacramento City College team that won the Valley Conference Championship, and signed with the Baltimore Orioles organization. A 1974 graduate of Hiram Johnson High School in Sacramento, Eric Cervantes was an All-City baseball selection and was picked in the ninth round of the 1974 draft by the Atlanta Braves. At times, players went on to play professional baseball in Mexico. For instance, Cuno played for the Puebla Pericos, while Eddie and Eric played for the Mexicali Aguilas in Mexico's Pacific Coast Winter League. Elk Grove native Buck Martínez was drafted out of Sacramento City College by the Philadelphia Phillies in 1967 and had a 17-year career in the major leagues. Buck Martínez has maintained his involvement in baseball through broadcasting by serving as the voice of the Toronto Blue Jays. This chapter chronicles the rich and exciting history of Sacramento's Mexican American players who went on to play professional baseball.

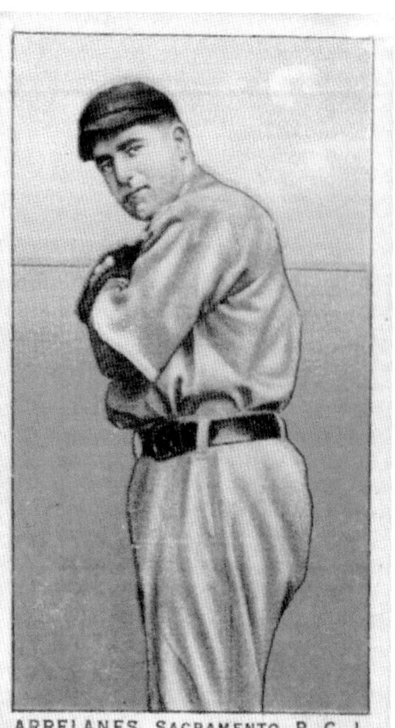

Frank Arrellanes was born in Santa Cruz, California, on January 28, 1882, and died on December 13, 1918. He played professional baseball for 14 years for teams that included the San Francisco Seals, San Jose Prune Pickers, Fresno Raisin Eaters, Santa Cruz Sand Crabs, Denver Bears, and Vernon Tigers. In 1908, Arrellanes became the first Mexican American to play in the major leagues when he pitched for the Boston Red Sox. He posted a 24-22 win-loss record for Boston from 1908 through 1910. Late in the 1910 season, Arrellanes joined the Sacramento Senators in the PCL. He had a 60-65 record with the Senators between 1910 and 1914 and moved with the team near the end of the 1914 season when they became the San Francisco Missions. (Courtesy of Alan O'Connor.)

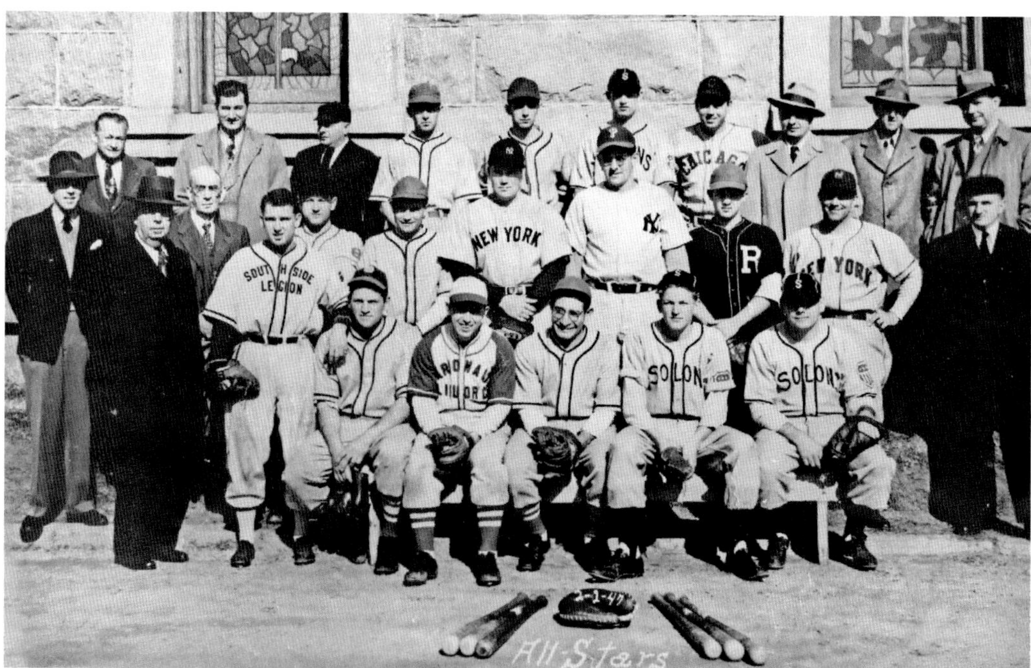

Fibo Herrera (first row center, with glasses) played on the MAC teams of the 1930s and went on to play for the PCL Sacramento Solons. This 1947 all-star team of locals who made the major leagues played a game at Folsom Prison. Solon players are joined by various players from the Chicago Cubs and New York Yankees. (Courtesy of the Mexican American Hall of Fame Sports Association.)

Born in Sacramento on June 20, 1932, Facundo "Cuno" Barragán is one of six children of Mexican immigrant parents. He is widely recognized as the first Mexican American from Sacramento to make it into the major leagues. As a kid, he and his friends would sneak into Edmonds Field on Broadway and Riverside Boulevard to watch Sacramento Solons games. Barragán played ball at Sacramento High School, graduated in 1950, and played baseball and football for Sacramento City College. (Courtesy of Cuno Barragán.)

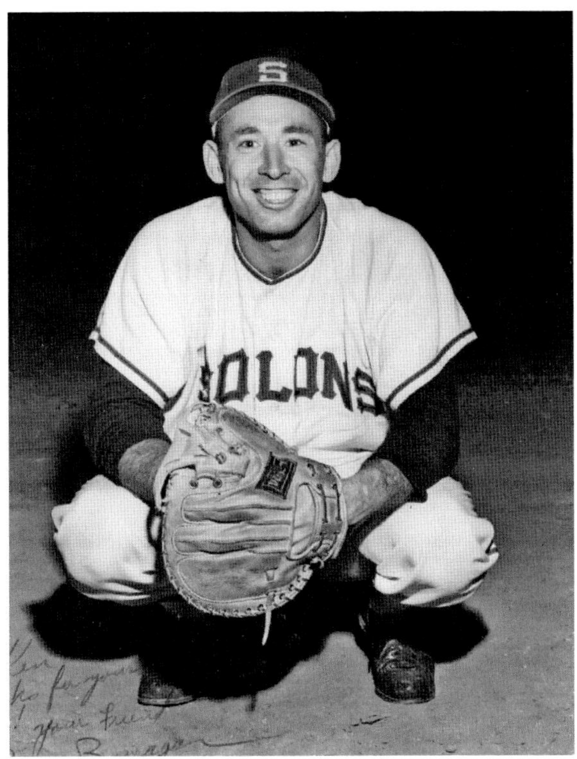

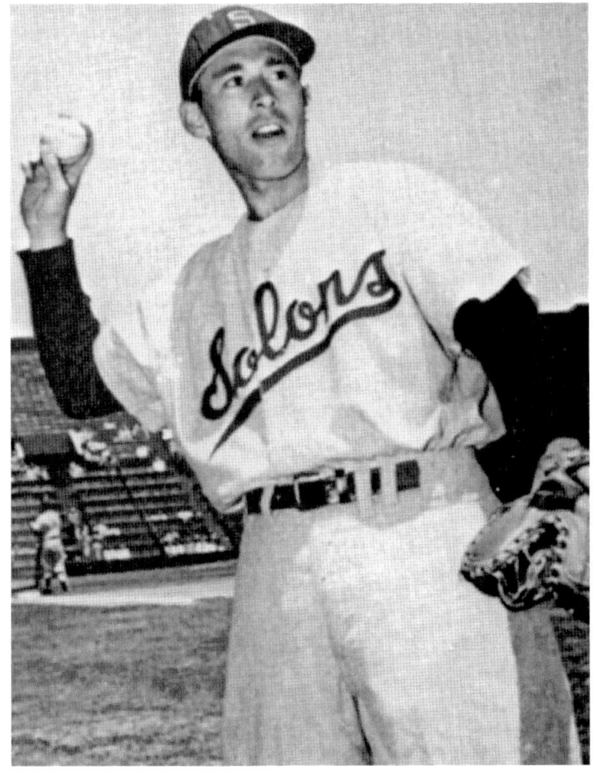

Cuno Barragán played 108 games for the Solons in 1957. After finishing the season, he played in the Winter League of the Mexico Central League with the Puebla Pericos. Playing with the hometown PCL team was a thrill, but as the 1958 spring training closed, the Solons sent him to the Atlanta Crackers of the Southern Association to work on his hitting. Feeling that he had paid his dues by catching 108 games the previous season, he did not want to leave his family and refused to go. He was suspended and went back to work setting tile. (Courtesy of Cuno Barragán.)

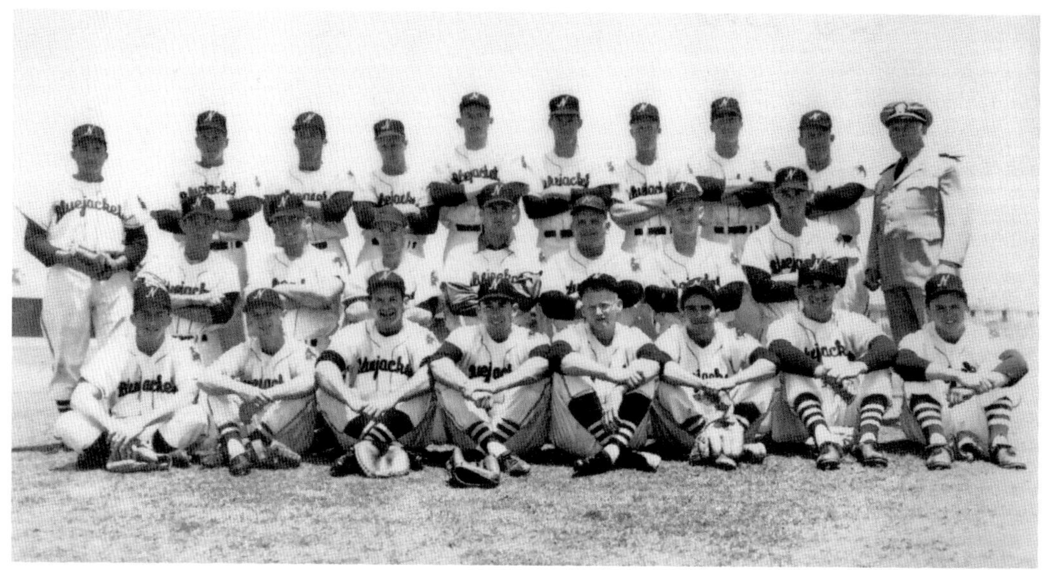

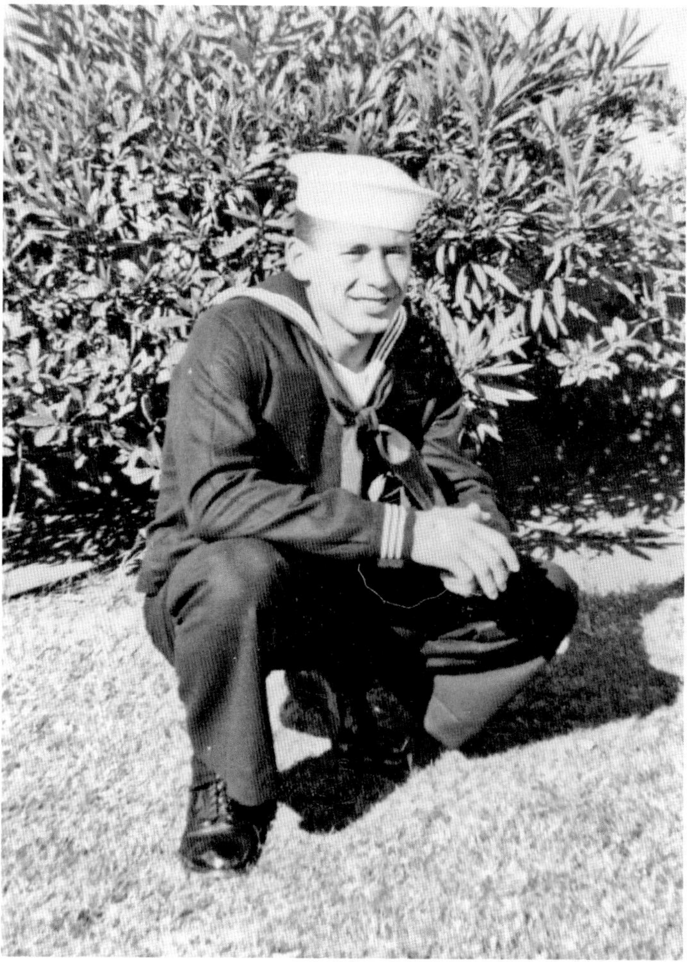

Cuno Barragán (first row, fourth from left above) joined the Navy Reserves during the Korean War and trained at the Naval Training Center in San Diego. He was transferred to the 13th Naval District in Idaho. Barragán played baseball in the military for the San Diego Navy Bluejackets. He later played for the Chicago Cubs and even had a hit off of Sandy Koufax. Raymond Hernández (first row, second from right above) pitched for the University of Southern California in the early 1950s. (Both, courtesy of Cuno Barragán.)

This photograph shows Cuno Barragán's half-brother Ernesto Galarza as a child in the 1910s. In 1947, Galarza received his PhD in history from Columbia University. He became one of the preeminent Mexican American scholars and activists of the 20th century. Galarza wrote a renowned novel in 1971 entitled *Barrio Boy* that described his family's journey from Nayarit to Sacramento during the Mexican Revolution. In 1979, Dr. Galarza was nominated for the Nobel Prize in Literature. (Courtesy of Occidental College Special Collections and College Archives, Ernesto Galarza Collection.)

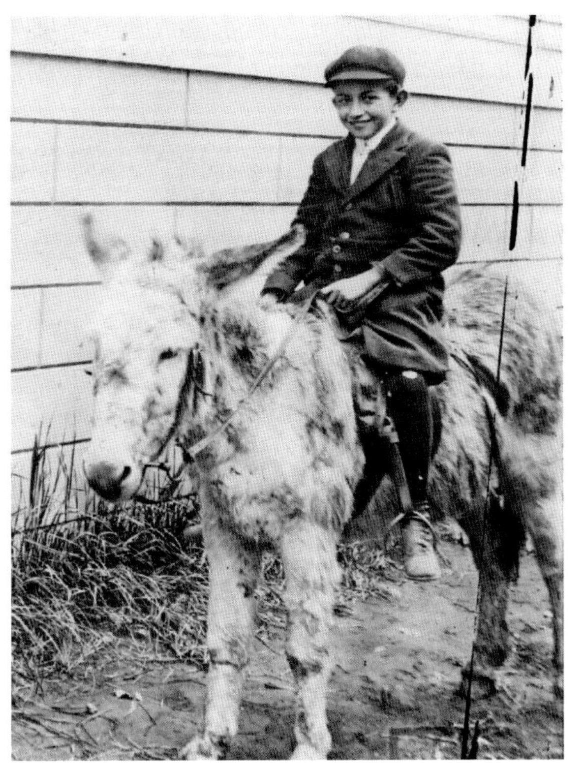

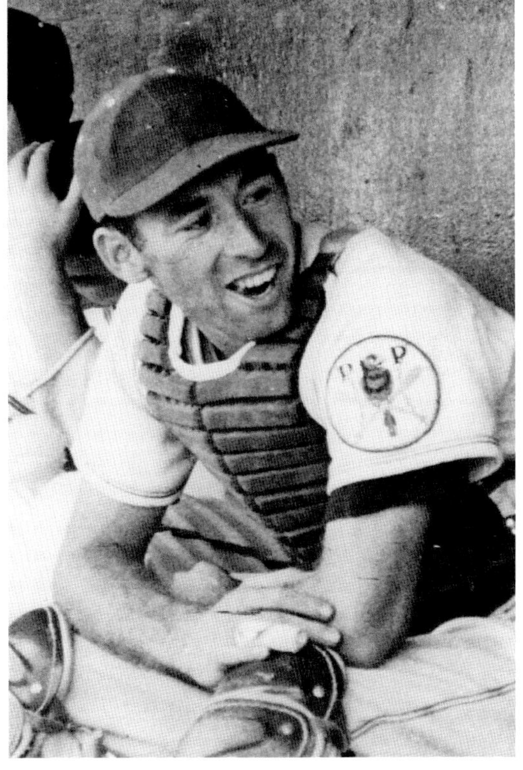

Cuno Barragán caught for the Puebla Pericos (Parrots) in the Winter League of the Mexico Central League from October through December 1957. Early scouting reports indicated that he would be a "very effective catcher," but a foul tip broke a finger on his throwing hand on opening day. The team's manager wanted him back in the lineup right away, but the team doctor held him out for a month to give the finger time to heal. Meanwhile, Dick Alejo, Cuno's cousin in Sacramento who caught for Sacramento City College, was called in to take Cuno's place behind the plate in October. Cuno is pictured in the Pericos dugout with his finger bandaged. (Courtesy of Cuno Barragán.)

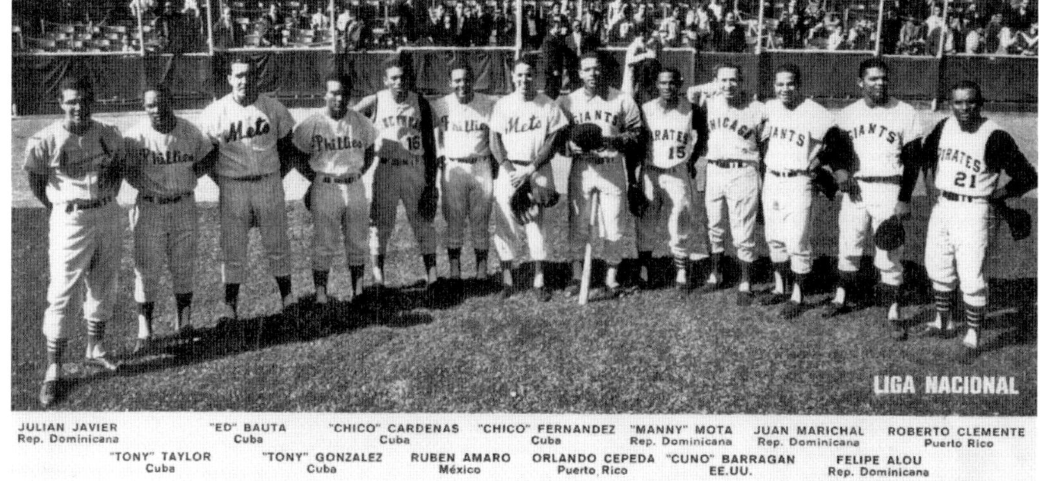

Barragán's last year in the major leagues was 1963. On October 12 of that year, the first and only Latin American All-Star Game was played at the Polo Grounds in New York City. Players included Felipe Alou, Luis Aparicio, Orlando Cepeda, Roberto Clemente, Minnie Minoso, Juan Marichal, Manny Mota, Tony Oliva, Vic Power, and Diego Seguí. Marichal was the starting National League pitcher, and Cuno caught the entire game, which ended in a 5-2 National League win. This was the last game played at the Polo Grounds. (Courtesy of Cuno Barragán.)

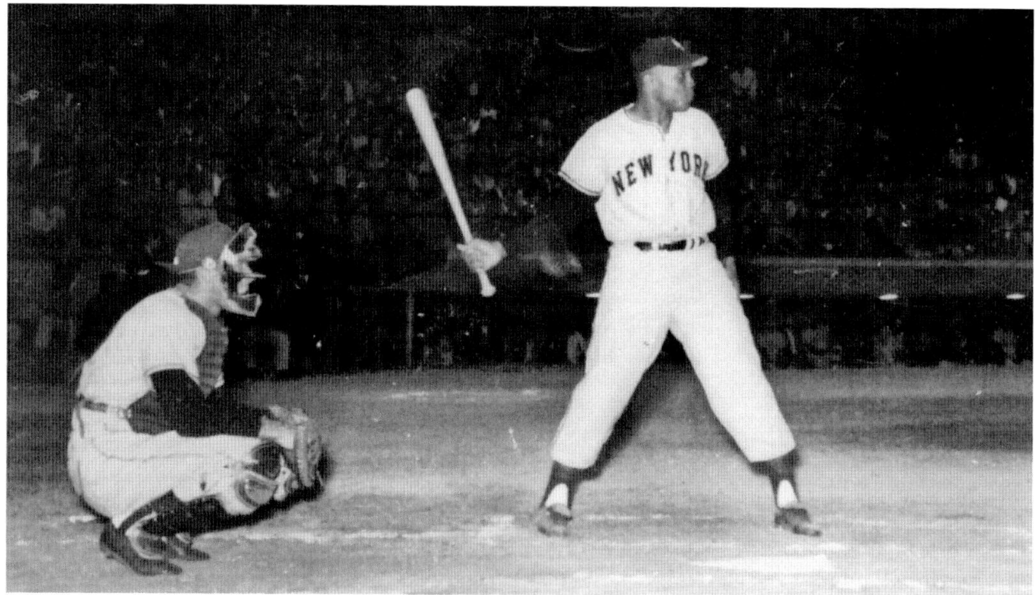

Cuno Barragán catches for Mexico's Central League All-Stars against the Willie Mays All-Stars on October 1, 1957, right before the start of Winter League, in front of 30,000 fans in Mexico City. Mays is shown batting. The Mays All-Star team included major-leaguers Bobby Avila, Gene Baker, Joe Black, Wes Covington, George Crowe, Elston Howard, Brooks Lawrence, Harry Simpson, and Al Smith. Barragán excelled defensively and went two for three at the plate. (Courtesy of Cuno Barragán.)

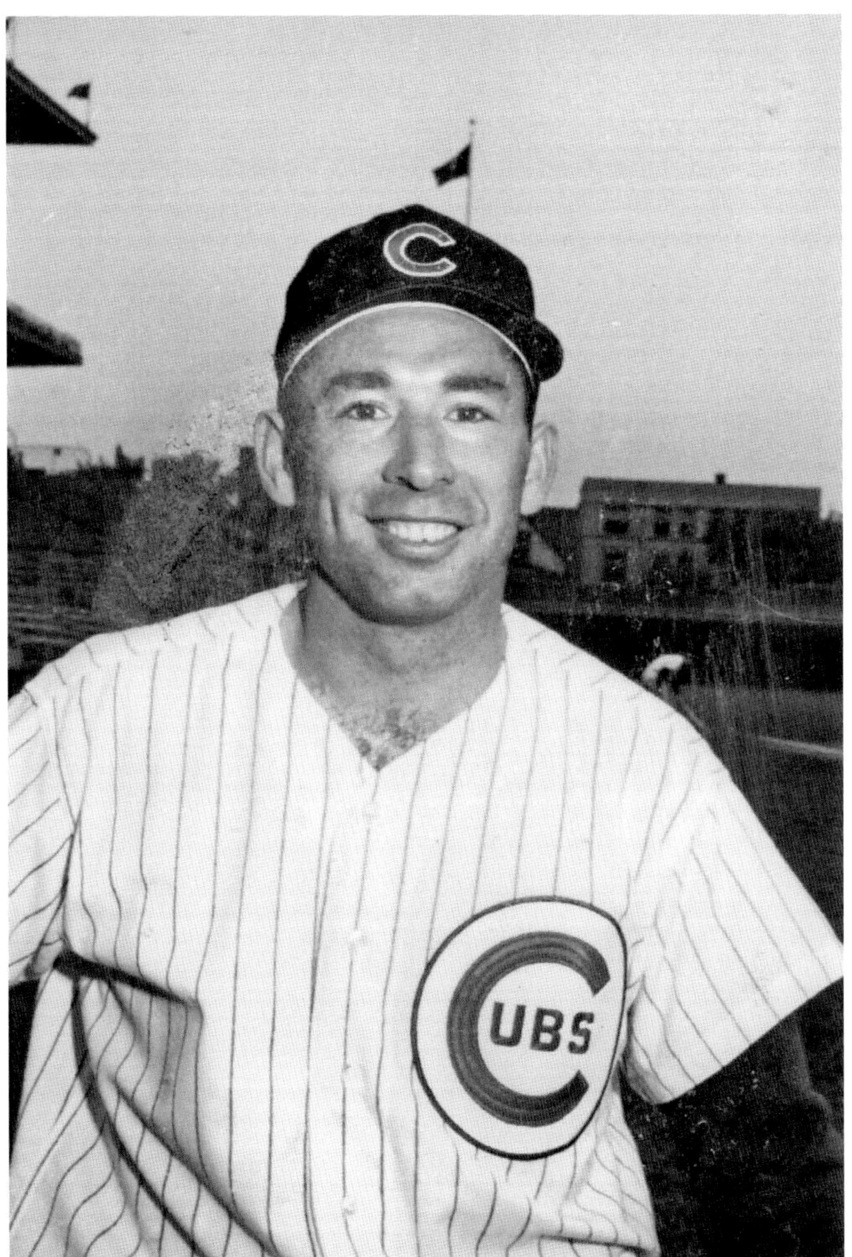

Cuno Barragán's performance with the 1960 Solons led to his being drafted by the National League Chicago Cubs, for whom he played from 1961 through 1963. On March 25, 1961, he broke his ankle sliding into third, and sat out most of the rest of that season. He got back into the Cubs starting lineup on September 1, 1961, against the Giants and hit a home run in his first major league at bat. In 1962, he had a good year on a bad Cubs team, getting into 59 games. During his years with the team, the Cubs lacked pitching but had some great position players, including Richie Ashburn, Ernie Banks, Lou Brock, Al Heist, Ron Santo, and Billy Williams. (Courtesy of Cuno Barragán.)

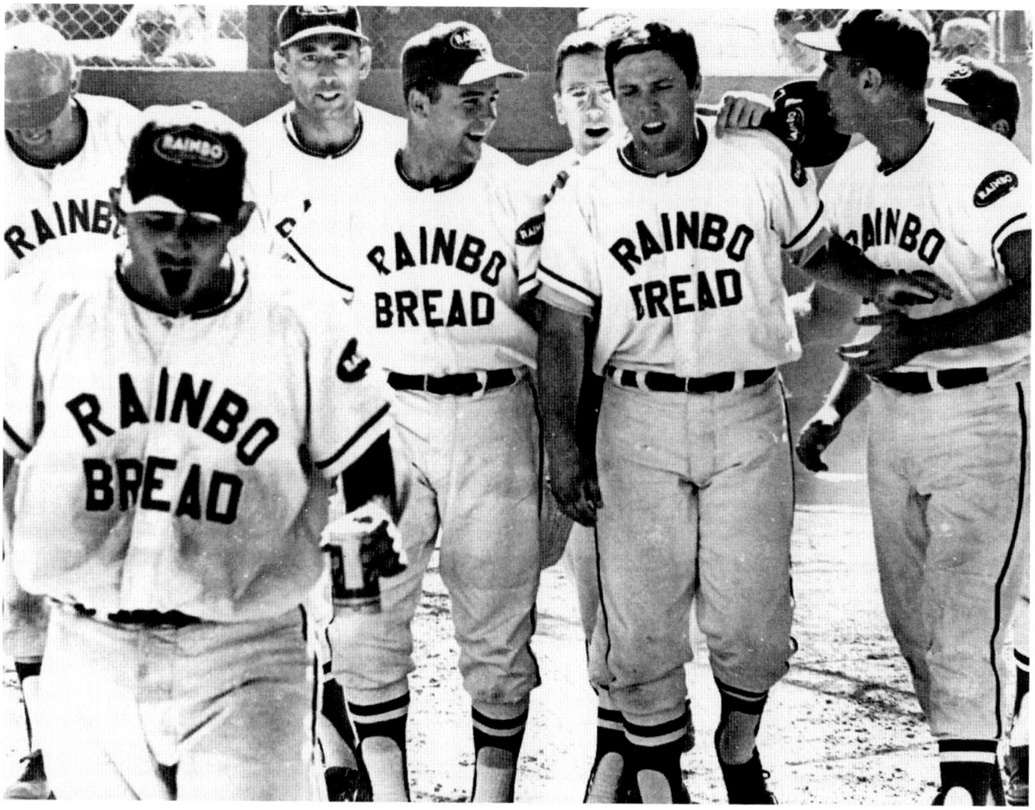

Cuno Barragán (third from left) celebrates with the team he managed after retiring from the Chicago Cubs in 1963. He secured sponsorship from the Rainbo Bread Company. Eventually, Barragán managed La Fiesta, another Sacramento baseball team. (Courtesy of Rick Cabral and Cuno Barragán.)

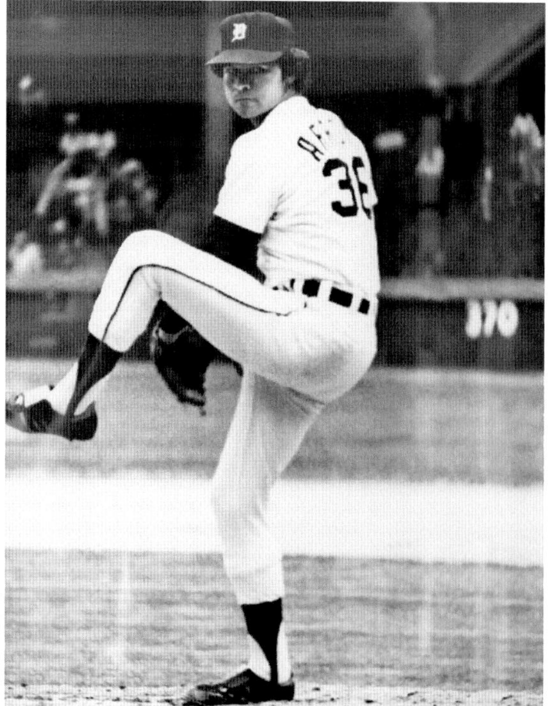

Shown here is Fred Arroyo of the Detroit Tigers. He was coached by Cuno Barragán while playing for La Fiesta. (Courtesy of Cuno Barragán.)

In 1971, Eddie Cervantes starred on the Sacramento City College team that won the Valley Conference championship. He was co-MVP and made All Conference as a shortstop hitting .362. He signed with the Baltimore Orioles and was assigned to Bluefield, West Virginia, in the Appalachian League. This was the beginning of seven years that took him to the Florida State, Northwest, and California Leagues. In the Northwest League, he played with an independent team, the Portland Mavericks, owned by Bing Russell. Bing's son, actor Kurt Russell, was a teammate along with Jim Bouton, an ex–New York Yankee and the author of *Ball Four.* Cervantes played seven more years in the Mexican Professional Leagues. (Courtesy of Eddie Cervantes.)

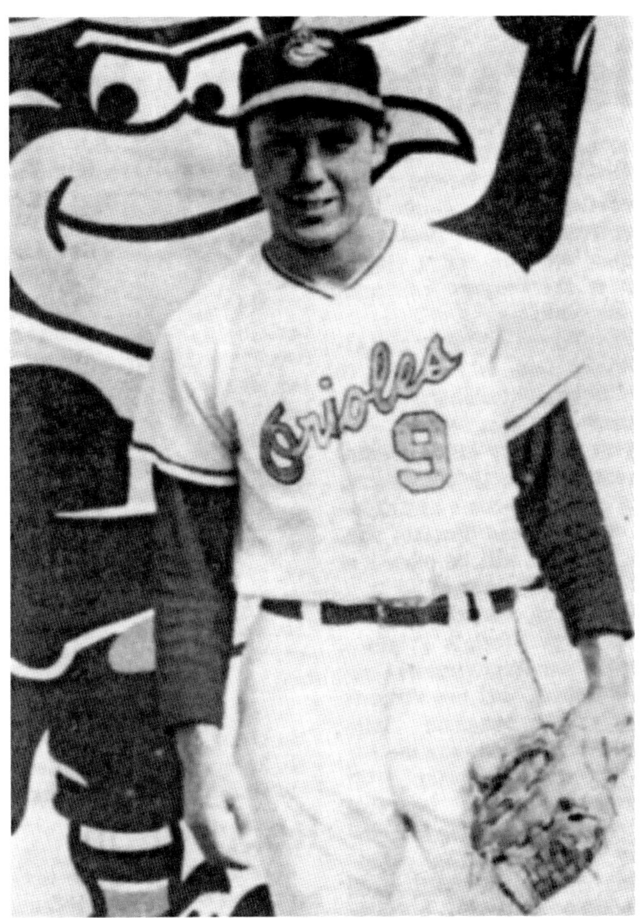

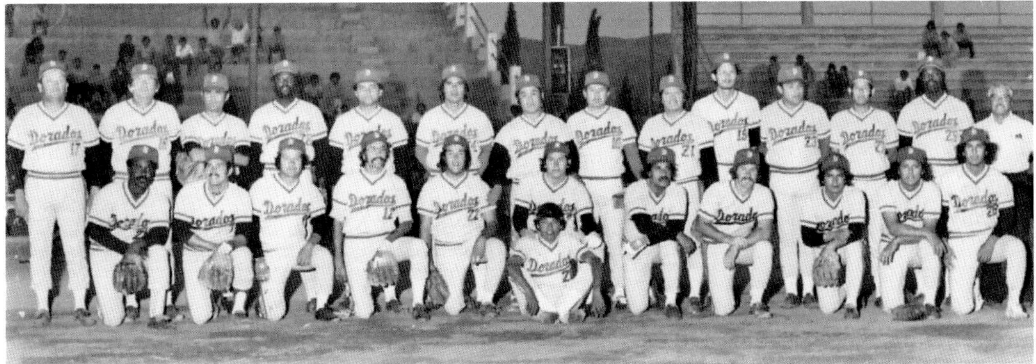

Released by the Atlanta Braves in 1976, Eric Cervantes was invited to spring training in Acapulco, Mexico, with the Chihuahua Dorados of the AAA Mexican League. His brother Eddie joined him on a tryout situation, not realizing his contract was still held by a Portland baseball club. Both made the team, and when the National Association of Professional Baseball Leagues realized the conflict in contracts, they ordered Eddie back to Portland. They are both shown in this team photo; Eric is at far right in the first row, and Eddie is next to him. (Courtesy of Eddie Cervantes.)

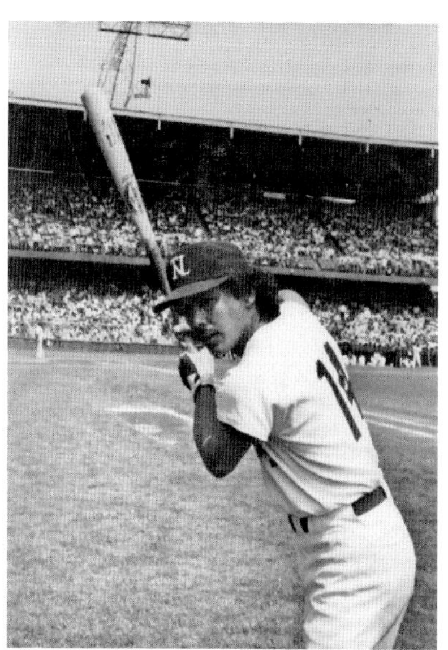

After a brief stint in 1976 with the Chihuahua Dorados, Eddie Cervantes returned to the Portland Mavericks. His contract was sold in 1977 to the Iowa Oaks, the AAA franchise of the Chicago White Sox. He went to spring training in 1978, and the Sox were going to option him out to a lower club. He instead asked for his release and rejoined his brother Eric that year in the AA Tabasco State League. Eddie played two seasons with the Macuspana Parrots before his contract was sold to the Nuevo Laredo Owls of the AAA Mexican League. He is pictured before a game in Mexico City at the Estadio Seguro Social. (Courtesy of Eddie Cervantes.)

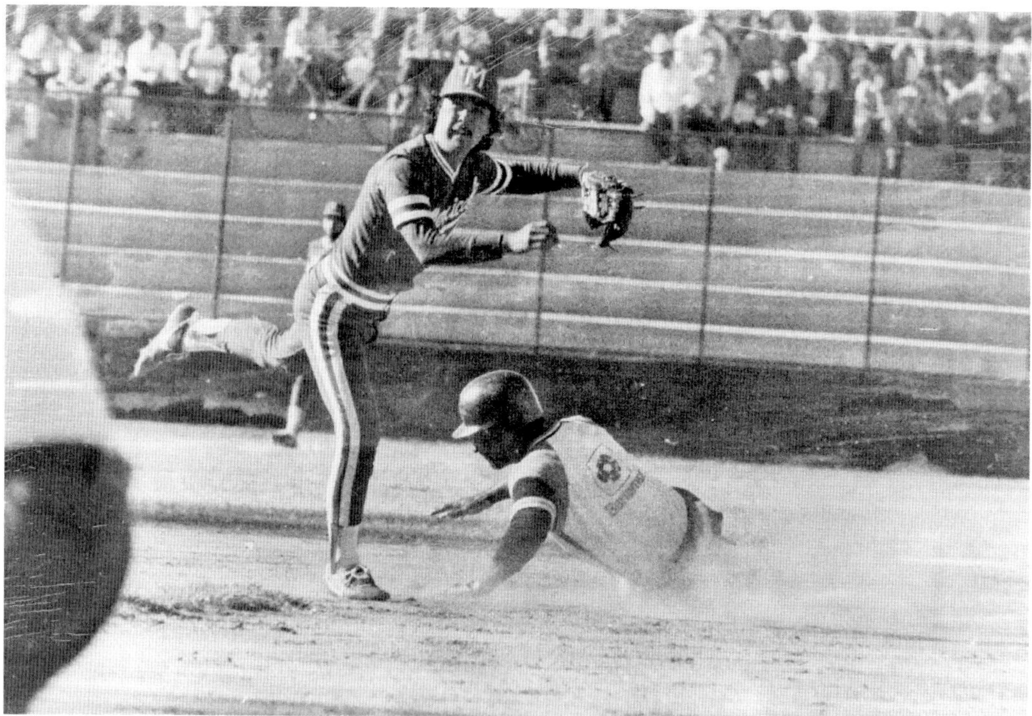

In October 1979, Eddie Cervantes began a four-season stretch with the Mexicali Aguilas (Eagles) in Mexico's Pacific Coast Winter League. He played in one all-star game, and this photograph shows him turning a double play while Alvin "Junior" Moore (Atlanta Braves and Chicago White Sox) slides into second base. Known for his elegant style of defensive play, "Silky" also produced with the bat. On November 11, 1980, he hit a two-run home run to end what could still be the longest game in Mexican Winter League history in the bottom of the 20th inning. (Courtesy of Eddie Cervantes.)

A 1974 graduate of Hiram Johnson High School in Sacramento, Eric Cervantes was an All-City baseball selection in 1973 and 1974. He was picked in the ninth round of the 1974 draft by the Atlanta Braves. He is pictured in the on deck circle for the Kingsport Braves (an Atlanta affiliate) before having the game of his career: he hit for the cycle (single, double, triple and home run) against the Pulaski Phillies (a Philadelphia Phillies affiliate). In 1976, he was invited to spring training with the Chihuahua Dorados of the AAA Mexican League. He played for five seasons in Mexican professional baseball. (Courtesy of Eddie Cervantes.)

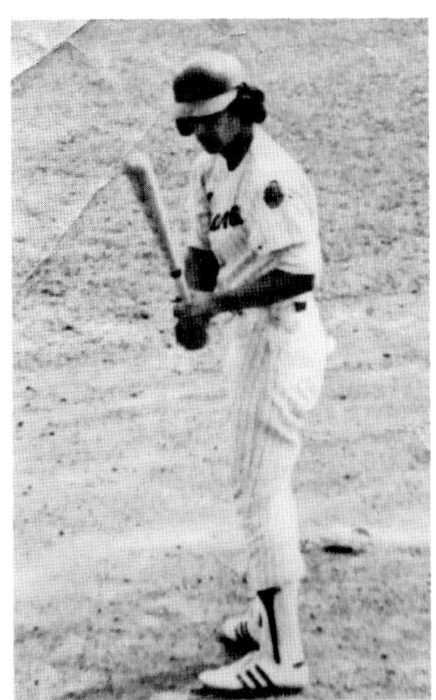

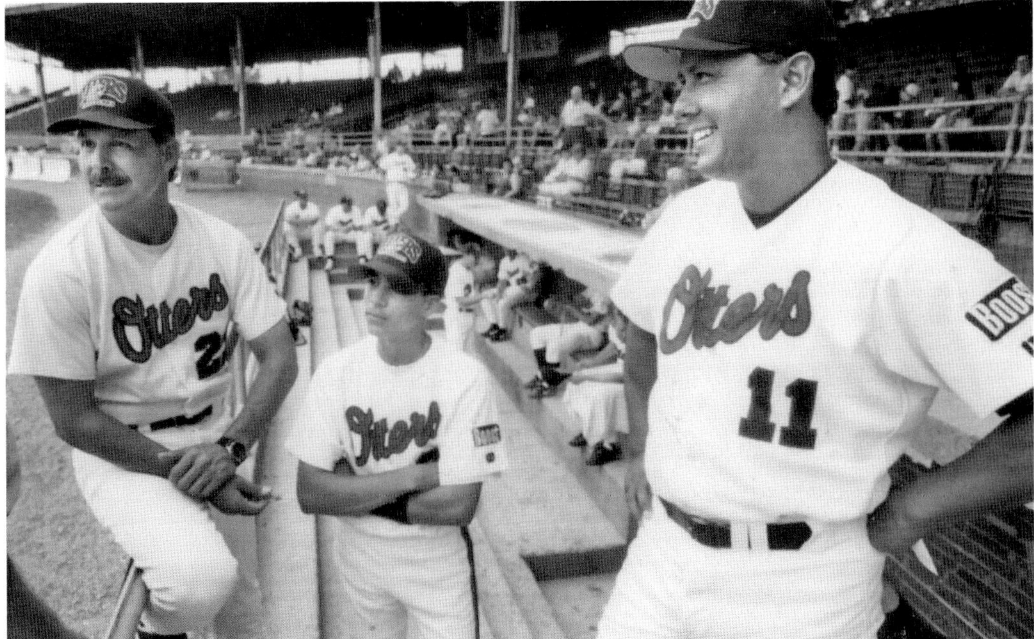

This photograph was taken in the dugout in Evansville, Indiana, in 1996. The team is the Evansville Otters, an independent pro team in the Frontier League. The manager is Fred "Fernando" Arroyo (far left). The infield and hitting coach is Eddie Cervantes (No. 11). Fernando and Eddie played against each other in Little League, high school, and American Legion baseball in Sacramento and during their professional careers in Mexico. Arroyo pitched for eight years in the major leagues, mostly with the Detroit Tigers. The Evansville stadium was used for filming parts of *A League of Their Own*, the story of women's professional baseball during World War II. (Courtesy of Eddie Cervantes.)

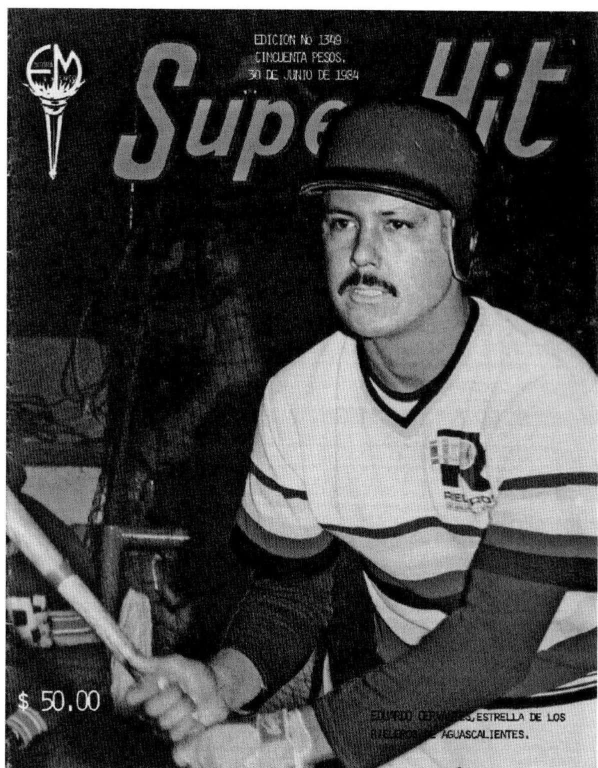

This is a 1984 issue of *Super Hit*, a baseball magazine in Mexico. Eddie Cervantes is featured on the cover after playing in the All-Star Game held in Aguascalientes, Mexico. He played for the Rieleros baseball club of Aguascalientes. (Courtesy of Eddie Cervantes.)

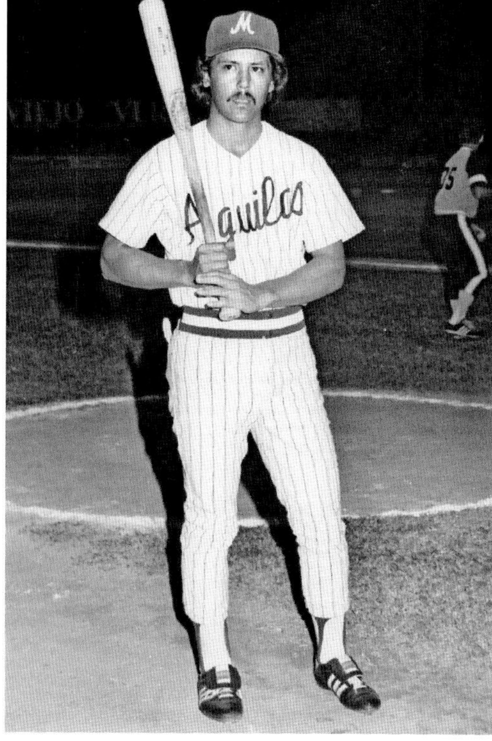

Eddie Cervantes is pictured in his Mexicali Aguilas uniform in the late 1970s. Mexican American baseball players have a long history of playing south of the US-Mexico border. The game often allowed these players to forge transnational solidarity with their Mexican counterparts and strengthen their connections to Mexican history and culture. (Courtesy of Eddie Cervantes.)

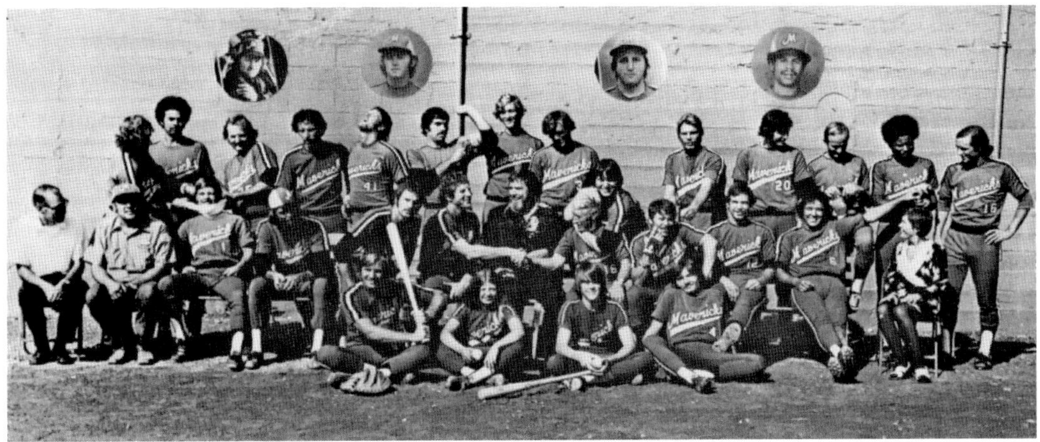

Eddie Cervantes (second row, second from right) is shown here with the Portland Mavericks. This team was part of the Northwest League and was owned by Bing Russell, father to actor Kurt Russell. (Courtesy of Eddie Cervantes.)

Cuno Barragán is shown in 1989 signing an autograph for a young fan. Barragán is wearing his Sacramento Solons cap and his Chicago Cubs jersey. This event was a fundraiser to aid the homeless and mentally ill. Former major-league players gathered to play local merchants, who paid a $250 donation to play against the ex-pros. (Courtesy of Mark Ocegueda.)

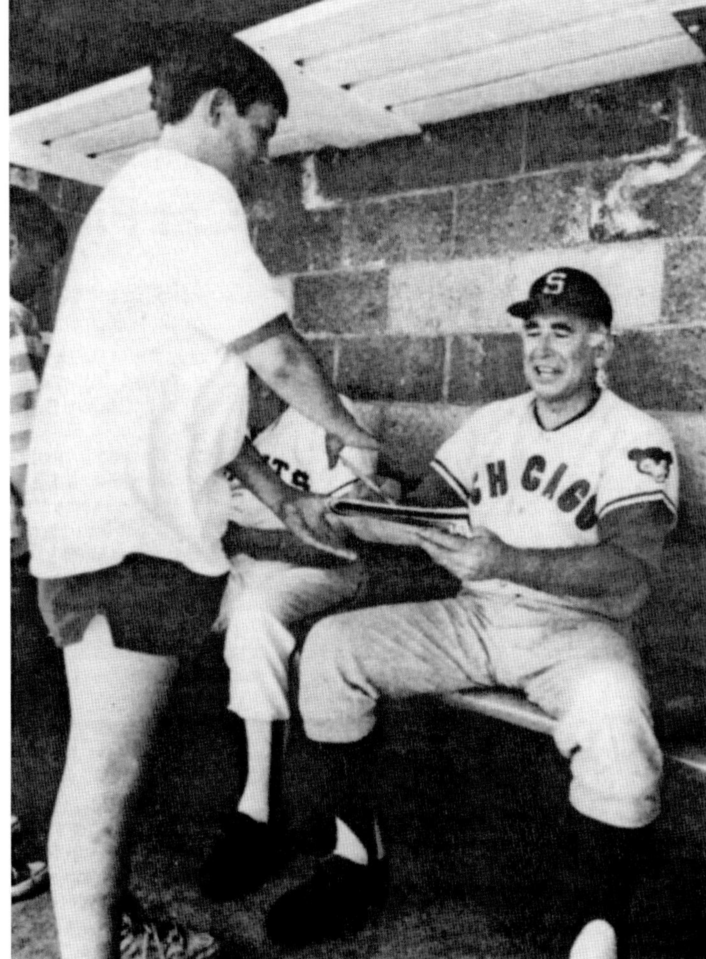

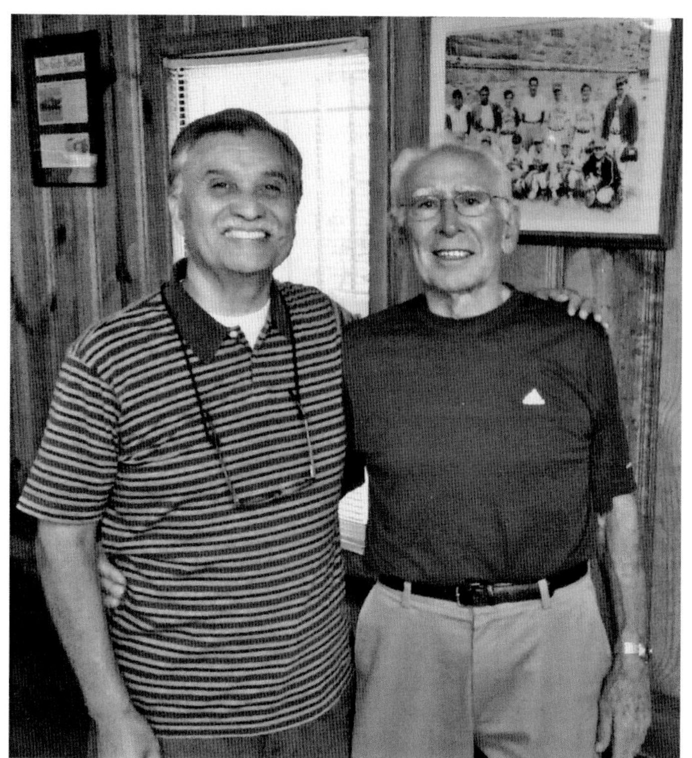

Prof. Richard Santillán (left) and Cuno Barragán, coauthors of this book, pose for a picture at the Mexican American Hall of Fame Sports Association building on Fruitridge Road. The hall of fame was an important site for the initial collecting of historic images featured in this book. It is still in operation and holds an annual induction ceremony for outstanding Mexican American athletes in the Sacramento area. The organization also fundraises for scholarships for young student-athletes. (Courtesy of Richard Santillán.)

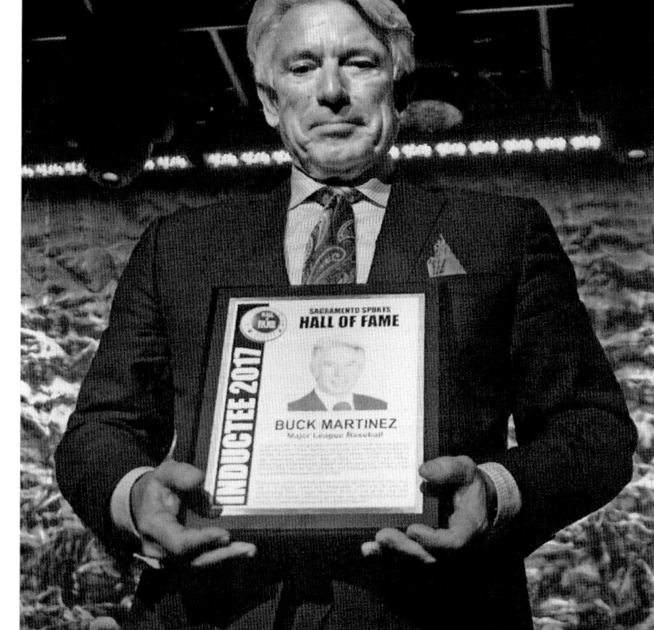

Elk Grove native Buck Martínez poses at the Sacramento Sports Hall of Fame induction ceremony in 2017. Martínez is the voice of the Toronto Blue Jays and had a 26 year career in the major leagues. (Courtesy of T.C. Martin and the Sacramento Sports Hall of Fame.)

The Upper San Joaquin Valley

Unlike in previous books in this series, the following chapters focus on one region of California: the San Joaquin Valley. Termed the "food basket" or "salad bowl" of the United States, the San Joaquin Valley stretches for about 8,000 to 10,000 square miles through the heartland of California. Wedged between the California Coastal Range to the west and the Sierra Nevada to the east, the valley is located south of the Sacramento–San Joaquin River Delta down to the Tehachapi Mountains in Kern and northern Los Angeles Counties. The upper San Joaquin Valley incorporates Merced, Stanislaus, and San Joaquin Counties.

In the early 20th century, teams played in Merced, Atwater, Livingston, Delhi, Turlock, Patterson, Modesto, Riverbank, Manteca, Tracy, and Stockton. Teams also existed in nearby areas throughout Northern California and the Bay Area, including Sacramento, Woodland, Grimes, Pittsburg, Martínez, Vallejo, Berkeley, San Francisco, San Jose, and Oakland.

In the upper San Joaquin Valley, incredible baseball pioneers dedicated their lives to the betterment of Mexican American sports and social life. They crafted community institutions that last to this day. Louis Villalovoz of Tracy constructed a baseball diamond in the 1930s on his farm to serve the town's Mexican American youth and helped organize the seminal Tracy Aztecas and Club Mexico Azules teams. Later in his career, he was instrumental in the construction of MacDonald Park and established the Guadalupe and Cristo Rey Centers in the Southside barrio.

Meeting in a Merced chicken coop in 1932, teenagers Salome Olivarez, Johnny Olivarez, Salvador "Chappo" Olivarez, Raymond Contreras, Dave Contreras, Jesse Padilla, and John Padilla created Club Mercedes. In response to a sense of isolation, the organization provided a much needed positive outlet for Mexican American youths. Club Mercedes welcomed all and was the first integrated team in Merced, including white and black players. Club Mercedes continues to support local Little League and high school sports. In addition, it awards college scholarships to local high school students among several other philanthropic activities.

Mexican Americans in Stockton responded similarly to a lack of integrated leagues in their city. In 1955, a group of managers transformed a decades-old San Joaquin Valley baseball network into a centralized league when they founded the Stockton California Mexican League. Esequiel "Tubby" Álvarez, Roy Álvarez, Frank Chico, Ray López, Del Ortega, Henry Perez, Henry Plata, and Frank Serrano sat on the board of directors that officially formed the league. Numerous others were essential in the growth of the league, including Jesús "Sue" Valverde, Ben Valverde, José "Mousey" Zaragoza, Primo Orosco, Sachus Orosco, and Reubén Limón. Their legacy lives on, as the Cal-Mex League currently fields 18 teams featuring current and former high school, college, and professional players who hone their skills every Sunday at Stribley Park.

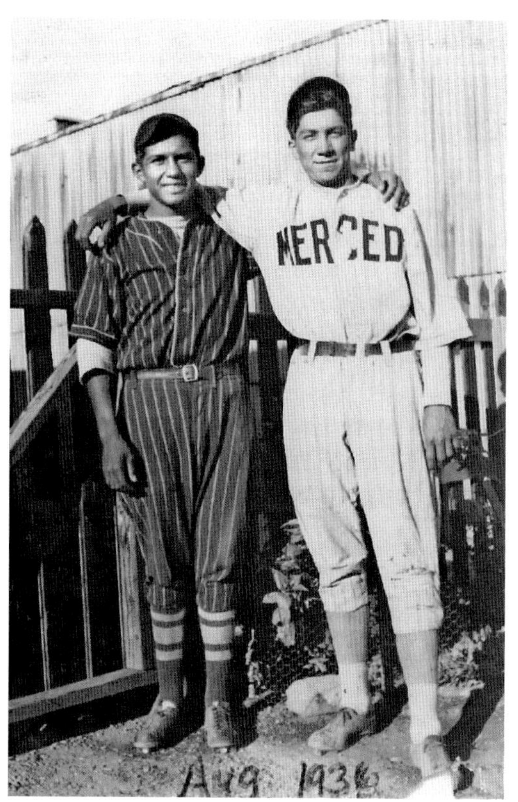

Merced players Dave Contreras (left) and ? Mojica pose in August 1936. Contreras was born in Stockton in 1920 and grew up in Merced, living with his family on Fourteenth Street. His mother, Estefana, was born in Hanford, California, and his father, Jesús, came from Mexico. Contreras played for the Eagles, while Mojica likely played for the rival Aztecas team. Players often interchanged between the Eagles and Aztecas, the earliest Mexican American teams in Merced. Contreras worked as a trucker and forklift operator at Cross Lumber Company for decades transporting lumber to the surrounding areas. Dave Jr. fondly remembers riding along with his father delivering lumber to Curry Village in the Yosemite Valley. (Courtesy of Dave Contreras Jr.)

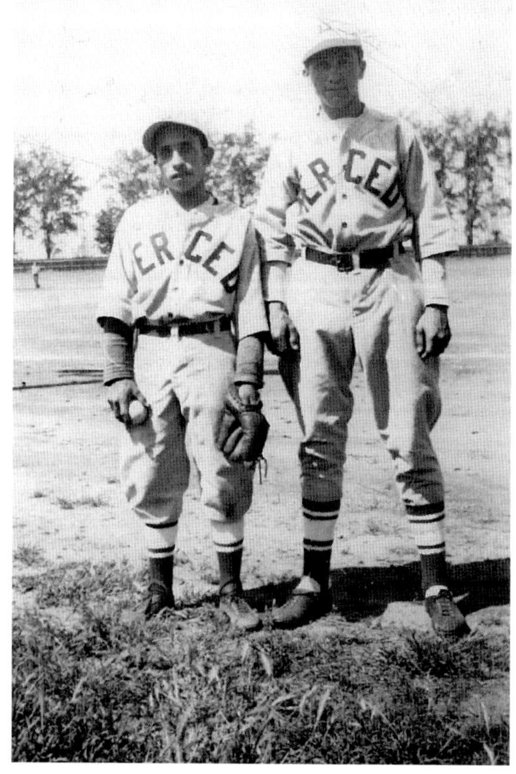

Merced Eagles players Johnny Olivarez (left) and Harold Arancibia are pictured in the 1930s. Arancibia was catcher, while the speedy Olivarez led off and played center field. Born in Jalisco, Mexico, in 1915, Olivarez moved with his family to Amsterdam in Merced County, California, where his father, Juan, worked for the Yosemite Valley Railroad. After moving to the city of Merced, Johnny and his father worked in the fields and for Stribling Nursery. His brother Salome was the ranch foreman. Olivarez and his close friends helped form Club Mercedes in the 1930s. In 2017, Johnny Olivarez was inducted into the Merced High School Athletic Hall of Fame (baseball and track, 1933–1934). (Courtesy of Dave Contreras Jr. and Raymond Olivarez.)

Brothers Dave (left) and Raymond Contreras of the Merced Eagles stand in the open landscape at Bear Creek Park in the 1930s. Merced maintained a rural identity at this time. Many families raised livestock and vegetables and hunted animals such as bear and duck. Mexican American teams played against white and black teams. After games, the wives of the hosting team's players cooked for everyone. These friendly feasts gave players the opportunity to try new food. The Applegate Park Zoo now stands on the former site of the Bear Creek Field. Dave Contreras was inducted into the Merced High School Athletic Hall of Fame in 2016. (Courtesy of Dave Contreras Jr.)

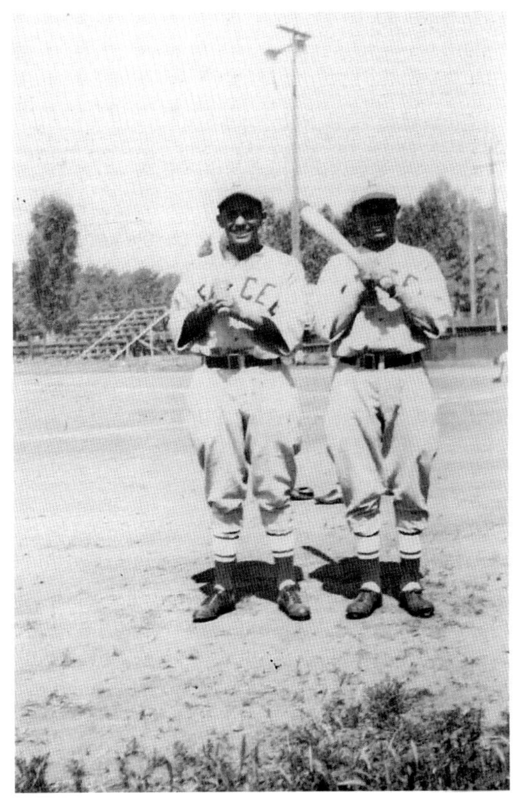

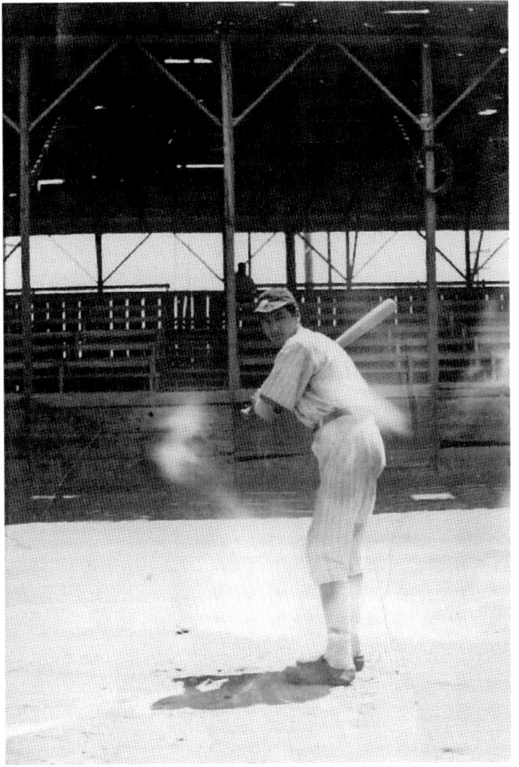

Jesse Padilla bats at Bear Creek Field in August 1936. Padilla was an acclaimed power hitter for the Merced Eagles. Born in Jalisco in 1919, he and his family immigrated in the 1920s to Gary, Indiana, where his father, Ricardo, worked for the railroad. After settling in Merced, Jesse worked in the fig orchards at Montgomery Farms. Major agricultural products in Merced at the time included cotton, figs, tomatoes, and corn. Jesse's brother John also played for the Eagles. The Padilla brothers, along with close friends Salome Olivarez, Johnny Olivarez, Salvador "Chappo" Olivarez, Raymond Contreras, and Dave Contreras, founded Club Mercedes in 1932. (Courtesy of Dave Contreras Jr. and Eddie Padilla.)

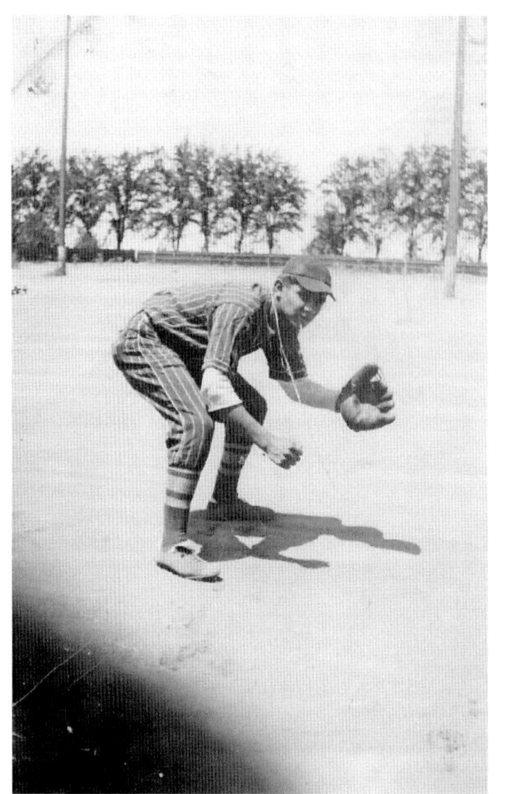

Merced Eagles shortstop Dave Contreras fields his position at Bear Creek Field in 1936. That year, he became the first Merced High School athlete to receive the All-America blanket award for football. In 1938, he received the All-America blanket award for baseball. Contreras married Evelyn Soria on the day before Pearl Harbor. He received an offer to play college baseball but soon embarked for the war, serving with the Army in the Aleutian Islands. In 1932, Contreras and his Eagles teammates formed Club Mercedes, an organization that provides athletic and social opportunities for the local youth. The Club Mercedes Hall opened in 1947 and is still located on the corner of Ninth and M Streets. Club Mercedes operates as a nonprofit service organization that supports the Merced community in several ways, such as raising money for the needy, holding socials, and providing student scholarships to Merced College and Cal State Stanislaus. (Courtesy of Dave Contreras Jr.)

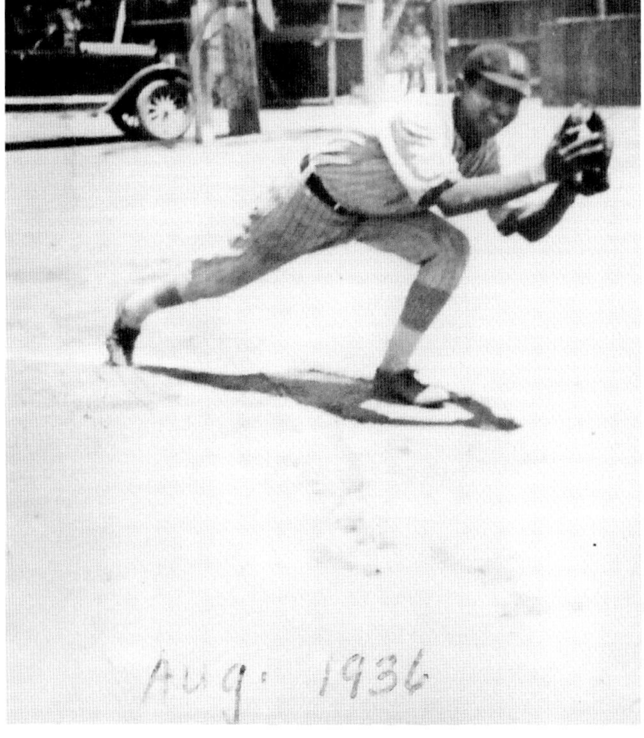

First baseman Raymond Contreras makes the play at Bear Creek Field in 1936. Brothers Raymond, Dave, and Danny Contreras were stalwart members of the Merced Eagles throughout the 1930s. During World War II, Raymond served as a Spanish translator for the military, Dave served with the Army in the Pacific, and Danny served on a battleship in the Navy. The tight-knit Contreras, Olivarez, and Padilla families, founders of Club Mercedes, lived next to each other on Fourteenth and Fifteenth Streets, their houses connected by an alleyway. The families were further connected through marriage. (Courtesy of Dave Contreras Jr.)

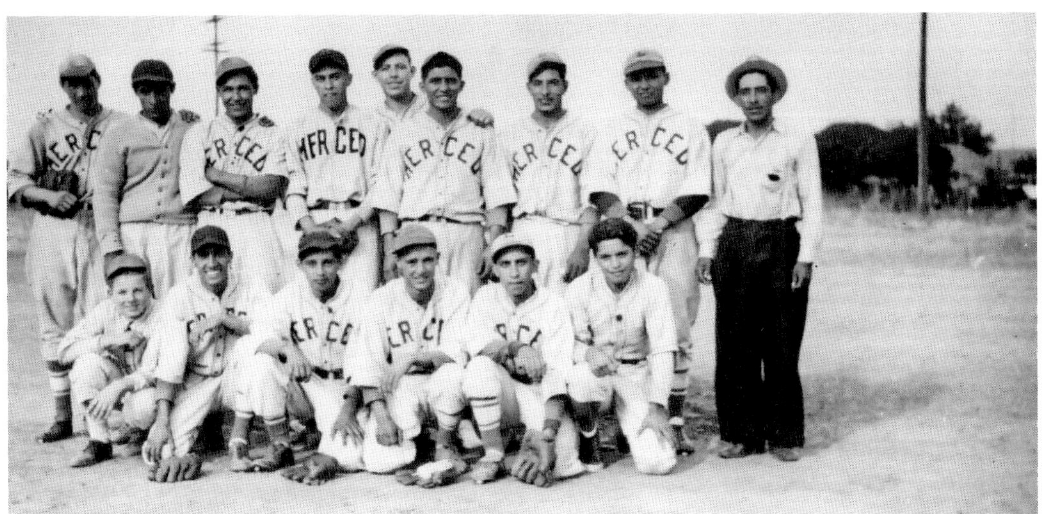

The Merced Eagles gather in this 1930s photograph. From left to right are (first row) unidentified, Ray Septién, unidentified, John Padilla, Johnny Olivarez, and unidentified; (second row) two unidentified, Jesse Padilla, Salvador "Chappo" Olivarez, Román Contreras, Dave Contreras, Mike Hernández, Raymond Contreras, and manager Salome Olivarez. Other Merced Eagles players of the 1930s were Eddie Gómez, Lester Martínez, Frank Martínez, Pete Buendía, Shuie Gonzáles, Tacho Moreno, Primo Chávez, Ysidro Mariscal, John Mariscal, Howard Cullen, Gail Phillips, Manuel Valverde, Harold Arancibia, Earl Nursement, and E.B. Alcorn. (Courtesy of Dave Contreras Jr.)

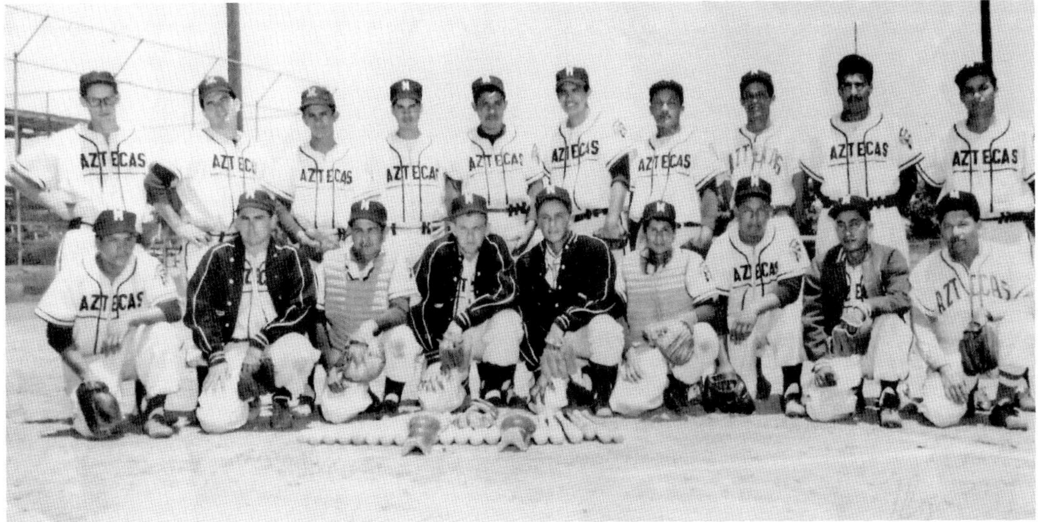

This mid-century Merced Aztecas team included Manuel Chávez (first row, third from left), Art Gutiérrez (second row, fifth from left), Seco Cárdenas (second row, fifth from right), and Frank Ybarra (second row, fourth from right). The Merced Aztecas date to the early 1930s. A 1931 Los Angeles *La Opinión* article reported that the Aztecas defeated the Fresno International club. Other Azteca players from the 1930s to the 1950s were from the Abercremaie, Apodaca, Espinoza, Faulkenberry, Flores, Gálvez, García, Gutiérrez, Haley, Mariscal, Martínez, Marvin, Mendoza, Ochoa, Ornelas, Orozco, Rocha, Santillán, Soriano, and Valdez families. (Courtesy of Dave Contreras Jr.)

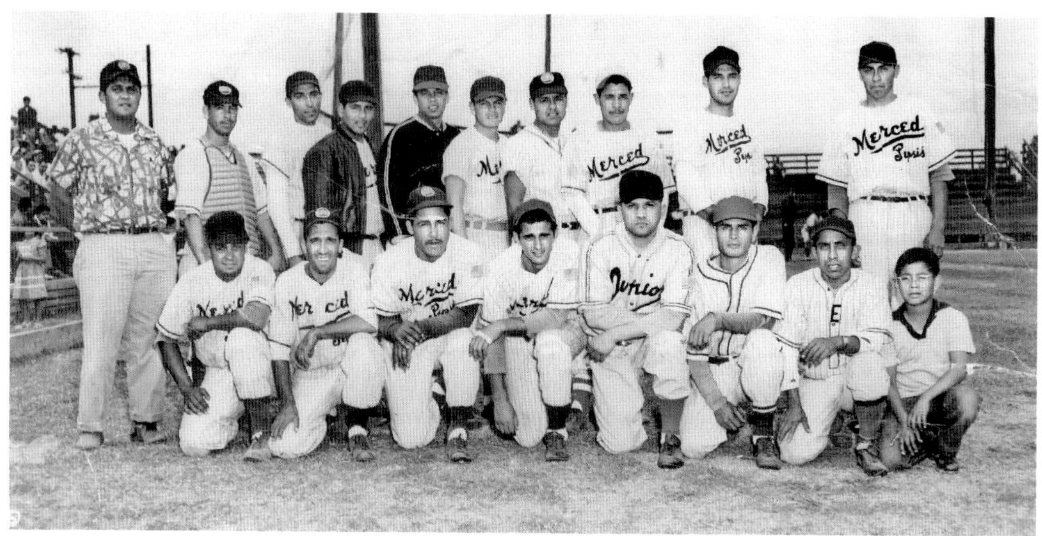

This 1950s Merced Pepsi team included, from left to right, (first row) Chava Sánchez, Ray Septién, Jesse Padilla, unidentified, Danny Contreras, unidentified, Johnny Olivarez, and Steve Contreras; (second row) manager Dave Contreras, Eddie Gómez, unidentified, ? Mariscal, Seco Cárdenas, Roy León, Rubén Padilla, Art Gutiérrez, unidentified, and Salvador "Chappo" Olivarez. Other players on 1950s Pepsi teams included Mike Hernández, Dick Kaylor, Larry Kaylor, and E.B. Alcorn. At the time, Pepsi operated two major bottling and distribution plants in Merced. (Courtesy of Dave Contreras Jr.)

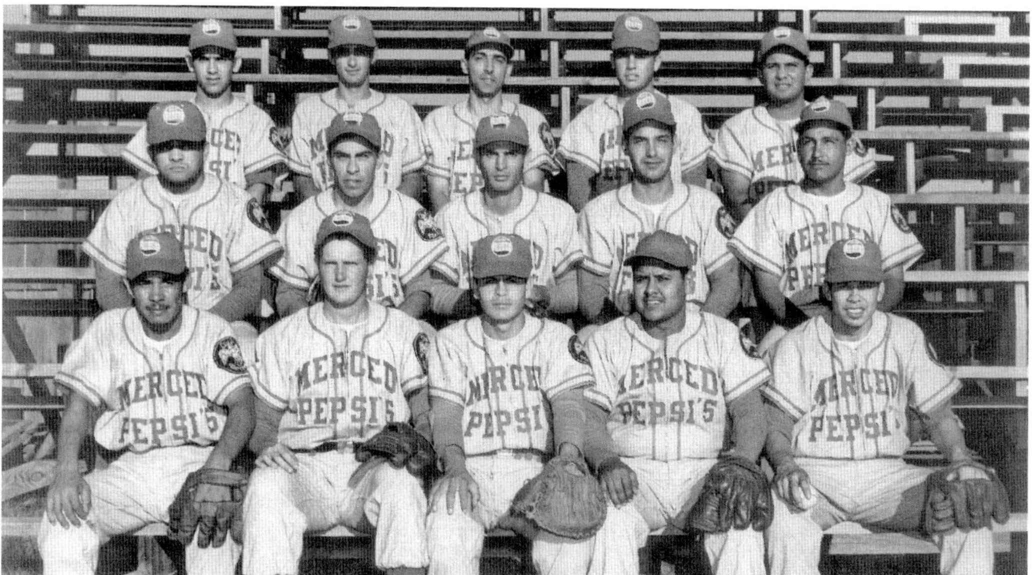

The Merced Pepsis participated in the 1953 California State Tournament. They are, from left to right, (first row) Art Gutiérrez, two unidentified, Rubén Padilla, and Seco Cardenas; (second row) Danny Contreras, Salvador "Chappo" Olivarez, two unidentified, and Jesse Padilla; (third row) two unidentified, Johnny Olivarez, unidentified, and Dave Contreras. Salvador "Chappo" Olivarez played for the prestigious Merced Bears professional team in 1941. (Courtesy of Dave Contreras Jr.)

Mercedes club batboy Bill Contreras shows off his baseball gear in the 1950s. He traveled with the team to Stockton, Modesto, and Sacramento. The son of Dave Contreras, Bill followed in the family baseball tradition, playing at Merced Junior College and for the Planada Latin American Club. He remains actively involved in Club Mercedes operations along with his brothers Dave, Les, and Fred and sons Chris and Willie. Club Mercedes continues to operate as an important institution in the Merced community. Some of the club's projects include its annual Thanksgiving Feed and Clothing Giveaway, awarding six educational scholarships every year, and cooking pregame meals for Merced high school football players. (Courtesy of Bill Contreras.)

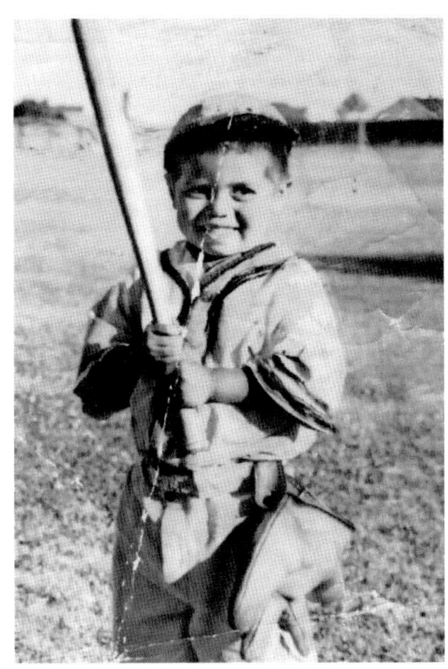

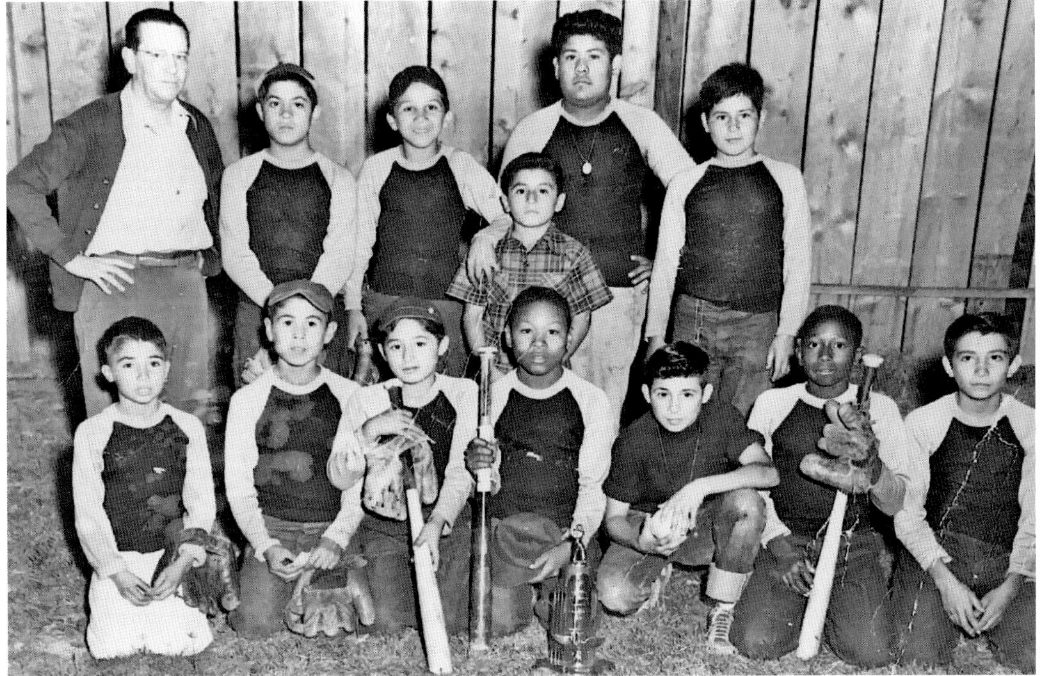

This Club Mercedes team from the late 1940s includes, from left to right, (first row) Johnny Olivarez Jr., Manuel Chávez, Sonny Ávila, ? Huddleston, two unidentified, and Jesse Montes; (second row) two unidentified, Nino Gutiérrez, Bob Ávila, Jesse Gonzáles, and unidentified. Founded in a chicken coop outside the Olivarez house in the early 1930s, Club Mercedes began as an athletic and social club that welcomed Merced youths from all backgrounds. They were the first team in Merced to include Mexican American, white, and black players from all sections of town. Johnny Olivarez Jr. became an outstanding quarterback and baseball player in high school. (Courtesy of Dave Contreras Jr.)

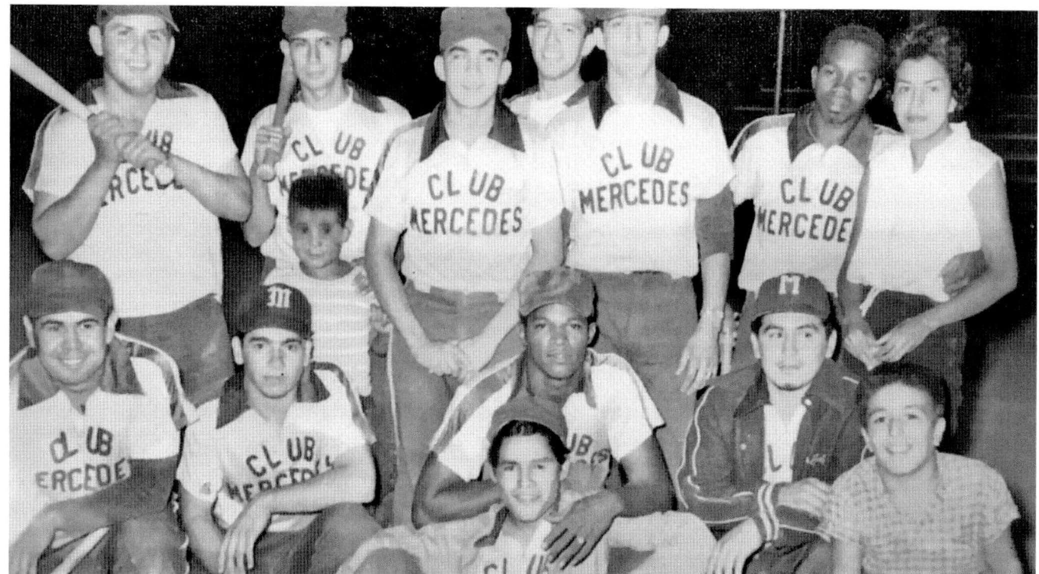

Players on this 1960s Club Mercedes team include Manuel Chávez, Bob Juárez, Vernon Wood, Mike Buena, Bob Ávila, Rubén García, Gil Torres, John Fernández, and ? Mendoza. In 1997 and 2007, the US Congress recognized Club Mercedes for its 50th and 60th anniversaries, praising the organization's purpose "to promote, carry on, and further the interest of the youth of the community; to carry on projects for the benefit of the fields of recreation, amusement, athletics, social relations, education, and American citizenship." (Courtesy of Dave Contreras Jr.)

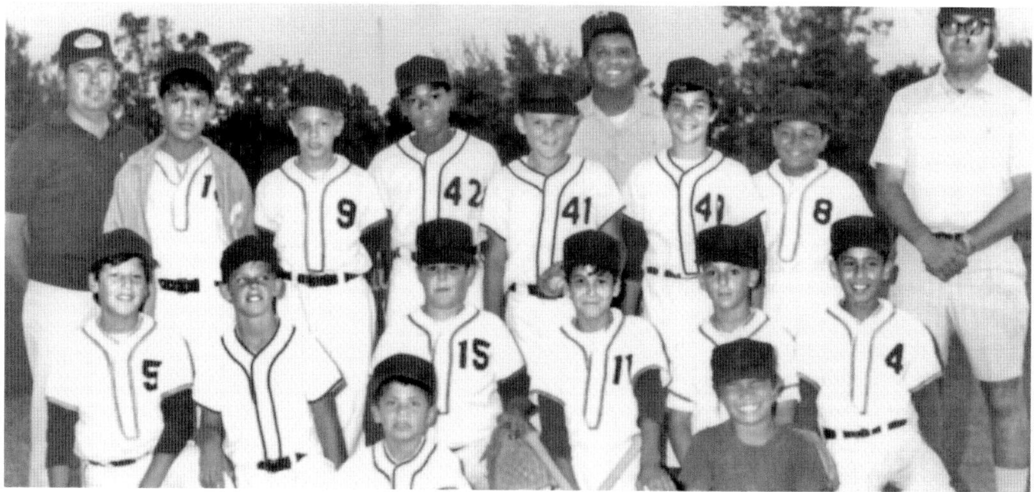

This 1960s Club Mercedes team includes, from left to right, (first row) Billy López, Whitey Watson, batboy Tommy Carrasco, unidentified, Andy Perezchica, Vic Macías, batboy John Contreras, and Robert Carrasco; (second row) coach Amado Castillo, unidentified, Mark Pazin, Corkie Harris, unidentified, coach Dave Contreras, two unidentified players, and an unidentified coach. In addition to managing Club Mercedes, Dave Contreras coached in the Babe Ruth League in the 1950s and in Little League in the 1960s. During the late 1960s, he built championship teams in the Central Valley Mexican American league. (Courtesy of Dave Contreras Jr.)

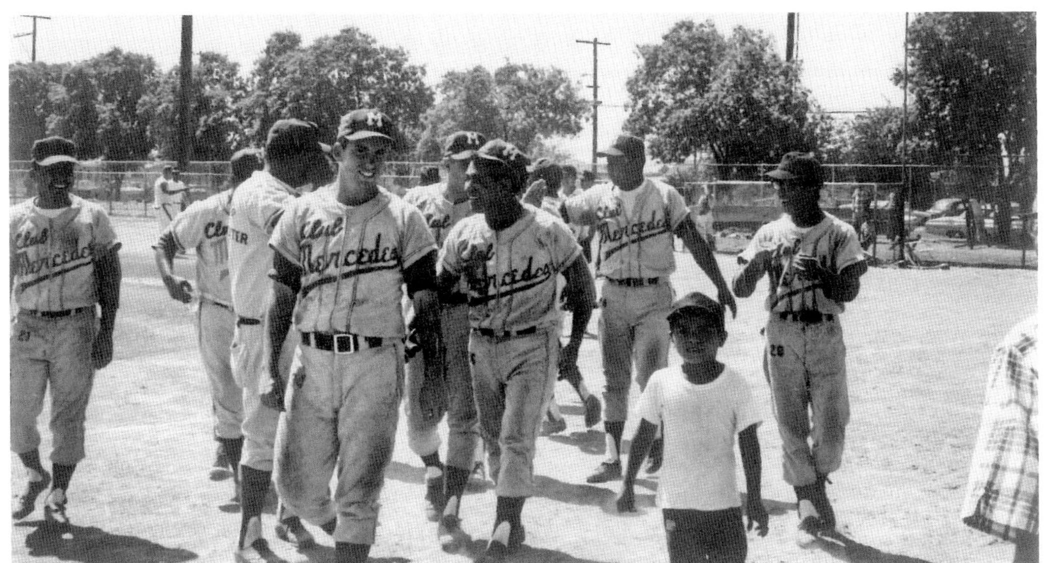

In 1967, Club Mercedes players celebrate after defeating the Madera Merchants in the Central Valley championship game at McNamara Park in Merced. The boy in front is John Contreras. The team roster featured manager Dave Contreras, coach Manuel Chávez, Bill Contreras, Steve Contreras, Les Contreras, Johnny Olivarez Jr., Jimmy Visher, Charlie Visher, Joe Pangelina, Dave Mendoza, Carl Mays, Danny Guzmán, Bob Rollins, Howard Cullen, and Eugene Breinig. Bill and Steve Contreras played at Merced Junior College, while Les Contreras played at the University of Nevada, Las Vegas. Danny Guzmán, Eugene Breinig, and Jimmy Visher later played professional baseball. (Courtesy of Dave Contreras Jr.)

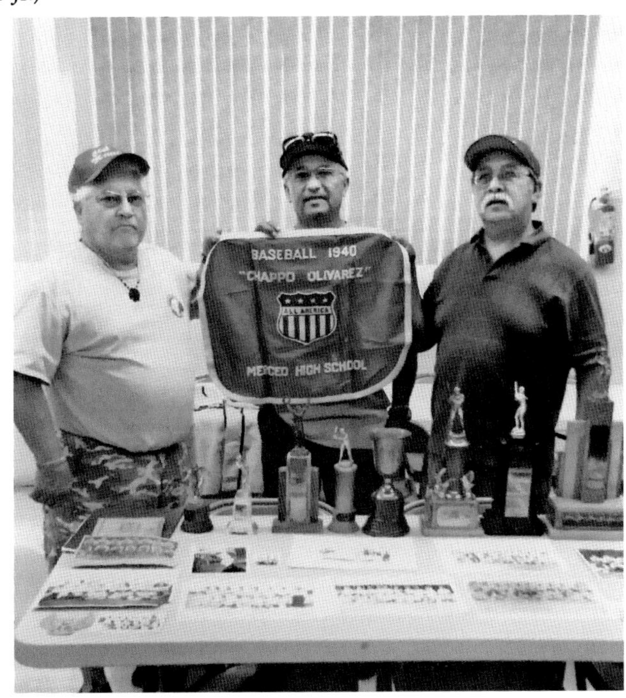

Seen in July 2015 at Club Mercedes Hall in Merced are, from left to right, Raymond Olivarez, Les Contreras, and Dave Contreras Jr. They are holding up the 1940 All-America award blanket belonging to their uncle Salvador "Chappo" Olivarez. A talented knuckleballer, Salvador would have signed a professional contract if not for World War II. His family and other club founders' descendants continue the legacy of Club Mercedes. The club currently awards college scholarships to local high school students, donates food and clothing to the needy, and sponsors Little League teams. (Courtesy of Richard A. Santillán.)

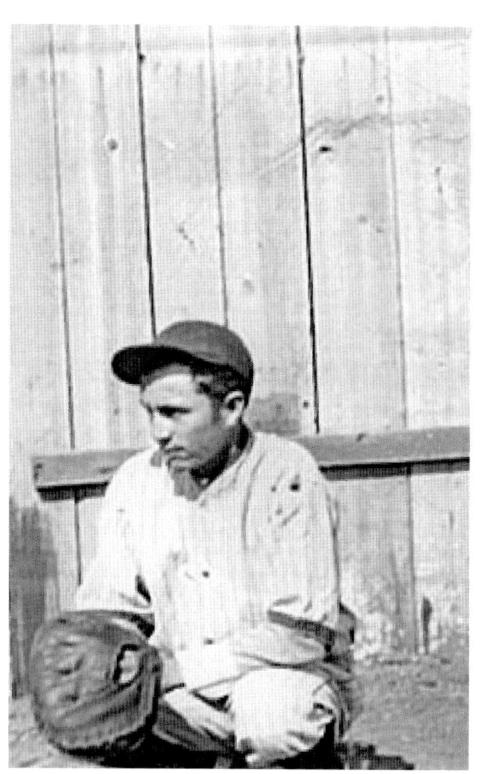

Tracy Aztecas catcher Louis Jurado Villalovoz warms up in the early 1930s. He was born in Solomonville, Arizona, in 1910 and grew up in the nearby town of Safford. In 1919, his family moved to California, caravanning in a new Ford Model T car and truck. They lived throughout the San Fernando Valley and South Bay regions of Los Angeles County, where Louis formed early teams. In 1930, his family moved to Tracy to pick prunes. Villalovoz worked hard and eventually owned over 30 acres. Since Mexican American teams in Tracy's Southside barrio had nowhere to play, he transformed part of his orchard into a baseball field, dragging the diamond with a railroad rail hooked to the back of the Model T. (Courtesy of Steve Villalovoz.)

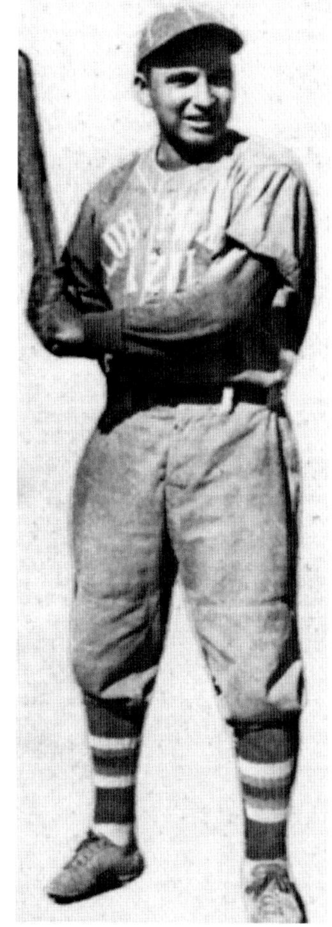

Louis Villalovoz, shown in 1941, cofounded the Tracy Aztecas and Club Mexico Azules baseball teams in the 1930s. For him, like many other Mexican Americans, sports were a gateway to civic leadership. Organizing teams provided valuable experience that helped shape him into the widely proclaimed "Mr. Tracy." Villalovoz subdivided 40 acres of land in Tracy, providing mortgages with no interest to low-income families. He founded and led the Guadalupe Society for several decades, served on the Tracy School Board from 1961 to 1973 and on the Tracy Recreation Commission, and acted as PTA president, among several other leadership positions. He worked in dairy farming, for the Southern Pacific Railroad, and at the Tracy oil refinery. His numerous honors include the San Joaquin County El Buen Vecino award, Latin Athletic Club Award, induction into the Tracy Sports Hall of Fame, and lifetime membership with the California Department of Parks and Recreation. Louis J. Villalovoz Elementary School opened in 1987. (Courtesy of *Tracy Press* and Virginia Villalovoz Vásquez.)

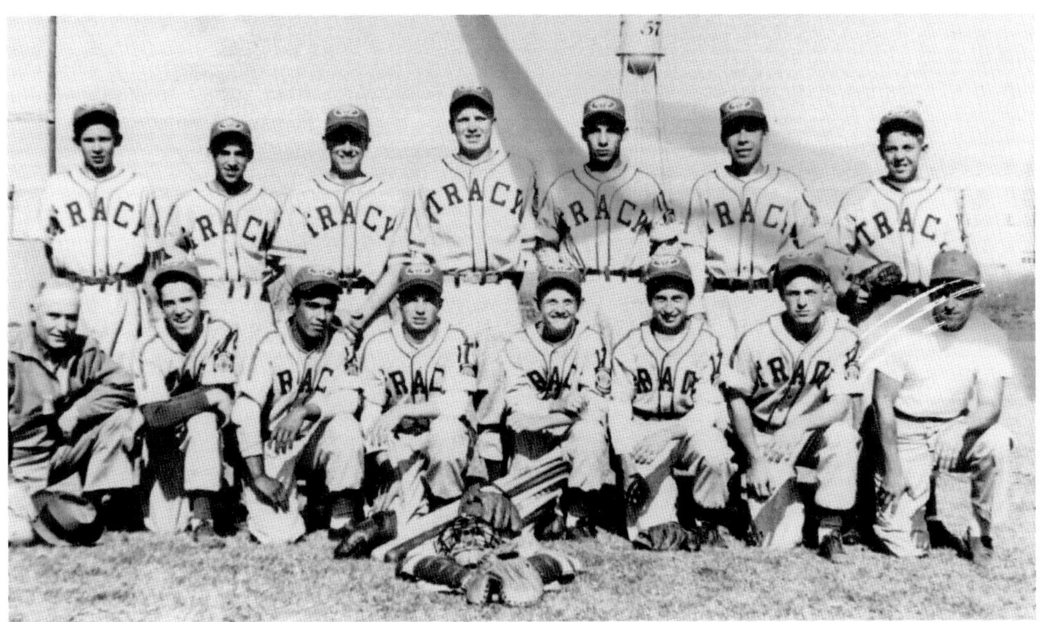

The 1948 Tracy Junior Legion district champions include, from left to right, (first row) John Philip Sousa, Al Cardoza, Al Moreno, Bob Couch, Bill Giffen, Jess Salas, Ed Pérez, and manager George Mandish; (second row) Henry Ottenstroer, Jess Gutiérrez, Stan Butolph, Russ Holcomb, Ray Ortega, Vince Osorno, and Jay Mattson. The Ortega family, the "first family of baseball" in Tracy, included six brothers: Del, Pete, Joe, and Ray Ortega and Jess and Bob Gutiérrez. They made up the backbone of many teams, such as the Tracy Aztecas, Tracy Club Mexico Azules, Spanish Caballeros, Latin Vets, Latin Athletic Club, Mi Ranchito, and Sun Valley Creamery. (Courtesy of Steve Villalovoz.)

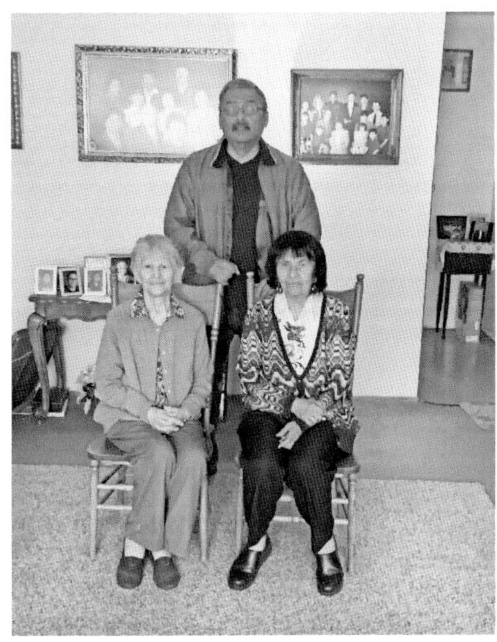

From left to right, Virginia Villalovoz Vásquez, Steve Villalovoz, and Maxine Villalovoz Gonzáles meet in Tracy in April 2018. In the early 1930s, Louis Villalovoz married Lucy Gutiérrez, who hailed from Canoga Park. Their children were Virginia Villalovoz Vásquez, Maxine Villalovoz Gonzáles, Louis Villalovoz Jr., David William Villalovoz, Diana Villalovoz, Frank Villalovoz, and Steve Villalovoz. The family lived in a brick house on their 30-acre farm. They grew vegetables, fruits, almonds, and walnuts and raised chickens, rabbits, and cows. Louis Villalovoz Sr. worked for Southern Pacific and developed real estate. Virginia and Maxine played baseball and softball in town, including for the Tracy Defense Depot. (Courtesy of Christopher Docter.)

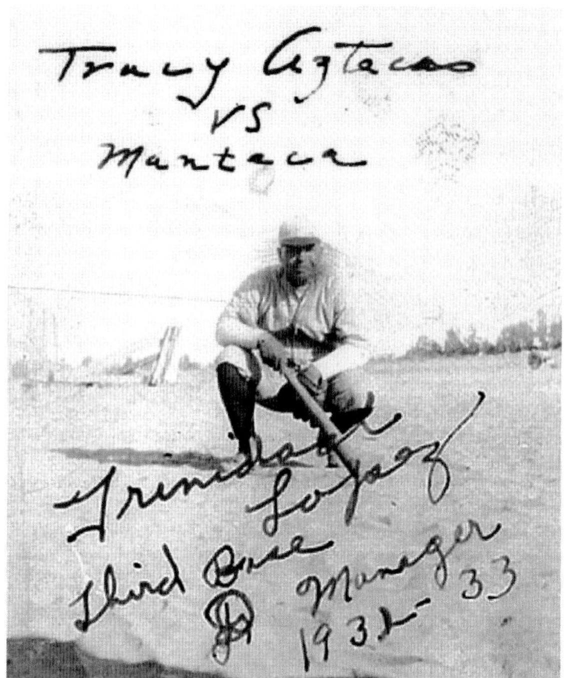

Trinidad López managed and played third base for the Tracy Aztecas in 1932–1933. Born in 1912 in Mexico to parents from Zacatecas, Trinidad López crossed the border with his family in the mid-1910s, settling in Tracy by the early 1930s. He worked as a maintenance foreman with the Southern Pacific Railroad for 34 years. López passed away on May 1, 2014, at the age of 101. The Aztecas of the 1930s and Club Mexico Azules of the 1940s included players from the Adame, Aguilar, Ávila, Bronich, Christian, Escobar, Flores, García, López, Martínez, Morelos, Moreno, Ortega/Gutiérrez, Pérez, Rangel, Romo, Villalovoz, and Zaragoza families. (Courtesy of Steve Villalovoz.)

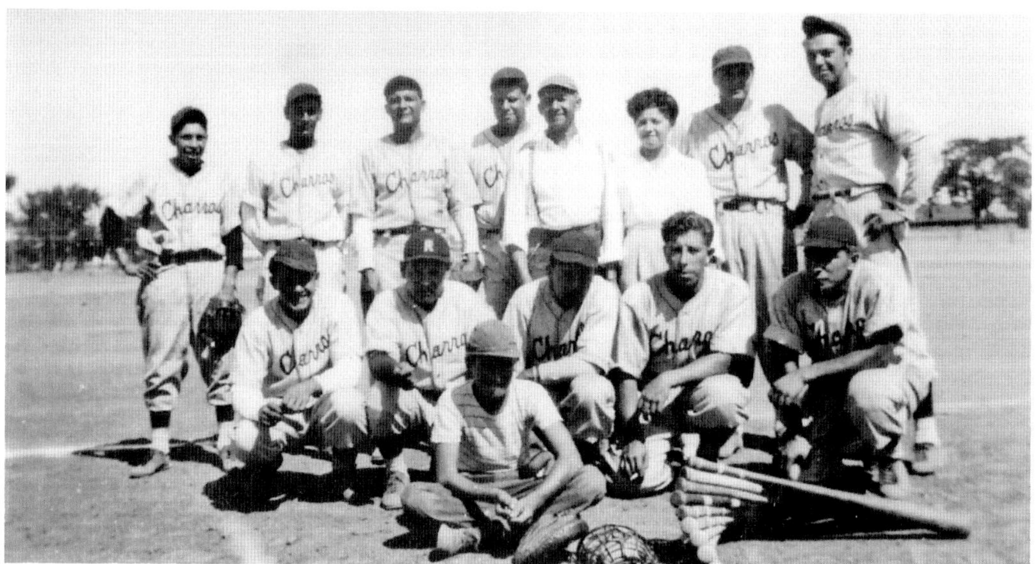

The Riverbank-Modesto Charros, photographed in the 1930s–1940s, competed throughout their home of Stanislaus County and all over California, even at Folsom Prison. The Charros and Merchants were the major Mexican American teams in Riverbank-Modesto. Players for these teams included A. Alfaro, L. Alfaro, L. Alonzo, J. Bordona, R. Cabrera, N. Carlo, M. Carrillo, ? Carrillo, Joe Estrada, Pete Estrada, W. Francisco, A. García, C. García, P. García, A. Gonzáles, A. Hernández, E. Hernández, T. Herriage, E. Jiménez, S. Jiménez, J. López, C. Martínez, John Monges, R. Monges, F. Navarro, F. Rodríguez, O. Sandoval, T. Tirado, J. Ulloa, and D. Vallo. (Courtesy of Cecelia Estrada and Félix Ulloa.)

As a teenager, Roy Álvarez left his home state of Sonora and moved to Stockton to pick asparagus. In the early 1930s, he was a charter member of the Stockton Mexico and Club Charro teams. Roy and brother Esequiel "Tubby" Álvarez worked for the Fibreboard Products plant in Stockton and played on the company team. They played on Mexico teams throughout the 1940s and 1950s and helped form the California Mexican League in 1955. Tubby served as the original league president and played on Club Mexico as a left-handed catcher. Roy was a gifted pitcher who received an offer to play for the Oakland Oaks of the PCL. He later managed Castillo Brothers, the first team to win the California Mexican League title in two games in 1959. (Courtesy of Roy Álvarez Jr.)

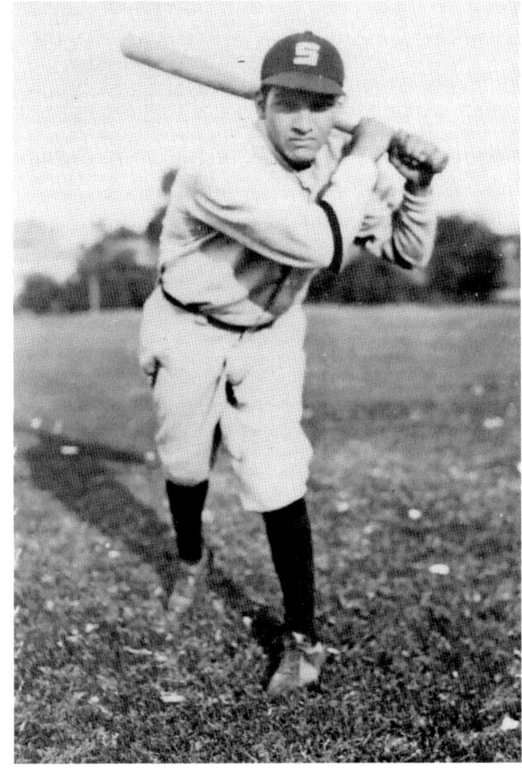

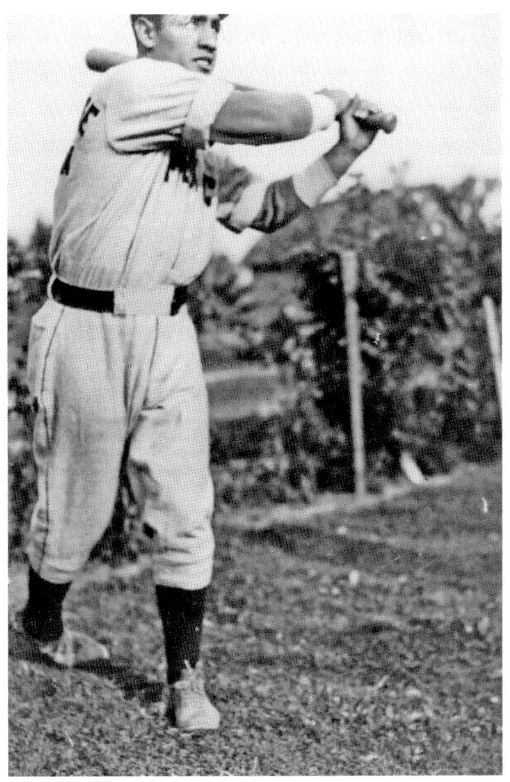

Jesús "Sue" Valverde, a tremendous power hitter for the Stockton Mexico team, demonstrates his swing in the 1930s. Valverde mostly played catcher and batted cleanup. He was born in 1910 in Chihuahua, Mexico, and arrived in the United States in 1919, moving to Stockton in 1920. He won awards as an outstanding athlete at St. Mary's High School, earning 11 varsity letters. Loyola Marymount, St. Mary's College, and Santa Clara University offered him football scholarships, but he chose baseball and received an offer from the Seattle Rainiers of the PCL. However, he had to turn down this opportunity in order to help support his family. He began working for Fibreboard Products in 1930. Valverde was inducted into both the Stockton Athletic Hall of Fame and the Stockton Mexican Sports Hall of Fame. (Courtesy of Louis A. Valverde.)

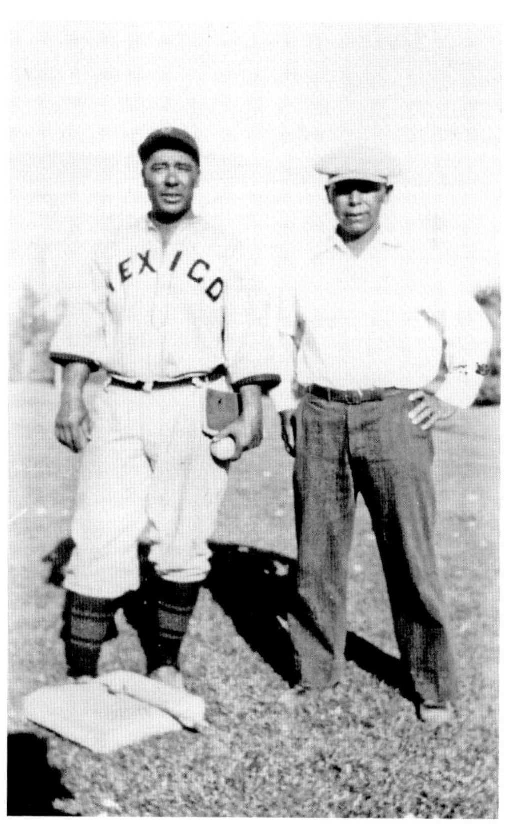

Seen in July 1933, Ralph Valverde (left) was the founder and manager of the Stockton Mexico team. The Stockton Mexico roster included Roy Álvarez; John Ávila; Fidel, Jess, Leo, and Pete Hernández; Lottie Herrera; Art Morotti; and Jesús and Tino Valverde. The team traveled all over Central and Northern California, playing in Sacramento, Modesto, Tracy, Manteca, Riverbank, Patterson, Turlock, and Livingston. In Amador County, they competed against an Ione Miwok Native American team. After games, hosting teams held parties, buying up to 10 cases of beer, and their wives served a buffet, typically consisting of tamales, chile verde, tortillas, and beans. (Courtesy of Louis A. Valverde.)

Close friends and Stockton Mexico teammates Jesús "Suc" Valverde (left) and Art Morotti pose in July 1933. The two met while attending St. Mary's High School. Morotti also played for American Legion Karl Ross Post No. 16 in Stockton. Jesús and his brothers started one of the finest athletic family dynasties in the San Joaquin Valley. In high school, Jesús and Manuel were accomplished baseball, football, and basketball players. Tino was an outstanding outfielder and Joe an excellent pitcher. Several members of the Valverde family were inducted into the Stockton Athletic Hall of Fame in 1973. In 1979, Delta College established the Valverde Scholarship, awarded to a deserving student each year. On July 18, 1981, Valverde Park opened in Stockton with 300 Valverde descendants in attendance. (Courtesy of Louis A. Valverde.)

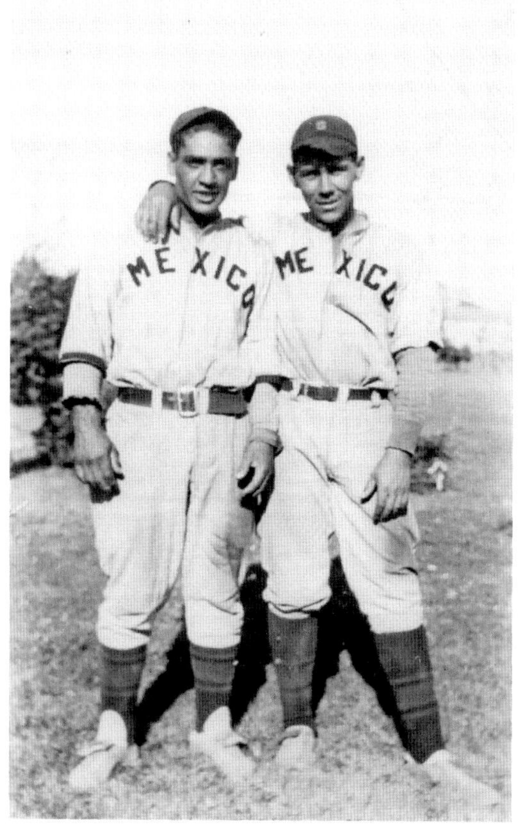

Stockton Mexico members and Stockton Athletic Hall of Fame inductees Manuel Valverde (left) and Jesús "Sue" Valverde are shown in the early 1930s. A revered figure in San Joaquin County and an active leader, Manuel was called the honorary mayor of Lathrop and owned a successful grocery in town. He was a generous man, giving people food on credit with no interest or expected time of payback. This credit honor system existed in many Mexican American businesses in the 1930s. He was instrumental in bringing Babe Ruth leagues to the area, helped build the Lathrop Park Community Center, and organized the Lathrop District Chamber of Commerce. Lathrop named a park and street after him. (Courtesy of Louis A. Valverde.)

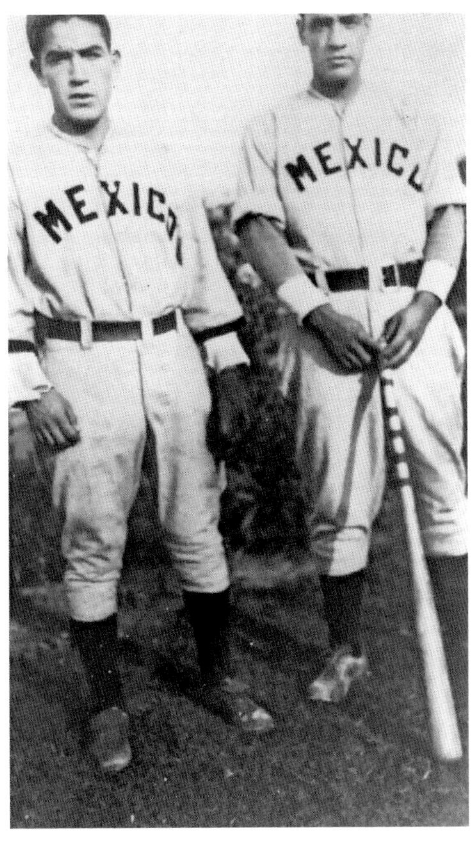

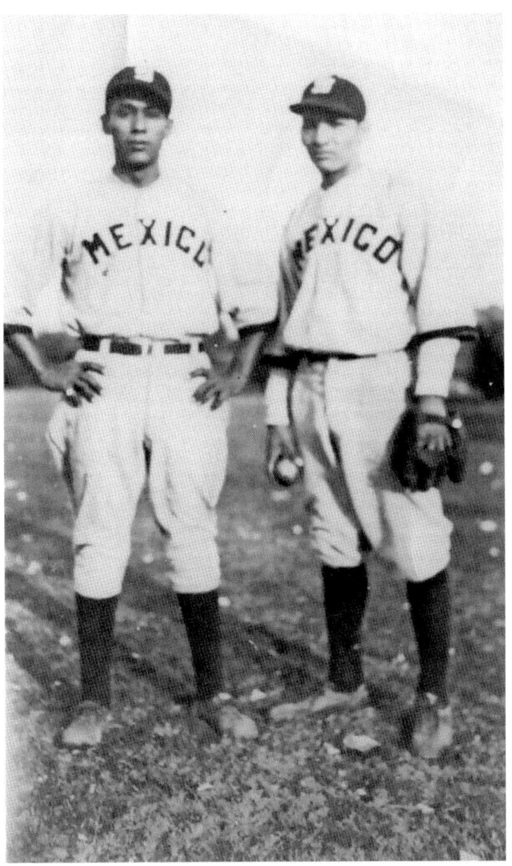

Pitcher Roy Álvarez of Stockton Mexico holds a baseball at right, likely at McKinley Park. According to a September 1932 *La Opinión* article, Álvarez pitched Stockton Club Charro to a victory over the Pittsburg Columbians in a tournament to decide the champion of Northern California. The following week, Club Charro played the Veracruz Eagles of Berkeley. The Charro team contained Roy Álvarez; Fred and Johnny Ávila; ? Castro; Manuel Gonzáles; Fidencio and Lottie Herrera; Bill, Jimmy, and Johnny Martínez; Juan and Ray Monges; Paul Morones; Raymond Múñoz; and ? Sandoval. Other regional Mexican American teams in the early 1930s were the Richfield Oilers, Martínez Druids, Grimes Aztecas, San Francisco Atlético Mexicano, Vallejo Cardinals, Berkeley Vagabonds, and Oakland Nuevo El Paso. (Courtesy of Roy Álvarez Jr.)

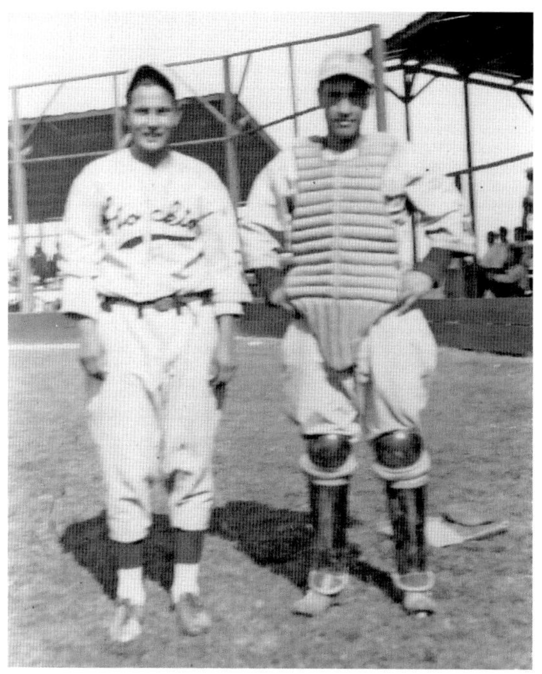

Stockton player Jesús "Sue" Valverde stands at right wearing his catching equipment in the early 1930s. This photograph was possibly taken at McKinley Park, which included the premier baseball diamond in the region and a swimming pool. Valverde worked for Fibreboard Products before becoming a beer distributor. He transported Lucky Lager and Hamms brand beers to the surrounding areas, including a bracero labor camp, in the 1940s. In the 1950s, he helped build the Club Mexico Hall, which became a popular dance hall during that time. The hall closed in the 1960s and was demolished in the 1980s. (Courtesy of Louis A. Valverde.)

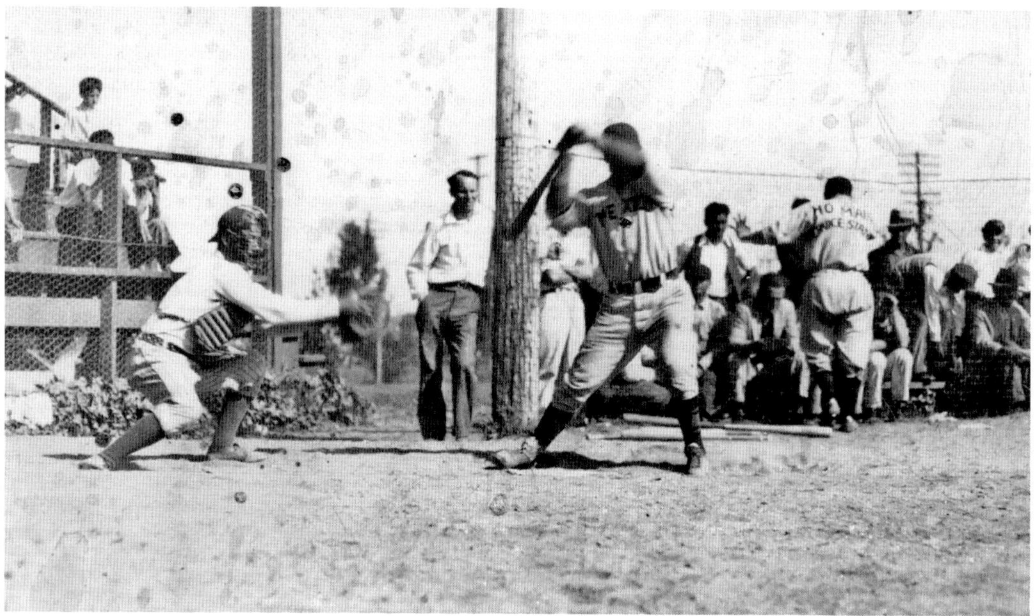

Jesús "Sue" Valverde reacts to an inside pitch while batting in the early 1930s at an unknown ballpark. His teammate's uniform in the background reveals one of the many team sponsors. Several Mexican American *tienditas* and other small businesses sponsored teams. Early Stockton sponsors included McKinley Service, Elmer R. Castillo Real Estate Insurance, Berg Clothiers, La Paloma, Farmacia Internacional, Mandarin Market, Yoshikawa Studio, and El Rancho Grande Foods. The diverse Stockton barrio, located on the south side of town, included Japanese and Chinese Americans. (Courtesy of Louis A. Valverde.)

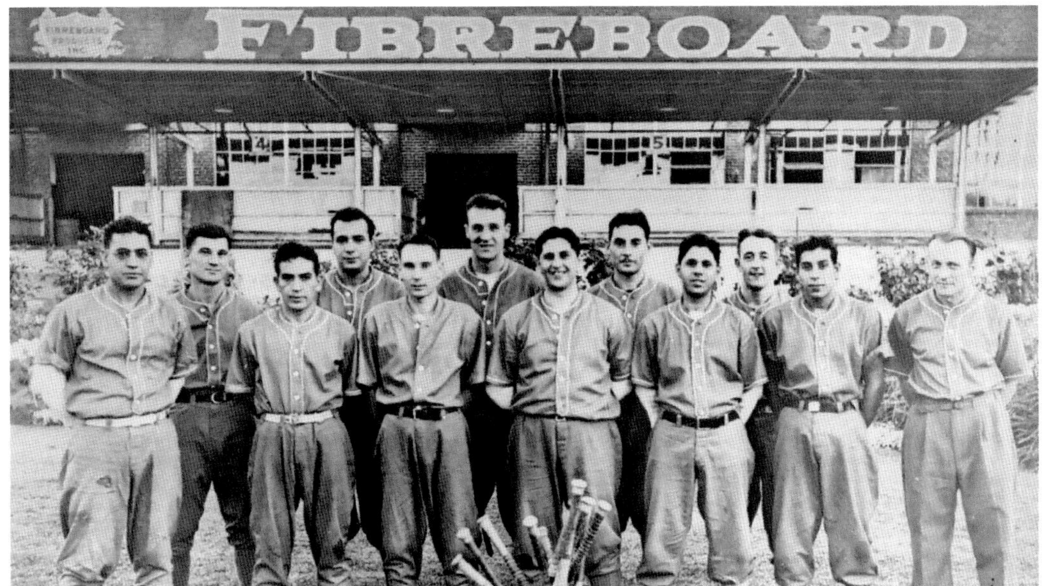

The 1941 Stockton Fibreboard team includes, from left to right, Jesús "Sue" Valverde, Bucky Yearicks, Manuel Valverde, Al Rogers, two unidentified, Art "Honey" Morotti, Jim Cashero, John Silva, Jim Camicia, Tony Romero, and "Inkie" Hodgson. Fibreboard-sponsored teams won titles throughout the 1940s. They won the industrial league crown in 1940 and 1941 and won the city open championship in 1942 and 1945. Fibreboard Products was the largest employer in the city of Stockton, with over 1,200 employees. The factory, which closed in 1972, produced shipping crates and food cartons for Sun-Maid Raisins, Kellogg's, and General Mills. (Courtesy of Louis A. Valverde.)

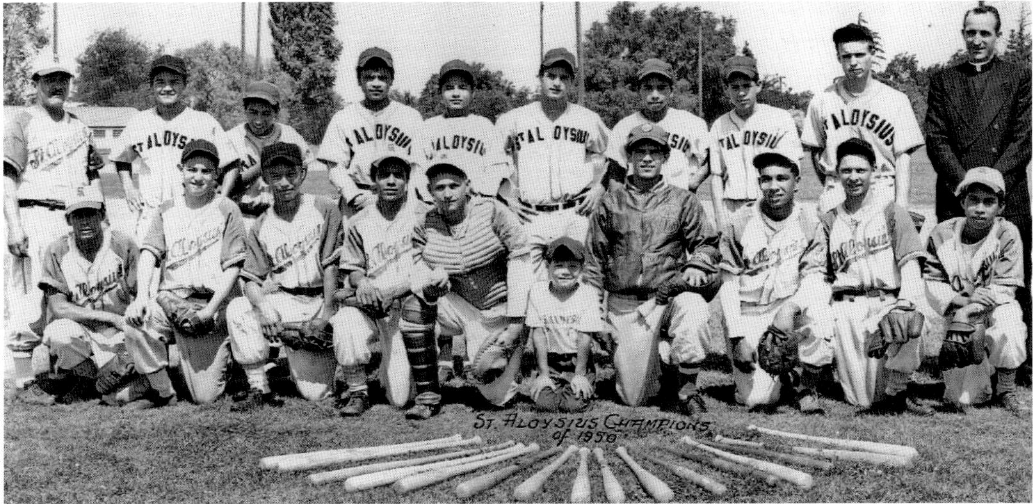

The 1950 Stockton St. Aloysius championship team includes, from left to right, (first row) Bill Ramírez, Matt Fish, Julio Romero, Robert Sánchez, Bill Bowman, batboy Dan Álvarez, Bob Álvarez, Jess Bustamante, Roy Álvarez Jr., and Julio Hernández; (second row) manager Esequiel "Tubby" Álvarez, Alex Leos, Tommy Fernández, Fred Alonzo, Rubén Fields, Sal Román, J. Fields, Bob Williams, unidentified, and Father Rolf. (Courtesy of Roy Álvarez Jr.)

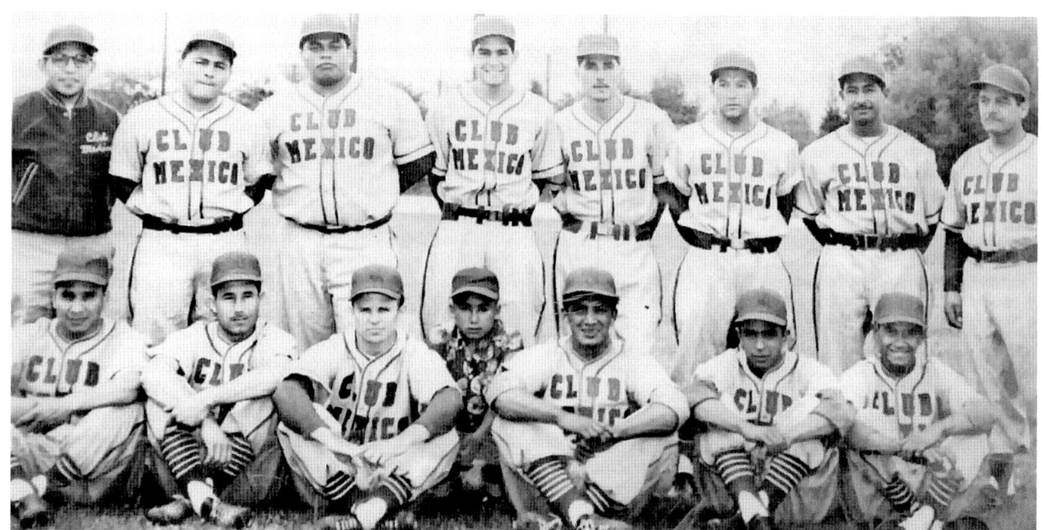

The 1955 inaugural Stockton Club Mexico team of the California Mexican League includes, from left to right, (first row) Pete Martínez, Leo Magdaleno, Billy Rue, batboy Michael Orosco, Primo Orosco, Richard Valverde, and Innocent Montalvo; (second row) Joe Zárate, Reubén Limón, Manuel Martín, José "Mousey" Zaragoza, Charlie Barral, Joe Águilar, Sachus Orosco, and manager Esequiel "Tubby" Álvarez. Most of the players carried over from the Pan Americans, an older team started by Primo Orosco, Sachus Orosco, Reubén Limón, and José Zaragoza. Sachus Orosco managed and announced games. He later became the California Mexican League commissioner. The league experienced immense growth during his tenure. (Courtesy of Louis A. Valverde.)

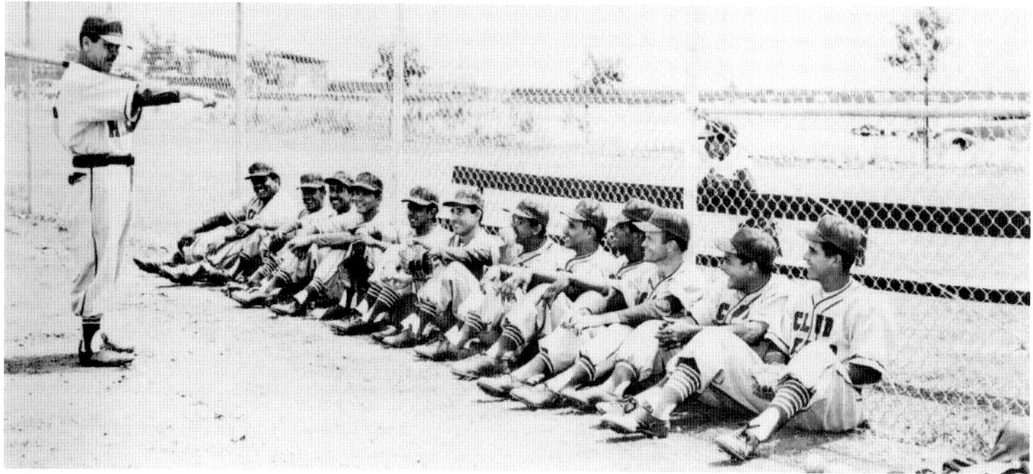

Manager Esequiel "Tubby" Álvarez instructs his Club Mexico team at Stribley Park in the 1950s. Sitting against the fence are, from left to right, Manuel Martín, Innocent Montalvo, Sachus Orosco, José "Mousey" Zaragoza, Richard Valverde, Leo Magdaleno, Joe Águilar, Pete Martínez, Primo Orosco, Billy Rue, Reubén Limón, and Bob Álvarez. Tubby Álvarez acted as the first president of the California Mexican League. In 1955, he sat on the board of directors that oversaw the formation of the league. The group included brother Roy Álvarez, Frank Chico, Ray López, Del Ortega, Henry Pérez, Henry Plata, and Frank Serrano. (Courtesy of Louis A. Valverde.)

Club Mexico player Bob Álvarez pitches during practice in the 1950s. A star pitcher at St. Mary's High School in Stockton, Álvarez also pitched in the US Marine Corps during the Korean War. His father, Esequiel "Tubby" Álvarez, uncle Roy Álvarez, Jesús "Sue" Valverde, Reubén Limón, Primo and Sachus Orosco, and Del Ortega were influential figures in the birth of the California Mexican League in 1955. Esequiel worked at Fibreboard Paper Products for almost 40 years and provided transportation for players to games in Northern California. In addition to his founding role in the California Mexican League, he organized the Saint Aloysius Boys Town and Laetare Club from Saint Gertrudes church. (Courtesy of Louis A. Valverde.)

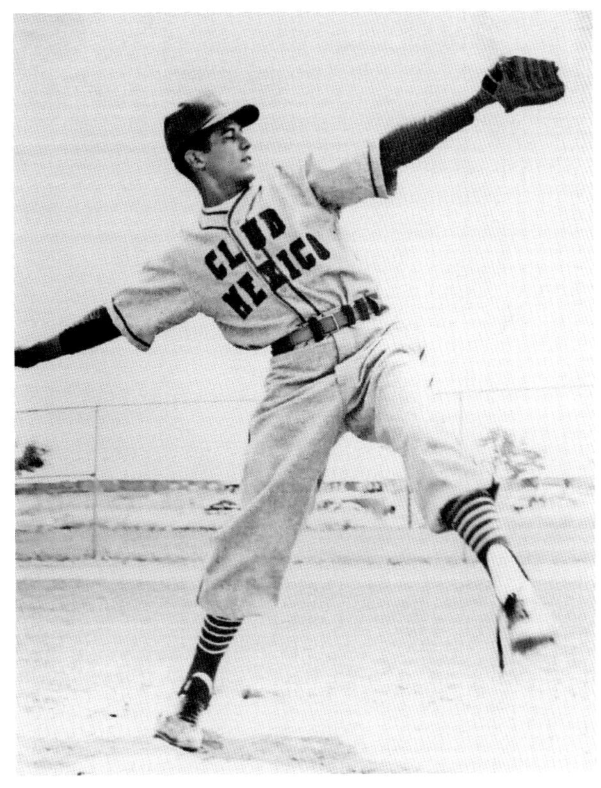

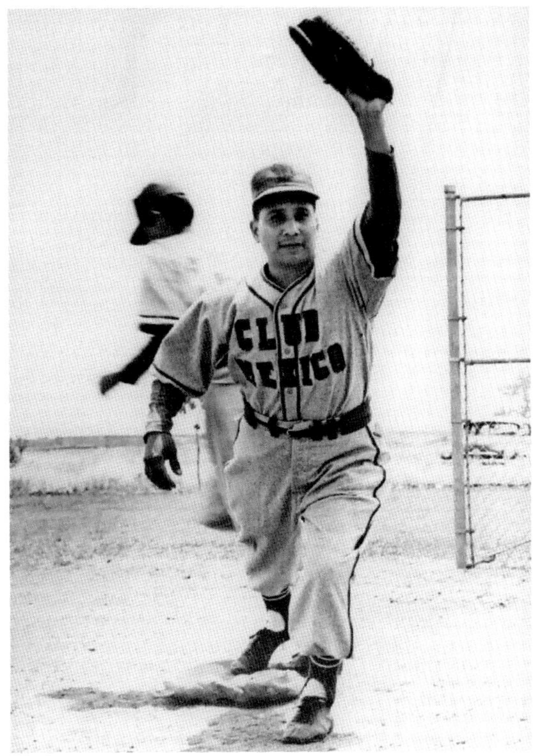

Club Mexico first baseman Pete Martínez stretches out to make the play in 1955. Club Mexico was the first champion of the California Mexican League, which formed as a welcoming, nondiscriminatory environment for Mexican American ballplayers. Some of the original teams were Club Mexico (Stockton), Club Azteca (Stockton), San Jose Merchants, San Jose Caballeros, Mi Ranchito (Tracy), Rancho Chico (Woodland), and Hi-Way Club (Sacramento). Though games were very competitive, players fraternized and made new friends in other cities. Son Pete Martínez Jr. received all-league awards as a pitcher at the University of the Pacific and holds one of the lowest career earned run averages in school history. (Courtesy of Louis A. Valverde.)

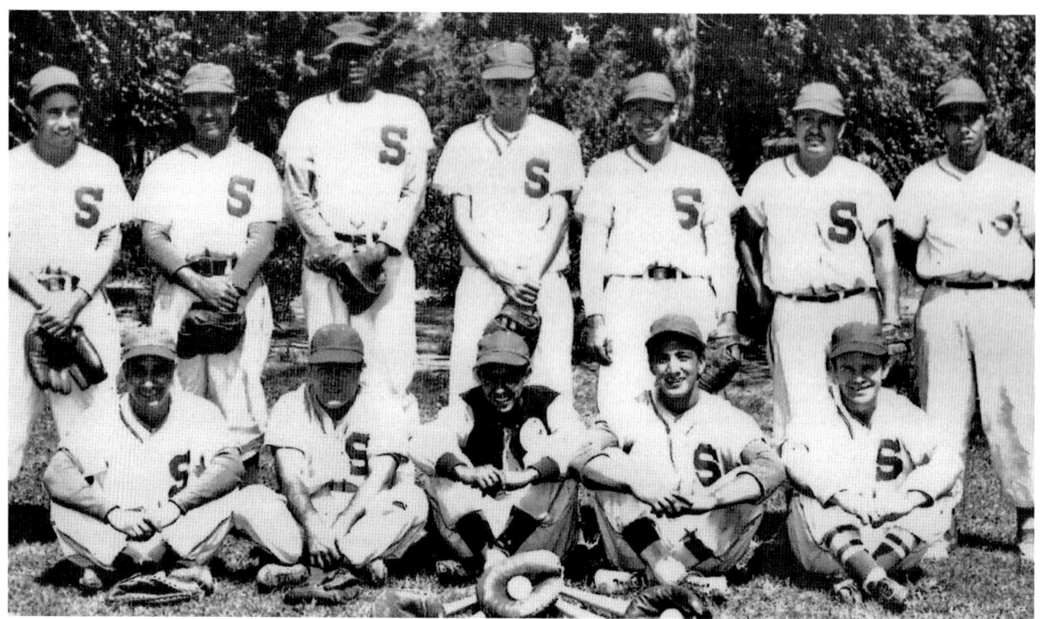

The 1951 Pan American baseball team of Stockton featured, from left to right, (first row) Pete Martínez, Reubén Limón, Richard Valverde, Primo Orosco, and Billy Rue; (second row) Leo Magdaleno, Sachus Orosco, Chester Fields, José "Mousey" Zaragoza, John Naranjo, Joe Sánchez, and Manuel Catario. Born in Bakersfield, José "Mousey" Zaragoza grew up and played baseball in Woodland before moving to Stockton. His son Randy played in Stockton youth leagues and for the Stockton Reds, an instruction team for the Cincinnati Reds. (Courtesy of Randy Zaragoza.)

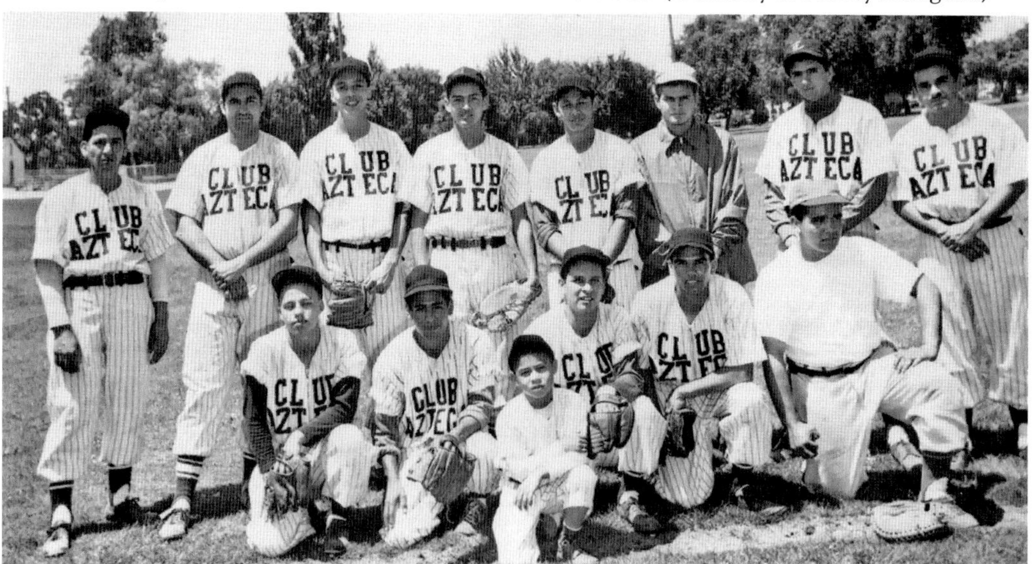

This 1956 picture of Stockton Club Azteca shows, from left to right, (first row) unidentified, John Bernado, batboy C. Álvarez, Roy Álvarez Jr., Rubén Padilla, and Joe Cortez; (second row) manager Roy Álvarez, unidentified, Gil Granados, Dave Pérez, Vince Ramírez, Frank García, T. Cuevas, and R. Moreno. (Courtesy of Roy Álvarez Jr.)

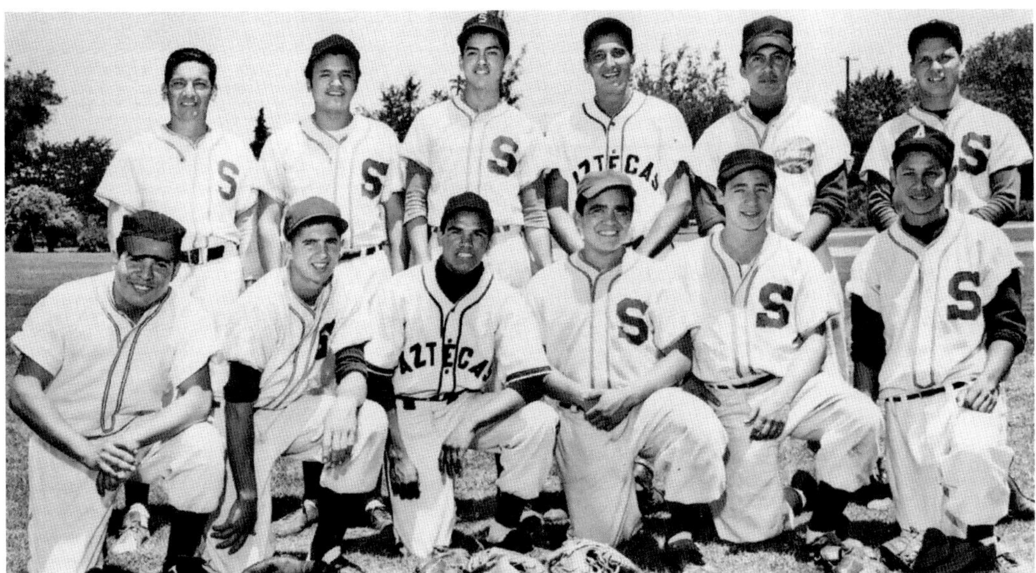

This 1950s Stockton Club Aztecas team consisted of, from left to right, (first row) Steve Mendoza, John DeCicco, Rubén Padilla, Joe Cortez, Rich Bottini, and Vince Ramírez; (second row) manager Roy Álvarez, Fred Alonzo, Dave Pérez, Ed López, Julio Hernández, and Roy Álvarez Jr. (Courtesy of Roy Álvarez Jr.)

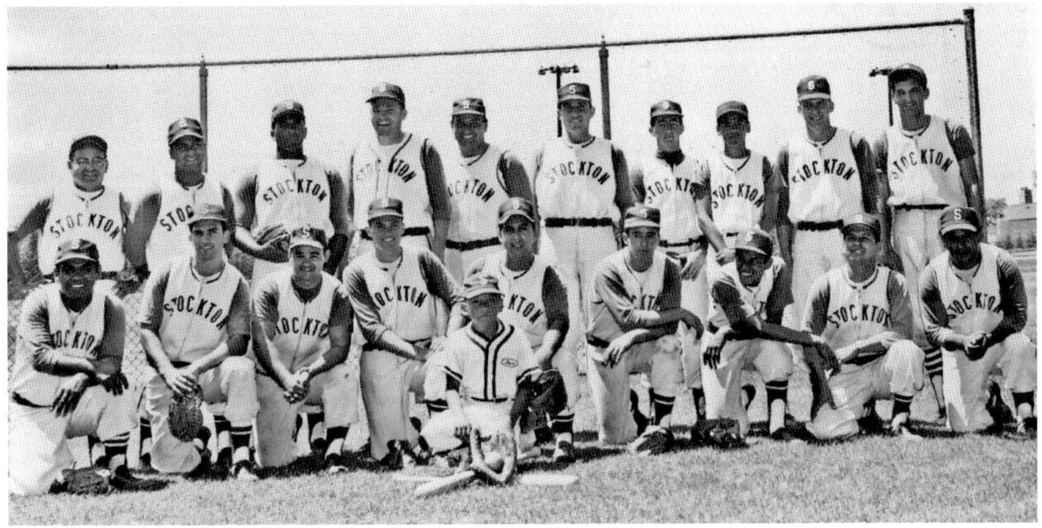

In the 1960s, this Stockton Club Mexico team included, from left to right, (first row) Al Moreno, Ernie Strauman, Alex Leos, Jack Vernon, batboy Davy Padilla, Julio Hernández, Louis A. Valverde, John Pina, Roy Álvarez Jr., and John Bernado; (second row) manager David Padilla, Dave Herrera, unidentified, Art Delmar, Walter Payne, Paul Devincenzi, Paul Oliver, Félix Rodríguez Jr., Ronnie Kuehl, and Emil Vaccarezza. Valverde played on the Third Army baseball team during his service in the Vietnam War. He remained involved in Army baseball upon returning to the United States, pitching in Georgia, Florida, and Alabama. He was inducted into the Stockton Sports Hall of Fame in 2003. (Courtesy of Roy Álvarez Jr.)

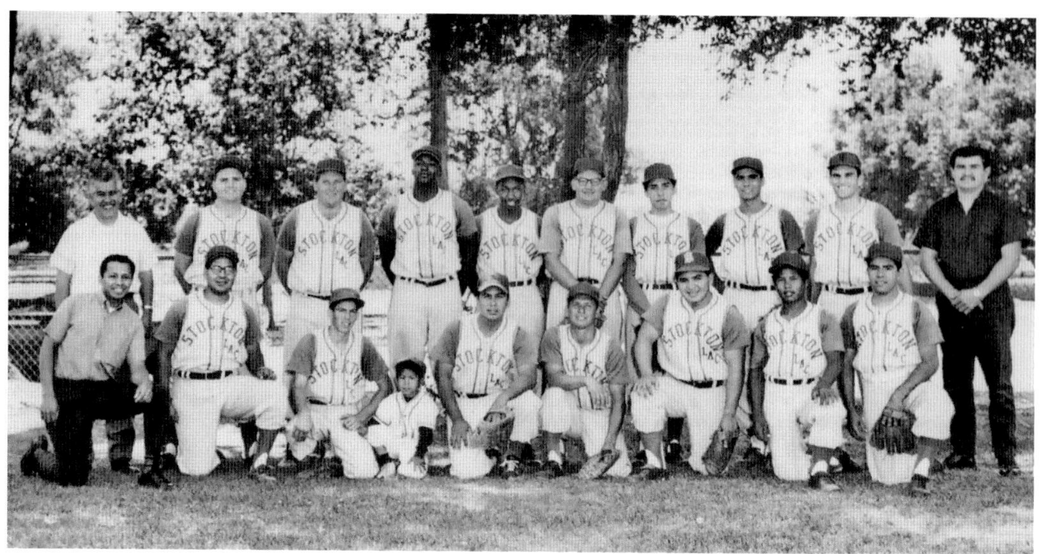

This 1960s Stockton Latin American Club is comprised of, from left to right, (first row) unidentified, Joe Aguilar, unidentified, Joe Aguilar Jr., Julio Hernández, Roy Álvarez Jr., Carl Agbulos, ? Aguilar, and Gilbert Montes; (second row) Bruno Cardona, Larry Burgess, Dave Zeller, unidentified, J.C. Fox, unidentified, Trini Ruíz, unidentified, Ernie Strauman, and unidentified. An inductee of the Stockton Sports Hall of Fame, Joe Aguilar won titles in 1965, 1967, and 1968 as manager of Latin American Club and Club Mexico teams. He also coached the Pi-Nays women's softball team for 17 years. (Courtesy of Roy Álvarez Jr.)

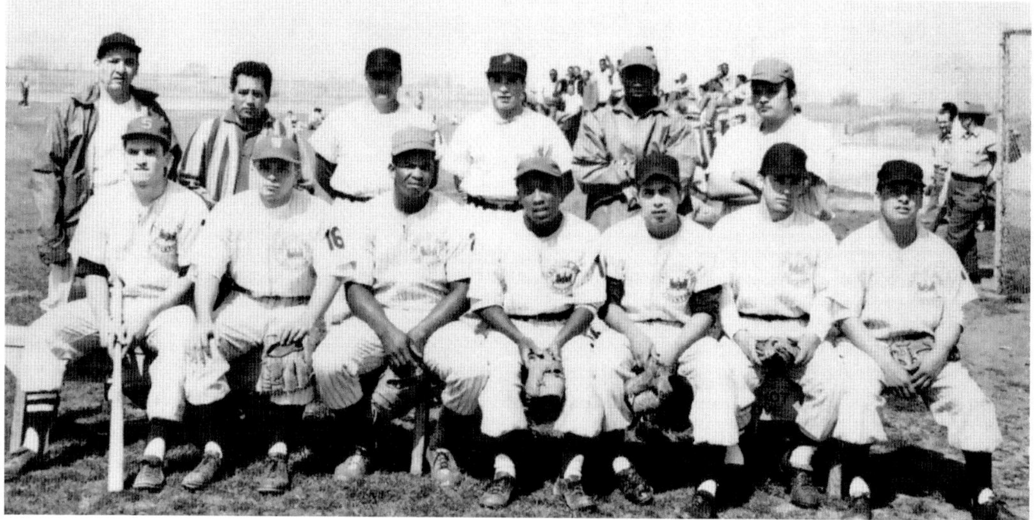

The 1959 Stockton Castillo Brothers team is, from left to right, (first row) Ernie Strauman, J. Madrid, Gene Nelson, Matt Wilson, Julio Hernández, George Centeno, and Roy Álvarez Jr.; (second row) manager Roy Álvarez, John Bernado, B. Alfonso, Juan Sánchez, J.C. Fox, and Fred Alonzo. Roy Álvarez Jr. was born in 1933 in Stockton and grew up in the town's passionate baseball environment, serving as batboy. He played on the Pan American and Latin American clubs. He later managed for three years and umpired for seven years. (Courtesy of Roy Álvarez Jr.)

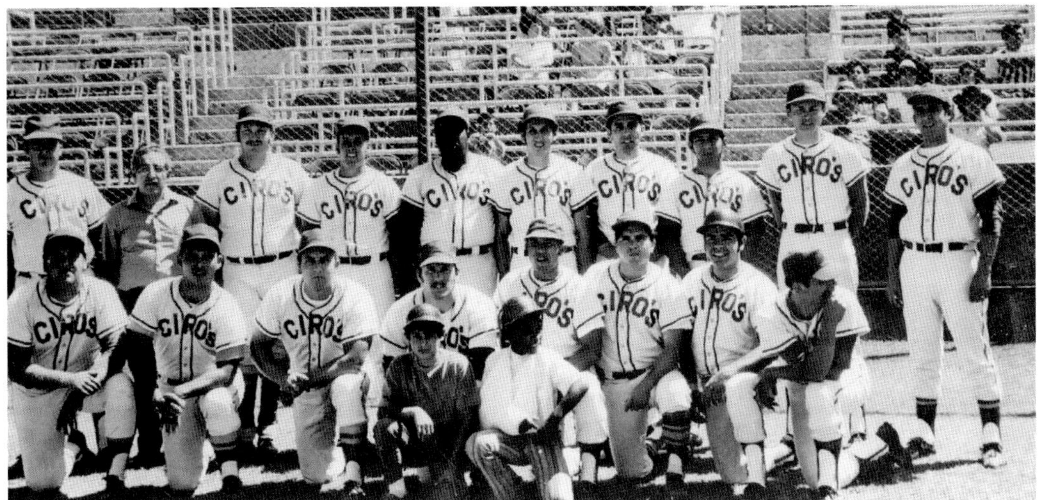

Ciro's Tavern won the 1970 California Mexican League championship. This picture at Billy Hebert Park shows, from left to right, (first row) Paul Buckley, Rick Arucan, Mark Kulhanek, Larry Matuska, batboy Charles Belasco, batboy Alonzo Owens, Sam Arong, Dan Peralta, Gilbert Montes, and John Piña; (second row) manager Louis A. Valverde, assistant manager Joe Zárate, Tim Loveland, Bob Guidi, George Hunter, Bob Guerrero, Trini Ruíz, Jess Barajas, Pete Martínez Jr., and coach Dave López. Son of Stockton sports legend Jesús "Sue" Valverde, Louis A. Valverde followed in his father's footsteps, excelling at baseball, football, and basketball at St. Mary's High School. (Courtesy of Louis A. Valverde.)

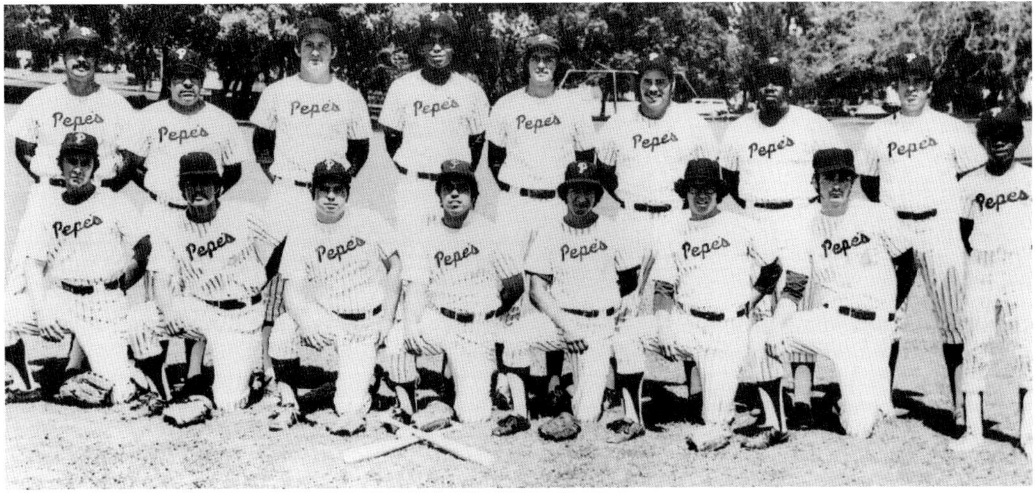

The 1972 Stockton team sponsored by Pepe's included, from left to right, (first row) Joe Tomingo, John Rodríguez, Dan Peralta, Ben Valverde Jr., Jess Barajas, David Lozano, Gary Ghan, and batboy Alonzo Owens; (second row) coach Dave López, Gilbert Montes, Lon Strom, Billy Sims, Gene Hernández, Jack Ojeda, George Hunter, and manager Louis A. Valverde. Louis A. Valverde, Gary Ghan, Gene Hernández, Dave López, David Lozano, John Rodríguez, and Joe Tomingo are inductees of the Stockton Sports Hall of Fame. Lozano played five years in AAA for the New York Mets. (Courtesy of Louis A. Valverde.)

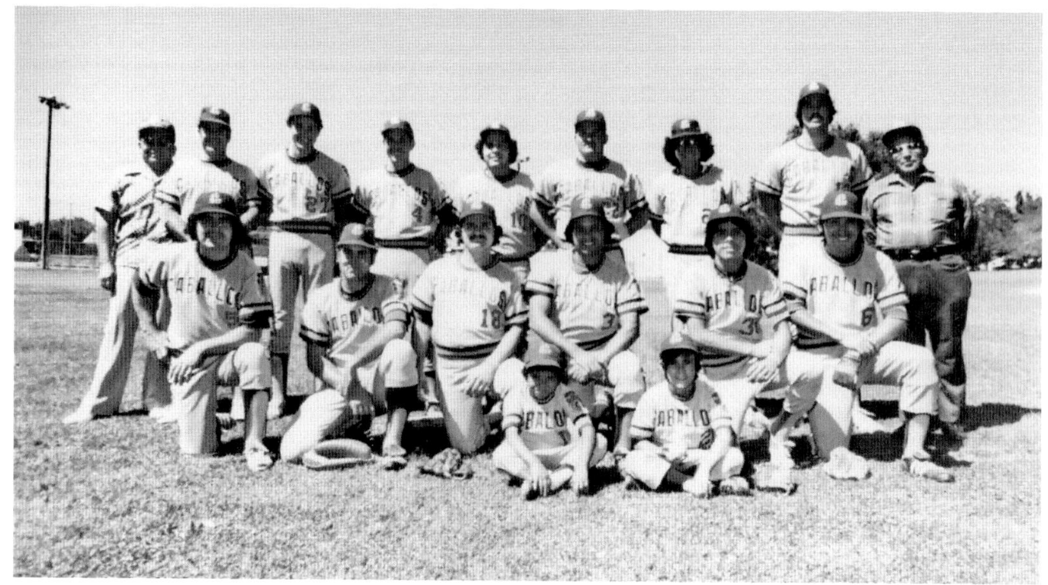

In 1975, Los Caballos reigned supreme in Stockton's baseball leagues. They were the first team to win the California Mexican League and Mexican American League titles in the same year. From left to right are (first row) batboys Mike Trujillo and Steve Trujillo; (second row) Steve Cardona, Nick Cecchetti, Anthony Jaime, Cedric Trujillo, Steve Escobar, and Julio Pérez; (third row) team sponsor David Padilla, manager Louis A. Valverde, Pete Martínez Jr., Eddie Hunt, Don Guerrero, Danny Dalonzo, Reuben Fields, Joe Budiselich, and assistant manager Joe Zárate. (Courtesy of Louis A. Valverde.)

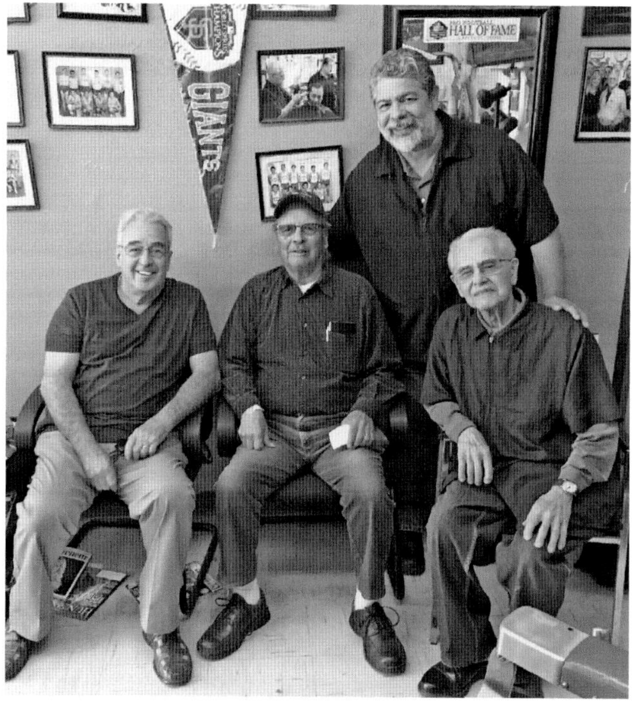

Pictured in April 2018 at Cal-Pine on the Ave barbershop in Stockton are, from left to right, Louis A. Valverde, Roy Álvarez Jr., Randy Zaragoza, and Frank Chavis. Louis A. Valverde and Roy Álvarez Jr. played, managed, and held leading roles in the California Mexican League for many years. Randy Zaragoza owns Cal-Pine on the Ave barbershop. Their fathers, Jesús "Sue" Valverde, Roy Álvarez Sr., and José "Mousey" Zaragoza, were admired pioneers of the California Mexican League. Frank Chavis, a World War II veteran, continues to work as a barber after 50 years. (Courtesy of Christopher Docter.)

The Lower San Joaquin Valley

The lower San Joaquin Valley encompasses Kern, Kings, Tulare, Fresno, and Madera Counties. Mexican Americans have been vital to the development of the lower San Joaquin Valley communities since the mid-19th century. Early on, many worked for mining and railroad companies or as *vaqueros*, herding cows, sheep, and wild horses on vast ranches. In the 1900s, those living in the Mexican "colonies" or barrios mostly worked in the burgeoning agribusiness industry. They continue to form the backbone of the nation's most productive agricultural region, which generates several billion dollars every year.

As a respite from the grueling work picking the region's staple crops of cotton and grapes, and facing a lack of municipal recreational opportunities, communities formed their own teams. By the early 1930s, newspaper records indicate that Mexican American teams existed in Randsburg, Tehachapi, Arvin, Taft, Bakersfield, Wasco, Delano, Alpaugh, Corcoran, Tulare, Tagus, Farmersville, Visalia, Hanford, Laton, Orosi, Dinuba, Reedley, Selma, Sanger, Fresno, Glorietta, Mendota, and Madera.

Several Mexican American leaders in the lower San Joaquin Valley spearheaded the creation of community baseball teams. In Dinuba, Felix Delgado organized the Dinuba Redskins, maintained the Tortilla Flats ballfield in the barrio, and led successful efforts bringing Little League and Babe Ruth baseball to the area. Frank Camacho helped found the Reedley Eagles and later funded local youth baseball, using his personal funds to make sure every neighborhood kid had the opportunity to play. Eddie Chapa formed the Madera Merchants as an opportunity for young men to play outside high school and college. Today, city parks and high school baseball fields carry the names of these remarkable figures.

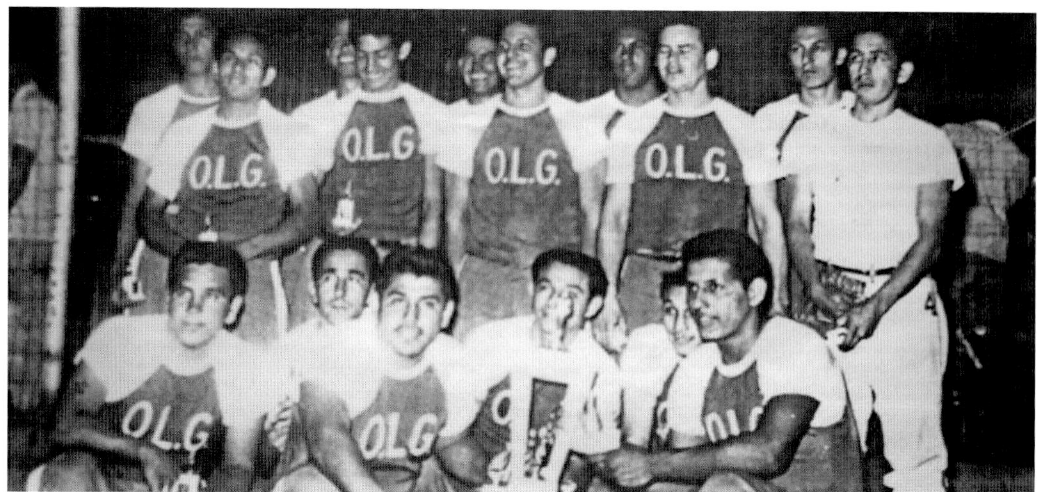

The Bakersfield Our Lady of Guadalupe players proudly show their trophies as 1959 champions of the A Class church softball league. From left to right are (first row) David Monsibais and Louie "Junior" Arias; (second row) Robert Lomas, Bobby Gardea, George Medina, and Joe Aguirre; (third row) Joe Medina, Pilar Colunga, Richard Sánchez, Frank Camacho, and Manuel Rocha; (fourth row) Johnny Aguilar, Leroy Hinojos, Robert Alvarado, Richard Andrada, and Raymond Solano. The team traveled extensively, forming ties with communities near and far such as Lamont, Arvin, Delano, Earlimart, Tehachapi, and San Fernando. (Courtesy of David Monsibais.)

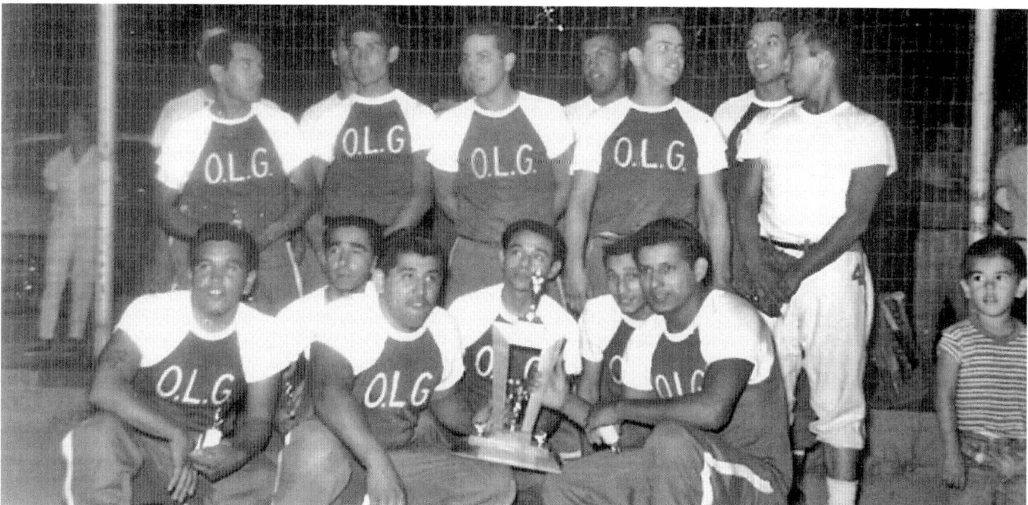

David Monsibais Jr. stands at far right in front along with his father's 1959 Bakersfield Our Lady of Guadalupe champion softball team. The two players holding the trophy in the first row are David Monsibais (left) and Louie "Junior" Arias (right). The rest of the team are, from left to right, (second row) Robert Lomas, Bobby Gardea, George Medina, and Joe Aguirre; (third row) Joe Medina, Pilar Colunga, Richard Sánchez, Frank Camacho, and Manuel Rocha; (fourth row) Johnny Aguilar, Leroy Hinojos, Robert Alvarado, Richard Andrada, and Raymond Solano. The earliest Bakersfield barrios of Little Tijuana ("the Barrio"), La Loma, La Colonia, Little Okie, and Texas Street all fielded teams. (Courtesy of Rachel Ozuna Arias.)

From left to right stand Bakersfield Our Lady of Guadalupe players Louie "Junior" Arias, Leroy Hinojos, and David Monsibais. Originally from the Jimtown section of Whittier, David Monsibais moved with his family to Bakersfield during World War II. His parents, Angela and Braulio, established La Loma Tortillería, which they operated from their house. David made deliveries and sold tortillas to local businesses. Many local companies supported Our Lady of Guadalupe softball, including Sanches Shell Service and Casa Moore Furniture. (Courtesy of Rachel Ozuna Arias.)

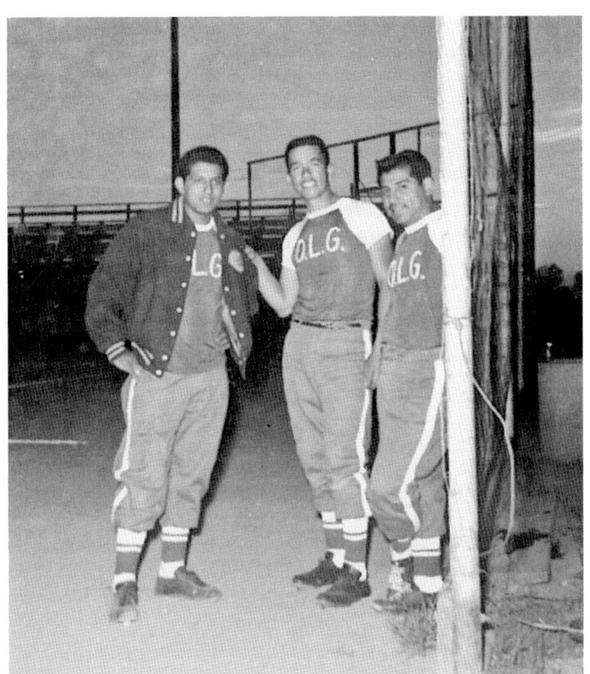

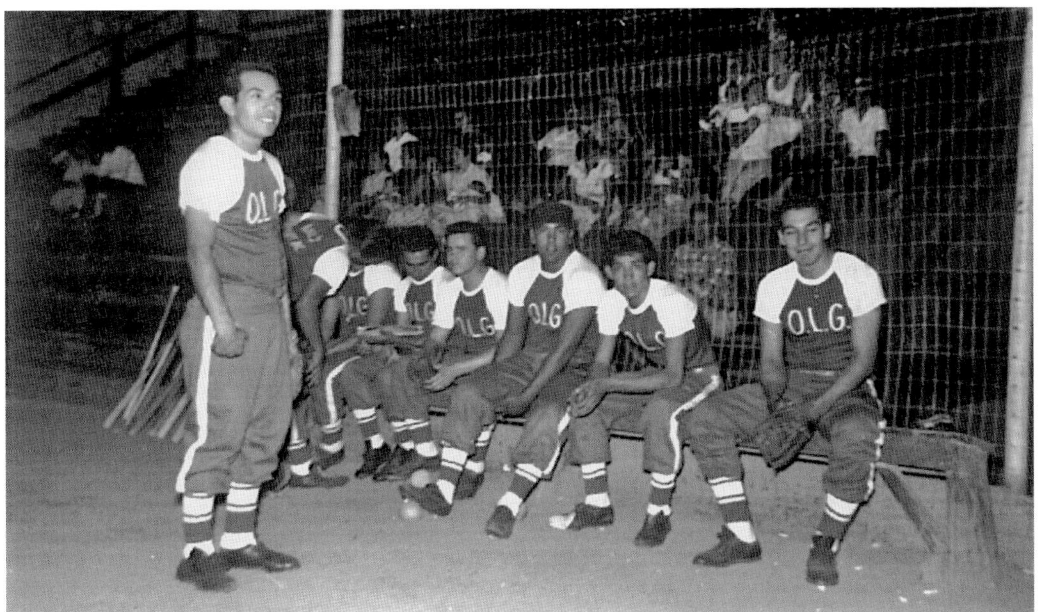

A 1950s Our Lady of Guadalupe team discusses its game plan. From left to right are Joe Medina (standing), two unidentified, Joe Aguirre, Frank Camacho, Richard Andrada, Pilar Colunga, and Raymond Solano. Games in Bakersfield were played on a vacant lot near the former Sacred Heart Church (the current site of San Clemente Mission). Along with San Clemente Mission Church, Our Lady of Guadalupe Church has remained a central part of Mexican American community life in Bakersfield. Our Lady of Guadalupe still stands at 601 East California Avenue. (Courtesy of Rachel Ozuna Arias.)

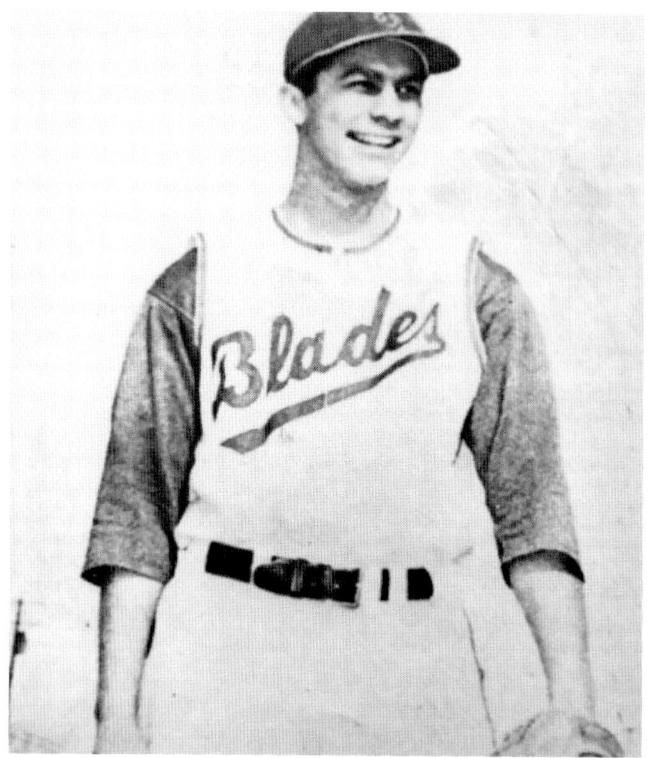

Ernie Morín, of Spanish and Native American ancestry, played for the East Bakersfield High Blades from 1964 to 1967. Morín received interest from college and professional scouts, including the Philadelphia Phillies. He married and started a family after high school. His brothers Leonard and Dan Morín also starred in baseball at the collegiate and professional levels. Leonard played at Cal State Northridge and for the Bakersfield Outlaws of the Class-A California League. Dan played at East Bakersfield High School and for Bakersfield College. (Courtesy of East Bakersfield High School and Ernie Morín.)

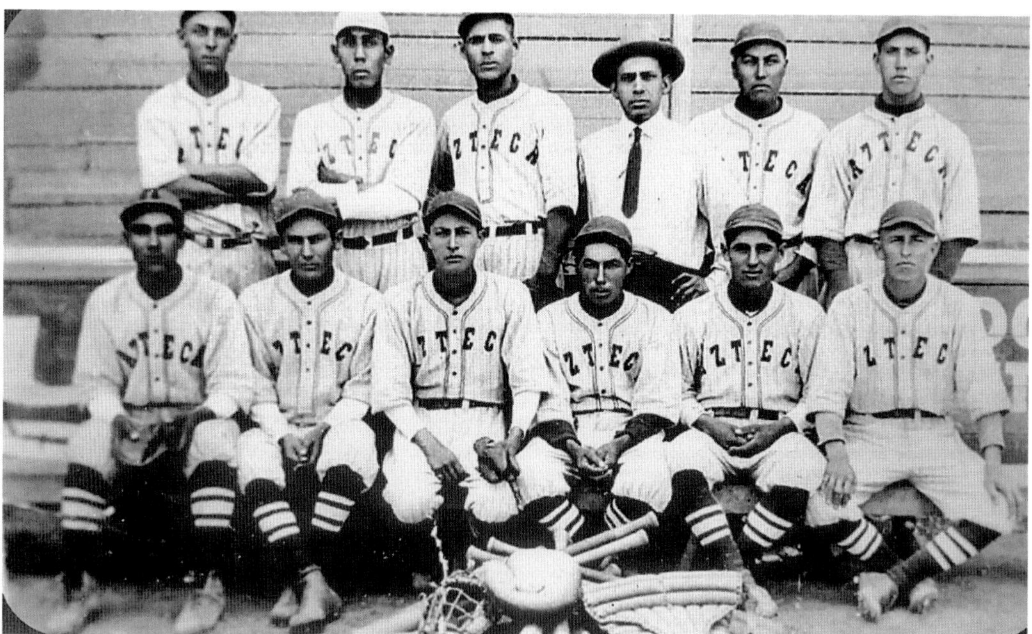

Pictured on July 4, 1924, this Hondo, Texas, Azteca team, from the San Antonio region, includes brothers Martín García (first row, second from left) and Víctor García (second row, second from left). Their aunt María de la Acensión moved to Bakersfield and married into the Morín family. (Courtesy of Frank García and Margaret Morín.)

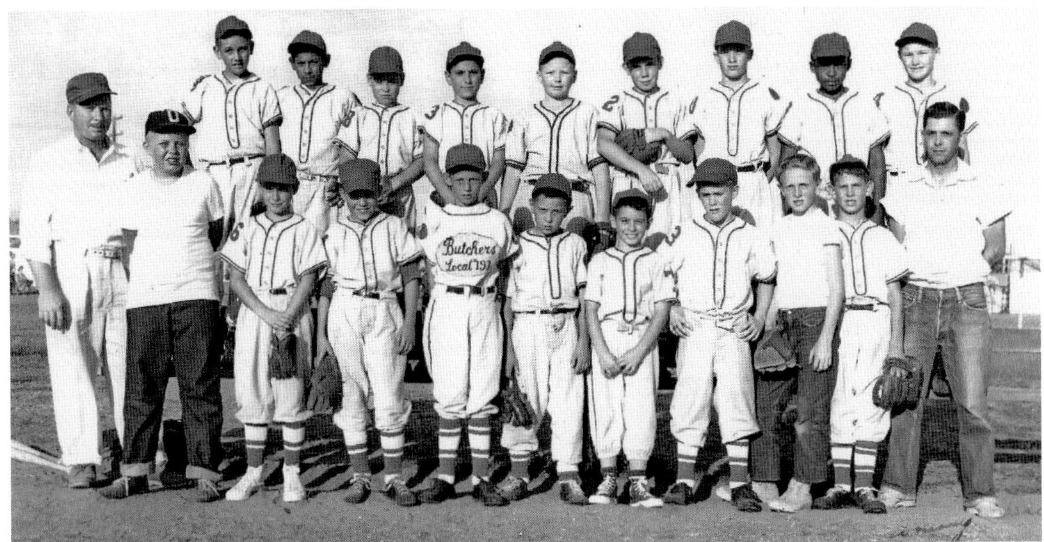

The Bakersfield Butchers Local 793 boys' team won its league championship in 1951. The team was led by coach Red Slater (first row, far left) and included players Mike Arias (second row, second from left) and Ted Slater (second row, far right). Mike Arias later played on several community baseball teams in Bakersfield and took part in basketball at Garces Memorial High School. He remained active in baseball after his playing days, organizing summer leagues for high school–age boys. (Courtesy of Evelyn Hernández Slater.)

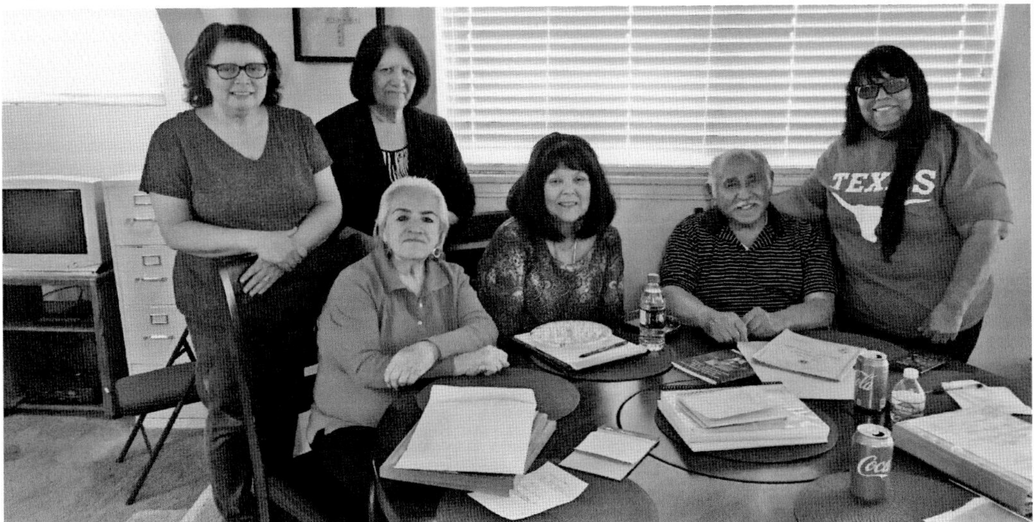

In April 2018, members of historical Kern County families met in Bakersfield. From left to right are (first row) Juana Pérez, Evelyn Hernández Slater, David Monsibais, and Margaret Morín; (second row) Teresa Martínez Vincent and Rachel Ozuna Arias. Rachel Arias has spent years researching the history of Mexican Americans in the region. Along with Lynda Finch, she produced several successful programs at the Kern County Genealogical Society, such as My Mexican and American Indian Ancestry, the Migration North (2013), The Sonoran Project, Parts I–III (2015), and Kern County Mexican Settlement (2016). (Courtesy of Christopher Docter.)

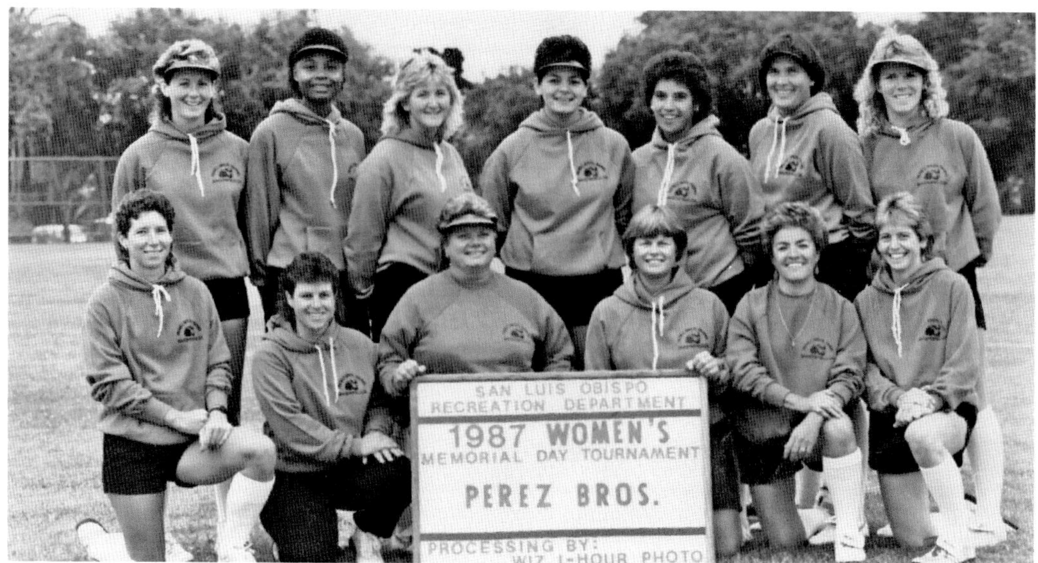

The Bakersfield Pérez Brothers women's softball team traveled throughout California and beyond, playing in San Luis Obispo, Santa Barbara, Edwards Air Force Base, Sacramento, Los Angeles, and Nevada. This competitive team featured many former collegiate players. From left to right are (first row) Kathy Welter, Pamela Clegg, Rhelda Hughes, Pam Savage, Juana Pérez, and Kathy Scatena; (second row) Cathy Turner, Gwen McRae, Jill Pylman, Minda Romero, Carolina Reyes, Cheryl Alexander, and Janice Heffernan. Kathy Welter won softball championships as a coach at Cal State Bakersfield. (Courtesy of Juana Pérez.)

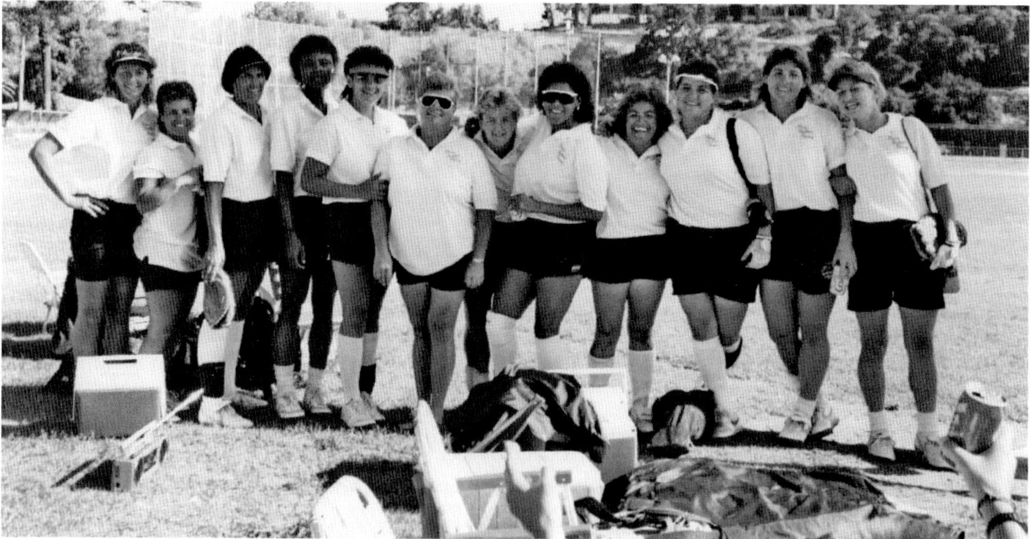

This late 1980s Bakersfield Pérez Brothers women's softball team includes, from left to right, Cathy Turner, Pamela Clegg, Cheryl Alexander, Gwen McRae, Minda Romero, Rhelda Hughes, Jill Pylman, Carrie Reyes, Juana Pérez, Barbara Santa Cruz, unidentified, and Tanya Warren. The athletic Juana Pérez pitched and played infield and also enjoyed playing rugby. (Courtesy of Juana Pérez.)

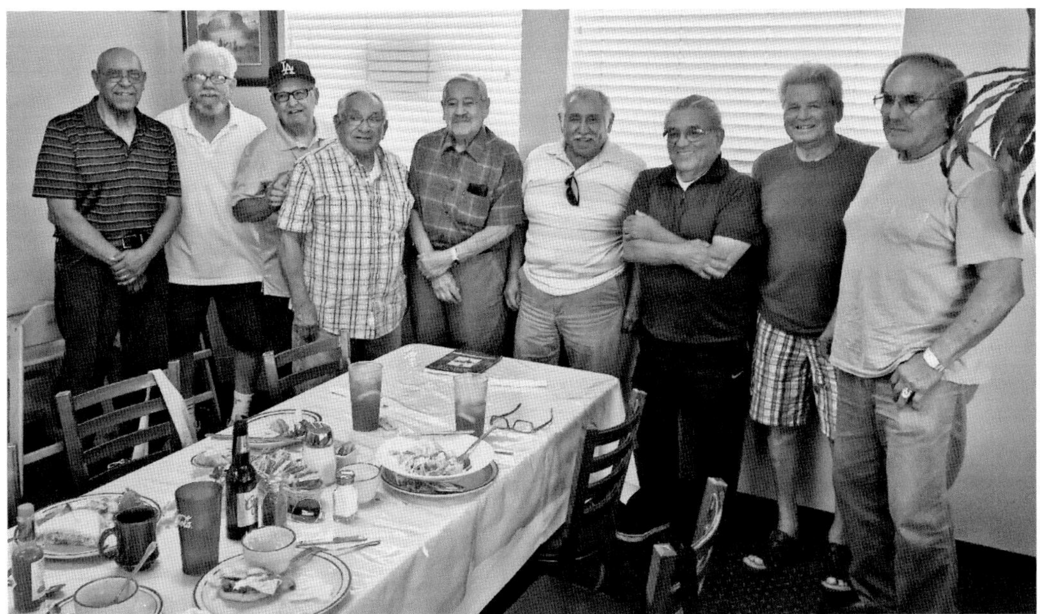

Every month, players from the 1950s Bakersfield Our Lady of Guadalupe softball team meet for lunch. The July 2016 meeting featured, from left to right, Richard Andrada, Leroy Hinojos, Robert Alvarado, Joe Medina, Fidencio Gaona, David Monsibais, Robert Lomas, Frank Camacho, and Ernie Albitre. (Courtesy of Christopher Docter.)

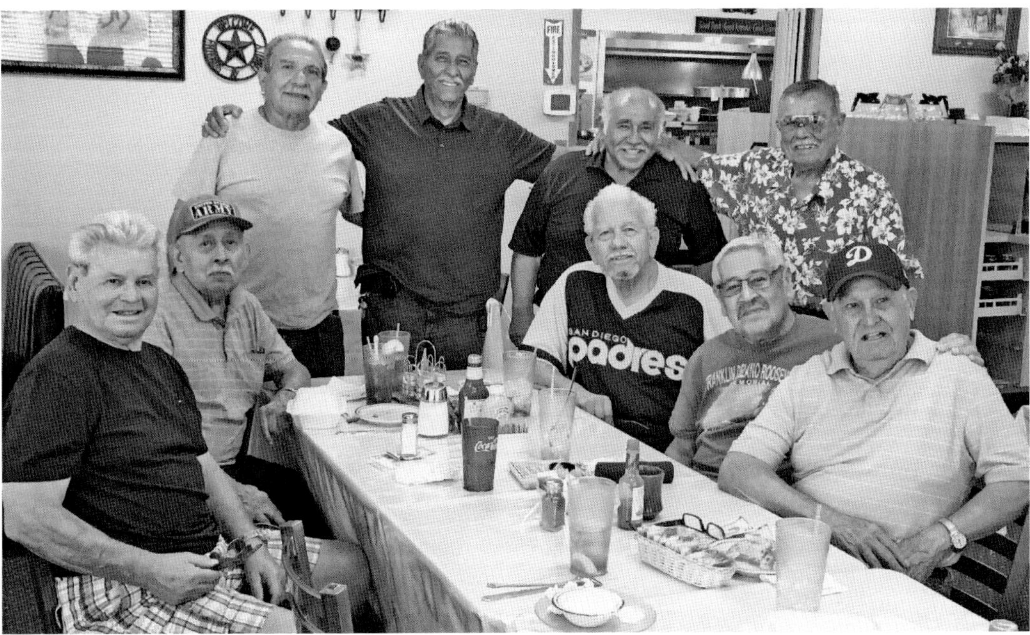

The August 2017 meeting of Bakersfield Our Lady of Guadalupe players included, from left to right (sitting at table) Frank Camacho, Manuel Rocha, Leroy Hinojos, Fidencio Gaona, and Robert Alvarado; (standing in back) Buddy Gallegos, Johnny Águilar, David Monsibais, and Rudy Arambula. (Courtesy of Christopher Docter.)

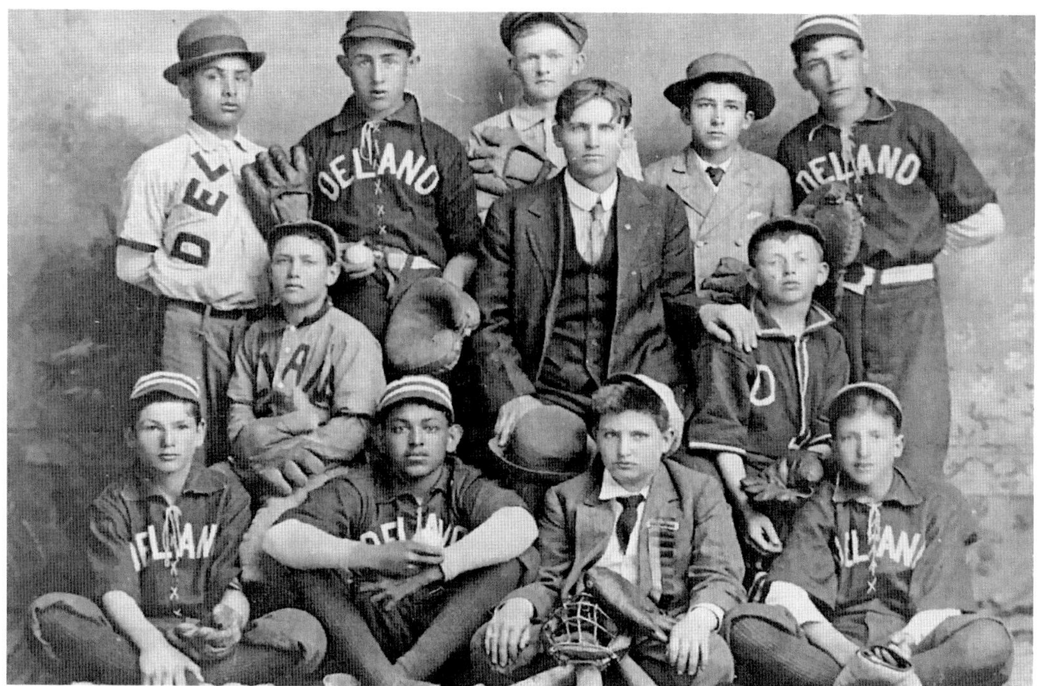

Descendants of longtime California settler families played for this late 1800s to early 1900s Delano team. They included Joe Núñez Jr. (first row, second from left) and Steve Núñez (top row, far left). The Núñez and Valencia families, linked through marriage, were among the earliest Mexican families in Delano. The Valencia family migrated from Sonora, Mexico, to Northern California in the 1840s and moved to Delano in 1876. They operated several businesses in Delano, including the Spanish Kitchen, a saloon, a barbershop, and a cigar store. Eddie Valencia played on the first organized baseball team in Delano in 1908. (Courtesy of Teresa Martínez Vincent and Delano Historical Society.)

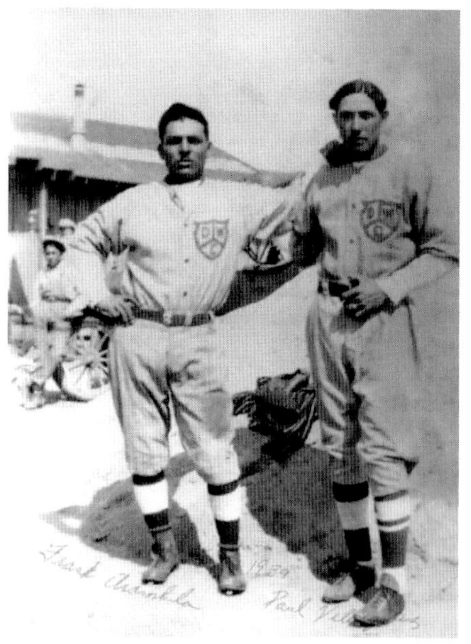

Delano baseball players Frank Arambula (left) and his brother in law Paul Velasquez pose in this 1939 photograph. Delano had a rich Mexican American baseball environment. Several Delano teams, including the Tigers, Aztecs, Wildcats, Monarchs, Merchants, Browns, Mexican Athletic Club, Honorary Mexican Commission, and Club Juvenil, formed in the 1930s and 1940s and played on the Southern Pacific baseball diamond. On Mexican Independence Day, September 16, 1939, the Honorary Mexican Commission held a two-day festival. The festivities culminated in a baseball game between the Delano Mexican Tigers and the Mexican YMCA team from Tulare. (Courtesy of the Velasquez family.)

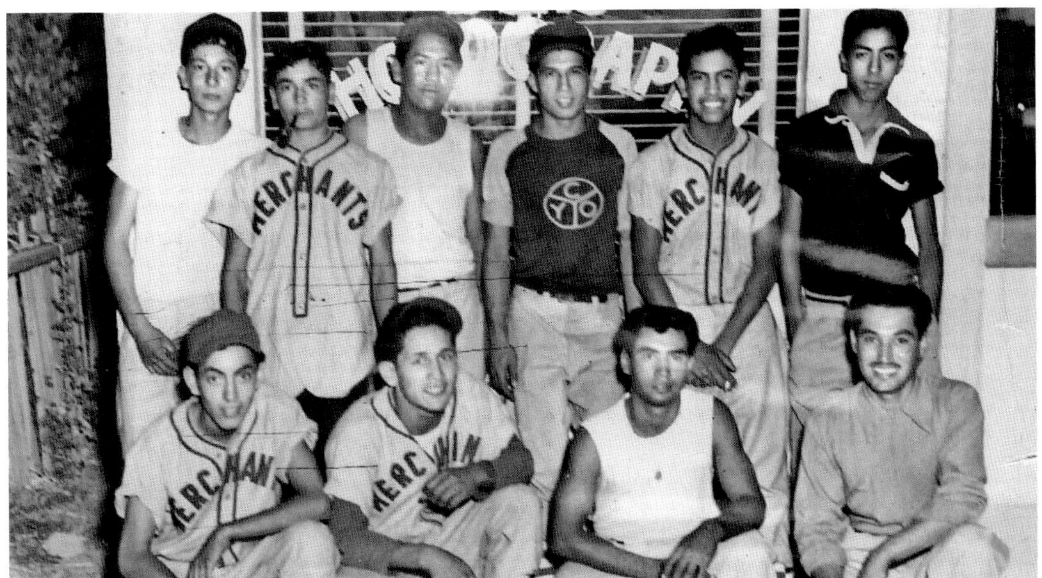

The Merchants team from Delano was led by coach Joe "El Grillo" (the Cricket) Soltero through the 1950s. Soltero openly admitted that his cousin Tony Márquez (first row, second from left) taught him the managerial skills necessary to coach this 1958 team. This squad placed third in a national tournament in New England. Márquez played third base for Delano High School, playing varsity as a freshman. Coach Soltero's son Karl (not pictured) currently serves on the board of directors of La Raza Historical Society of the Santa Clara Valley and also serves on the Santa Clara County Office of County Heritage. (Courtesy of Karl Soltero.)

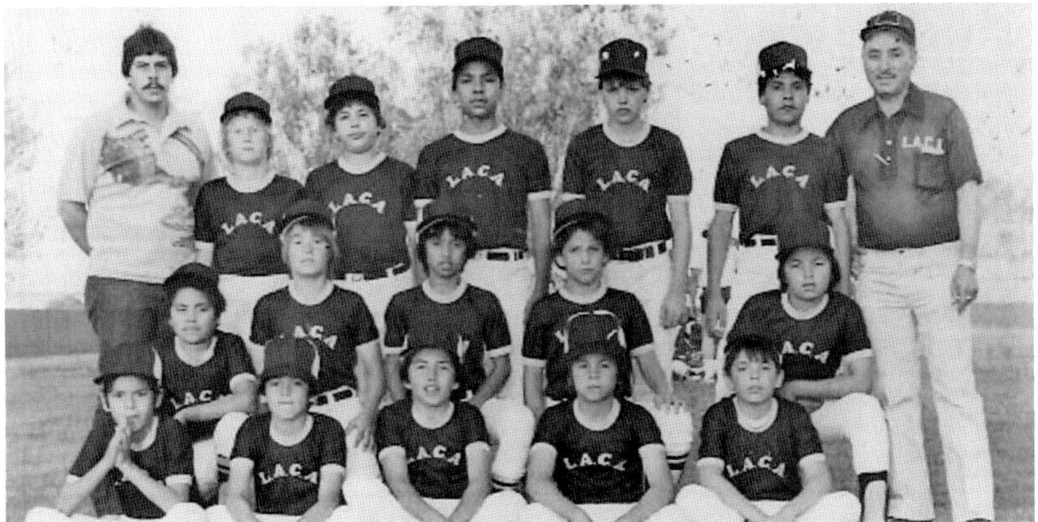

A generation after coaching the Merchants fast pitch softball team, Joe "El Grillo" Soltero was coaching Little League in Delano. He was now coaching the sons of former Merchants players. Unfortunately, the names of the players are not known. Besides the nickname "El Grillo," Joe was also known as "LACA Joe." Coach Soltero managed Little League for 37 years, appearing in 16 championship games and winning 12 of them. (Courtesy of Karl Soltero.)

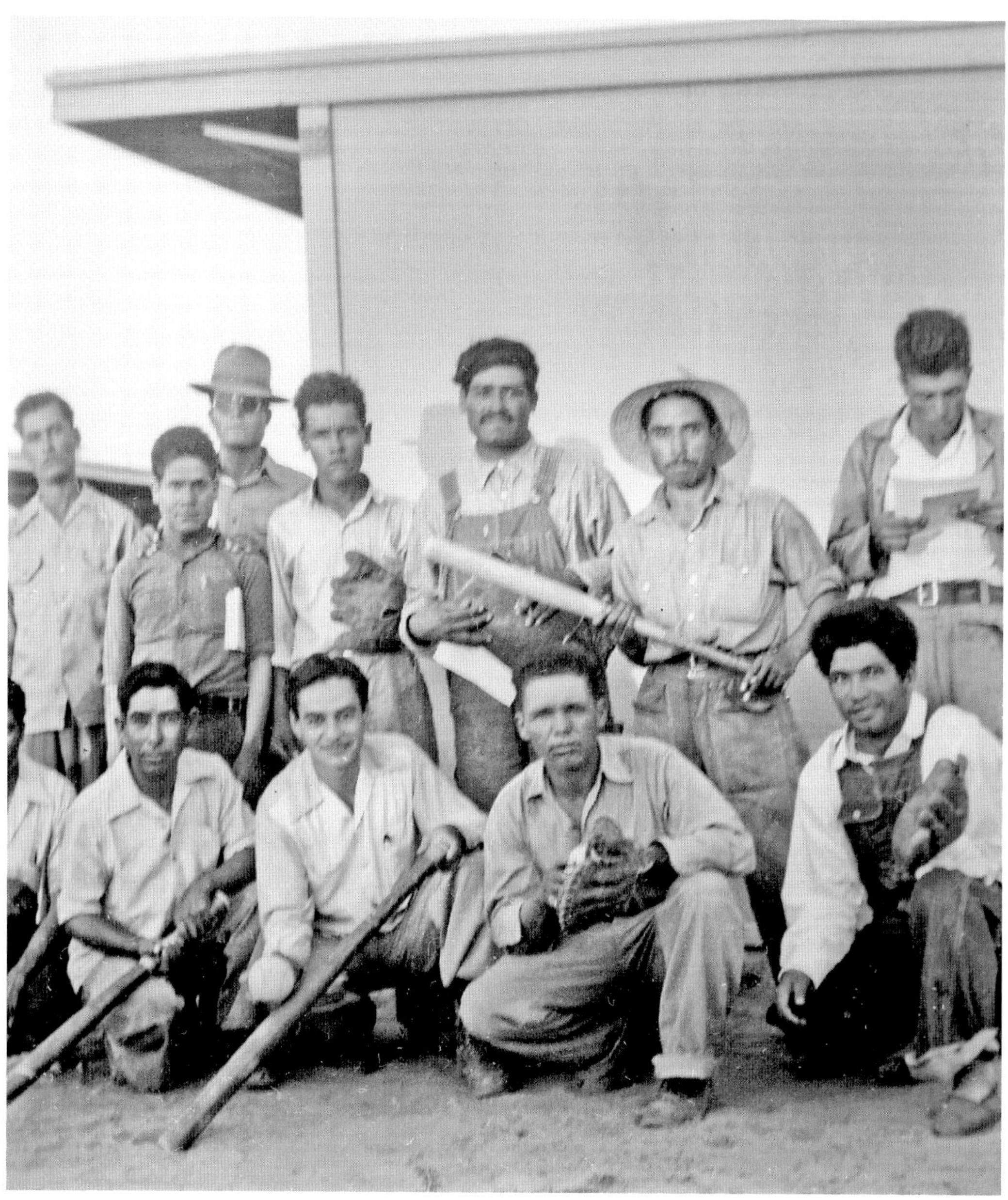

Mexican braceros display their softball equipment at the Wasco farm labor camp in 1943 as part of a physical education class. In the fall of 1942, Kern County growers called for the mass importation of Mexican braceros to fill the agricultural labor shortage during the war. By 1945, over a thousand braceros entered the multi-million-dollar agribusiness industry in Kern County, picking long-staple cotton, sugar beets, peaches, and grapes. In the nearby DiGiorgio labor camp in Arvin, workers lived in small, shabbily constructed boxcars with no sanitary facilities, away from the fine ranch homes of farm management. Since the 1930s, Mexicans and Mexican Americans who worked at the DiGiorgio labor camp had played on baseball teams. (Courtesy of Kern County Museum.)

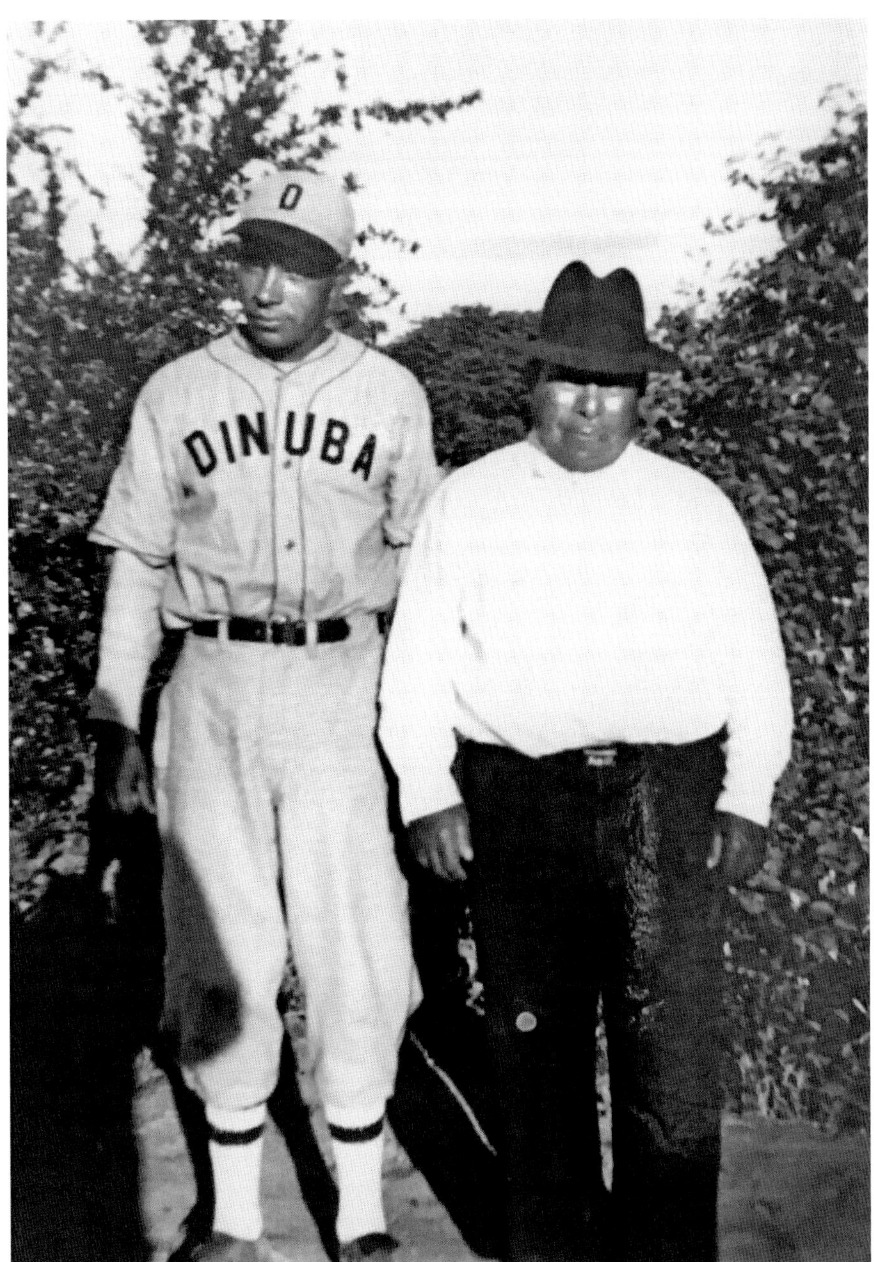

Lupe Delgado (left) and his father, José Delgado, stand among the crops in Dinuba. José Delgado was the first Mexican American to buy land in Dinuba in 1917, clearing out two lots full of wild grape vines. In the early 1930s, he managed the Dinuba Dons, one of the earliest Mexican American teams in the town. His sons Félix (centerfielder), Enoch (first baseman), and Lupe (shortstop) played for the Dons. Children of Dons players collected donations for the team, typically passing a hat around the bleachers. Delgado maintained the Legion Bowl baseball fields in Dinuba throughout the 1930s and 1940s. In 1943, he started Delgado's Café, which lasted for 47 years. (Courtesy of Isabel Delgado Ybarra.)

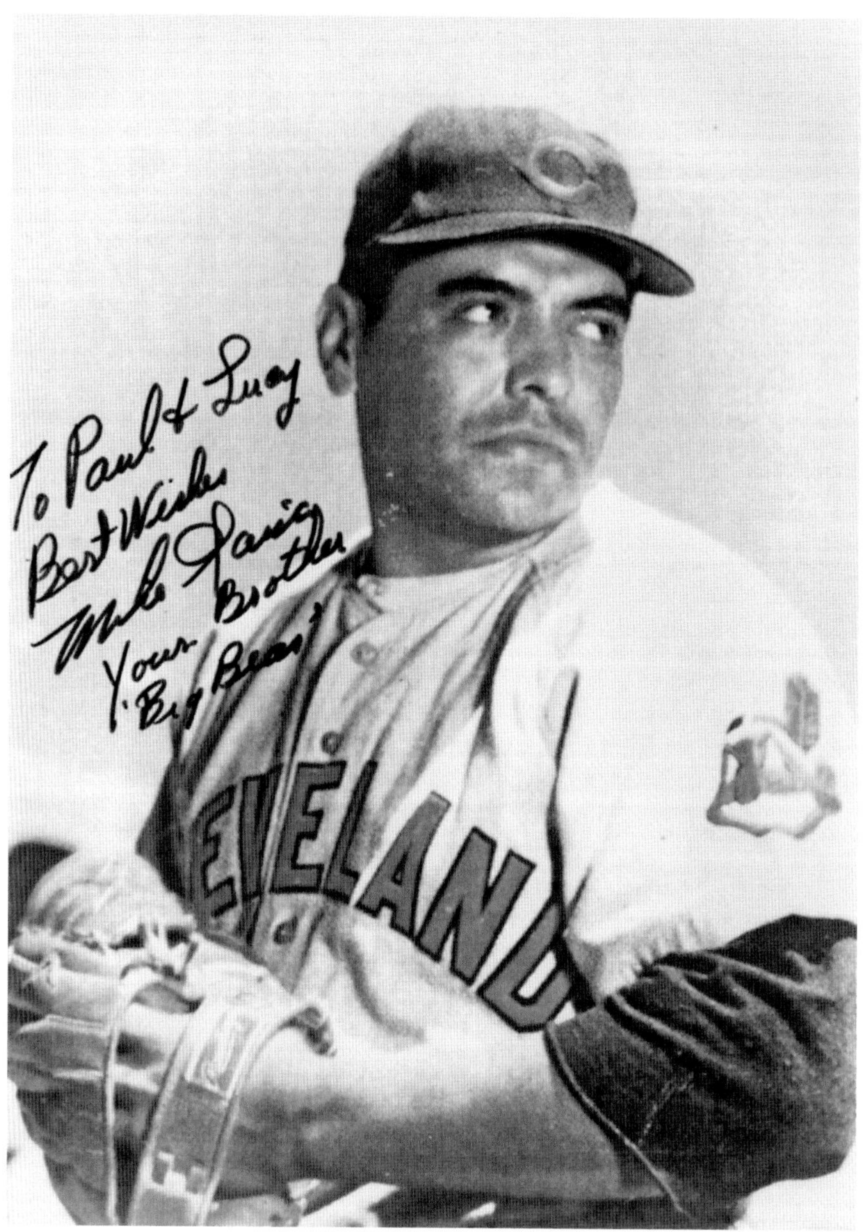

A power pitcher raised on a horse ranch in Orosi, California, Mike "Big Bear" García became one of the elite pitchers in Cleveland Indians history. In 1942, García pitched for a Tulare Mexican American community team when he caught the attention of professional scouts. After playing in the minors and serving in the Army Signal Corps during World War II, he made his debut in 1948 with the world champion Cleveland Indians, and pitched in the majors until 1961. His peak years occurred in the early 1950s as a key part of arguably the best pitching rotation of all time alongside hall-of-famers Bob Feller, Early Wynn, and Bob Lemon. Other Cleveland teammates included fellow Mexican American Rudy Regalado and Veracruz, Mexico, native Bobby Ávila. (Courtesy of Rudy Trejo.)

Simón Hernández was born in 1909 in El Paso, Texas. His family worked for the Southern Pacific Railroad and later moved west to work in the many farms of California, migrating between Brawley and Dinuba throughout the 1930s. Hernández settled in Dinuba in the 1930s and managed several teams, including the Apaches. In addition to the Dinuba Dons, other teams in the region included the San Joaquin Stars (Dinuba), Reedley Eagles, Fresno International, Guadalupe Victoria (Glorietta), Hanford Mohawks, López AC (Farmersville), Mendota, Tagus Rancheros, Delano Wildcats, Bakersfield Nacionales, El Porvenir (Selma), Laton Aztecas, Sanger Indians, Visalia MAC, Corcoran Bears, Arvin Aztecas, Tulare Monarchs, AHA Logia Esperaza Tehachapi, Wasco Bees, and Alpaugh Merchants. (Courtesy of Michael H. Estrada and Manny Hernández.)

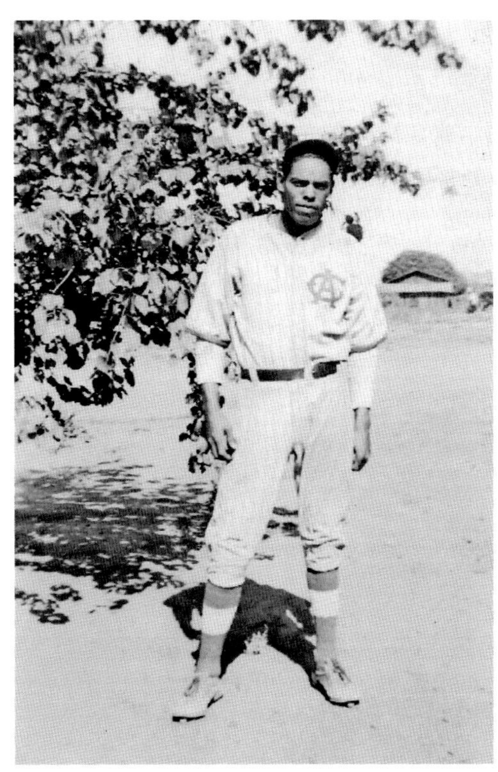

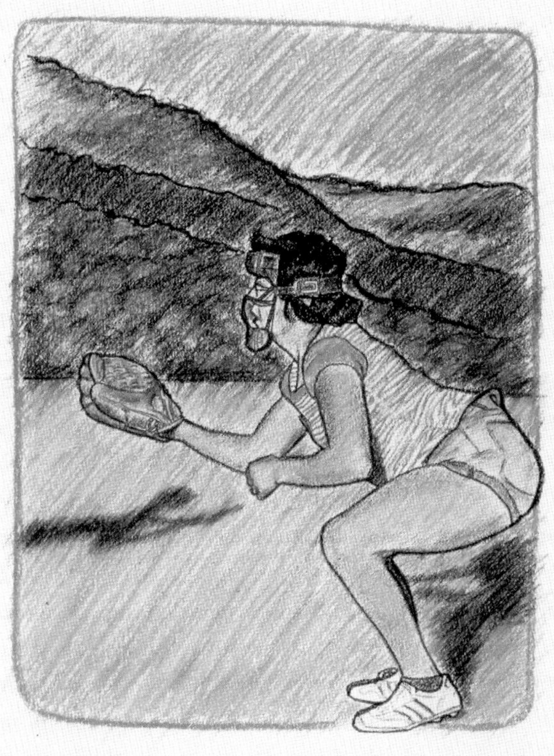

Ester Hernández, daughter of Simón Hernández, played for the Dinuba Chinatown barrio's women's softball team from the late 1950s to the mid-1960s. She is a world-renowned Chicana artist and activist. Her work, which prominently features women and frequently provides social commentary on issues related to farm workers, is included in the collections of the National Museum of American Art, the Smithsonian Institution, the Library of Congress, the Museum of Modern Art and the Mexican Museum in San Francisco, the National Museum of Mexican Art in Chicago, and the Frida Kahlo Studio Museum in Mexico City. This piece is from the 1980s and is entitled *Play Ball*. It features a Chicana softball player. (Courtesy of Ester Hernández.)

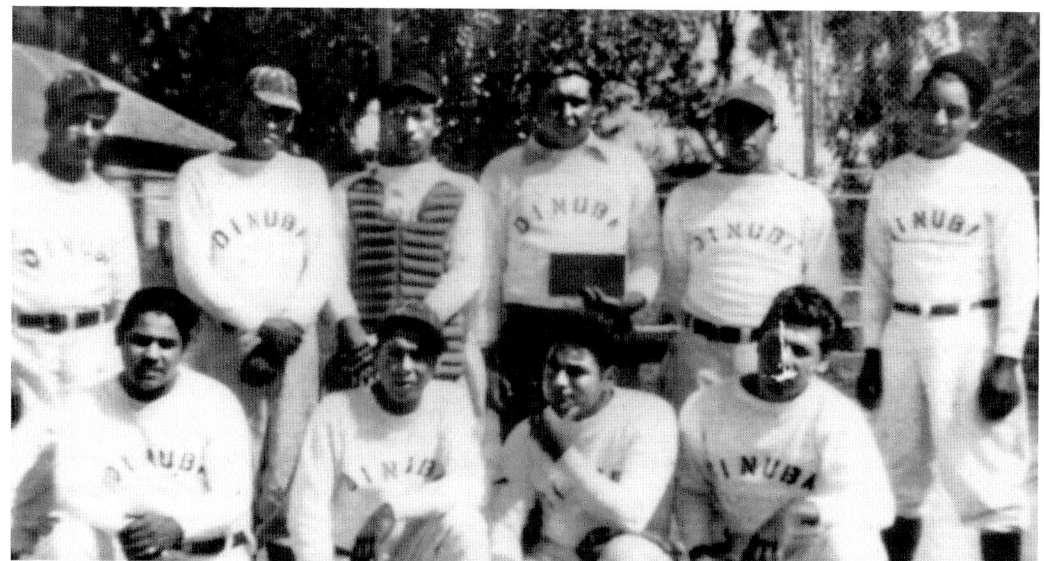

This early 1940s Dinuba Apaches team consisted of, from left to right, (first row) Charles Trejo, Wicho Moreno, Jess Tapia, and Ralph Aviles; (second row) Francisco Domínguez, Simon Hernández, Manuel Morales, Rito Trejo, Santos "Pee Wee" Morales, and Abundio Trejo. The Trejo family, originally from Chihuahua, lived in Fort Worth, Texas, before moving to Dinuba in 1937. Rito Trejo served as manager. During this era, men's and women's teams played at the Legion Bowl. Prior to closing in the 1950s, the Legion Bowl also held rodeos, fairs, and hot rod races. (Courtesy of Rudy Trejo.)

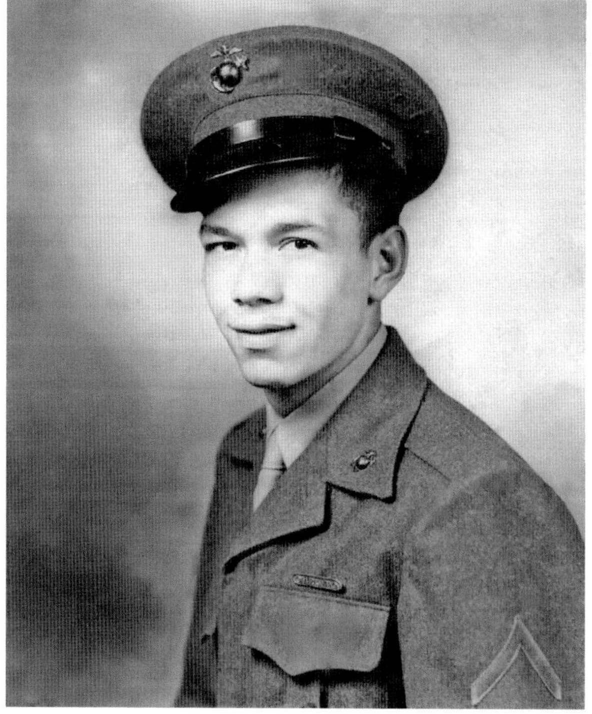

Michael H. Estrada was born in Dinuba in 1932, the oldest of Manuel and Manuela Estrada's seven children. He grew up playing and working in the vast fields and orchards of the San Joaquin Valley. Estrada later joined local baseball teams, playing on the Dinuba Apaches under his uncle Simón Hernández until enlisting in the Marine Corps during the Korean War. Beginning in October 1951, he served with the 5th Marine Regiment in Korea. Upon returning home, he married Leanore Soza, and the couple had five children. (Courtesy of Michael H. Estrada and Manny Hernández.)

John Garza is pictured in 1955 at his home in Dinuba next to his 1941 Chevy. Garza was a prominent pitcher for the semiprofessional Dinuba Redskins. The Redskins played against other Mexican American teams from the region, such as the Reedley Eagles, Reedley Panthers, Selma Braves, Orosi Lobos, Fresno Los Diablos, Cutler Tigers, Seville Colts, Tulare, Sanger, and McFarland. Dinuba also featured a team from the La Cuba labor camp. (Courtesy of John Garza and Linda Garza Ávila.)

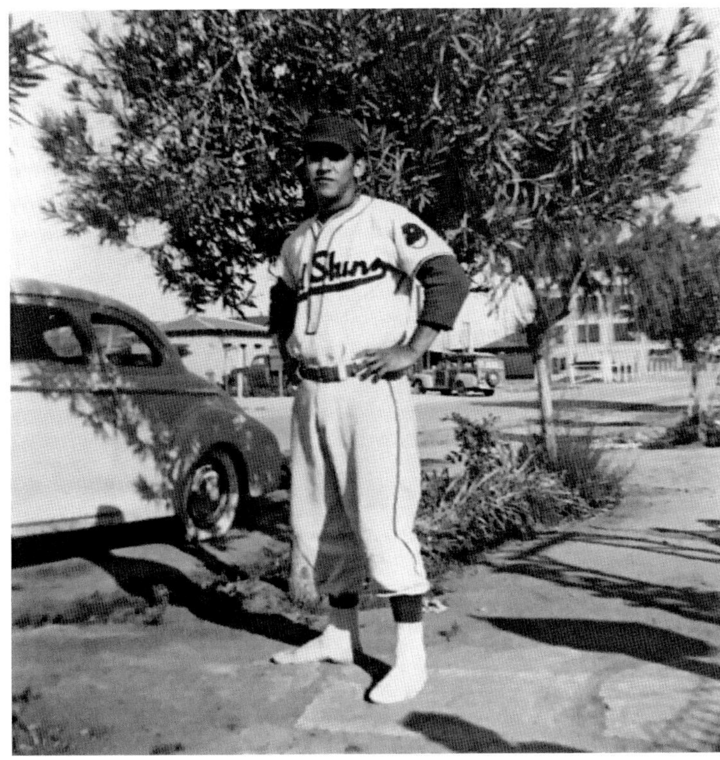

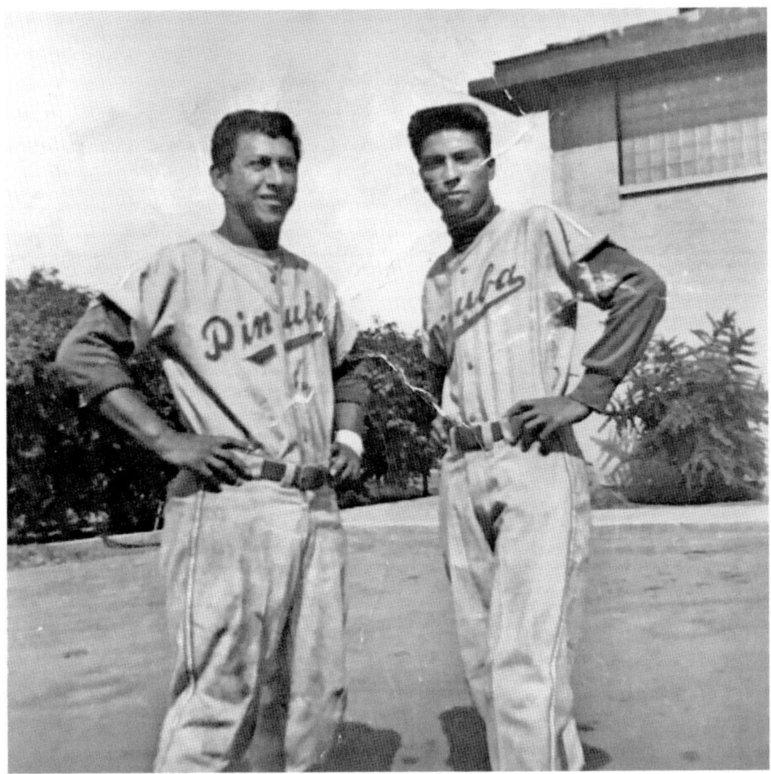

Dinuba High School players John Garza (left) and Richard Medina stand in this 1955 photograph after an incredible game. Pitcher John Garza struck out 29 batters from Lindsay High School, a record that still remains. Dinuba won the matchup between the two undefeated teams, with the final score of 1-0. Garza won pitcher MVP awards in high school in 1954 and 1955. (Courtesy of John Garza and Linda Garza Ávila.)

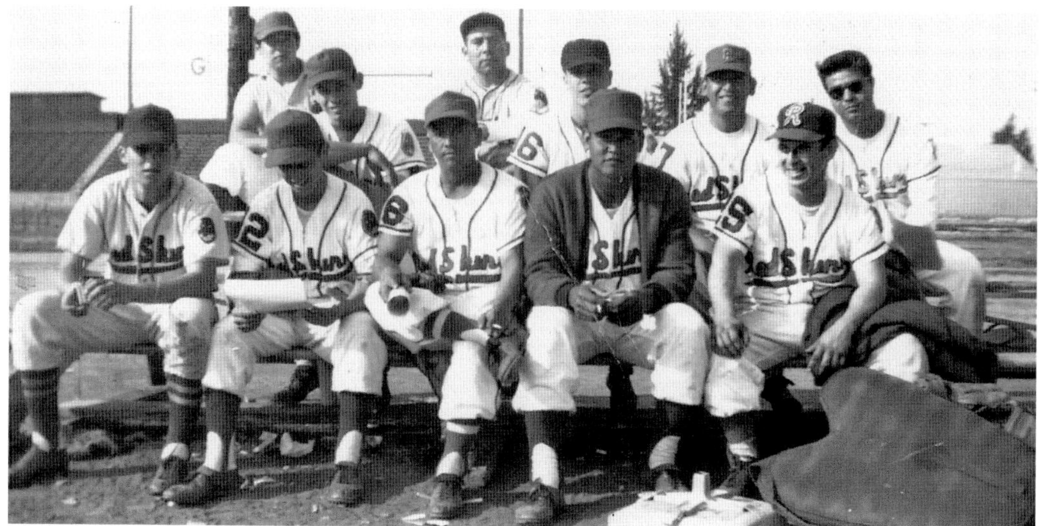

The 1961 Dinuba Redskins consisted of, from left to right, (first row) Jerry Pritchett, Eddie Vásquez, Lorenzo Morales, Rudy Trejo, and Chilo Arias; (second row) Louie Arias, Leroy Cervantes, John Garza, and Richard Medina; (third row) Charles Trejo and manager Félix Delgado. Talented catcher Rudy Trejo also played at Dinuba High School, where he caught John Garza. After graduating in 1957, he played baseball while in the Navy. (Courtesy of Rudy Trejo.)

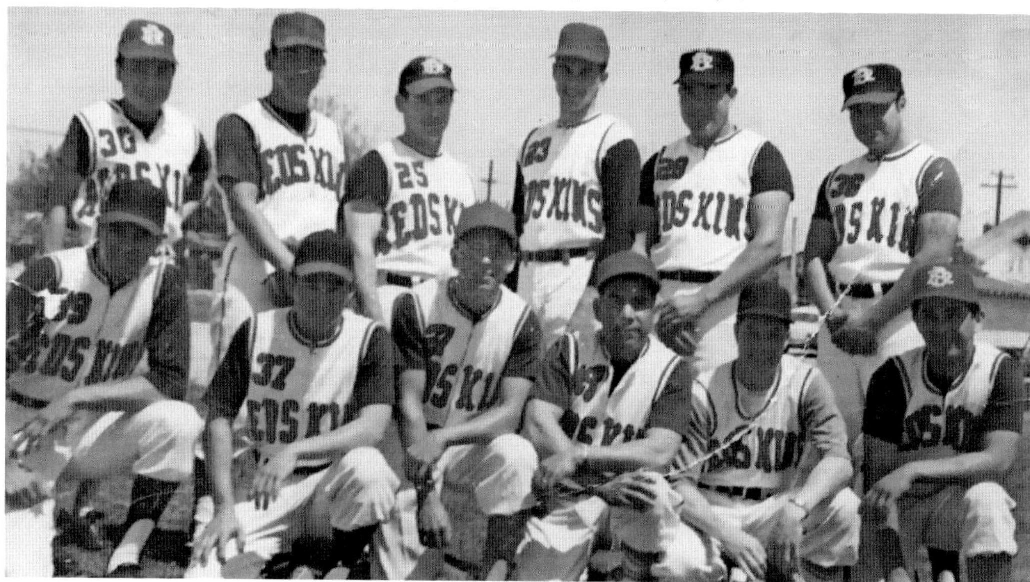

In the 1960s or 1970s, the Dinuba Redskins line up at the Tortilla Flats ballpark. From left to right are (first row) Louie Arias, Frank Kurijawa, Richard Delgado, Félix Delgado, Norman Krebs, and Eddie Vásquez; (second row) Joey Herrera, John Garza, Chilo Arias, Larry Green, Armand Mendoza, and Richard Medina. The diverse Dinuba barrio was called Tortilla Flats or Chinatown and included Mexican, Japanese, Chinese, Korean, and Filipino American families. The Tortilla Flats ballpark was renamed Félix Delgado Park in 1997. (Courtesy of John Garza and Linda Garza Ávila.)

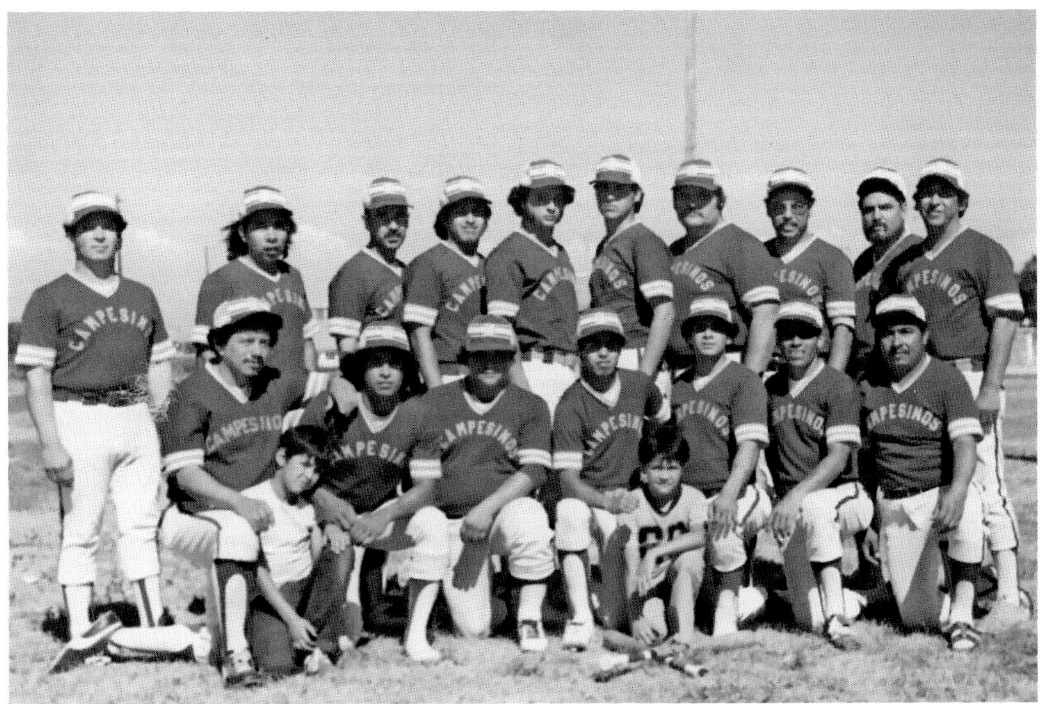

This 1976 Dinuba Campesinos team picture shows, from left to right, (first row) Pete Corona, batboy Jaime Vela, two unidentified, Art Quintero, unidentified batboy, Manuel Hernández, Cat Hernández, and Israel Morales; (second row) Pancho Garza, Pete González, Ray Alvarado, Harvey Quintero, Dave Gaston, Sony Santiago, unidentified, Ramos Pineda, Rubén Vela, and John Garza. The team name reflects the agricultural identity of Central Valley towns. (Courtesy of John Garza and Linda Garza Ávila.)

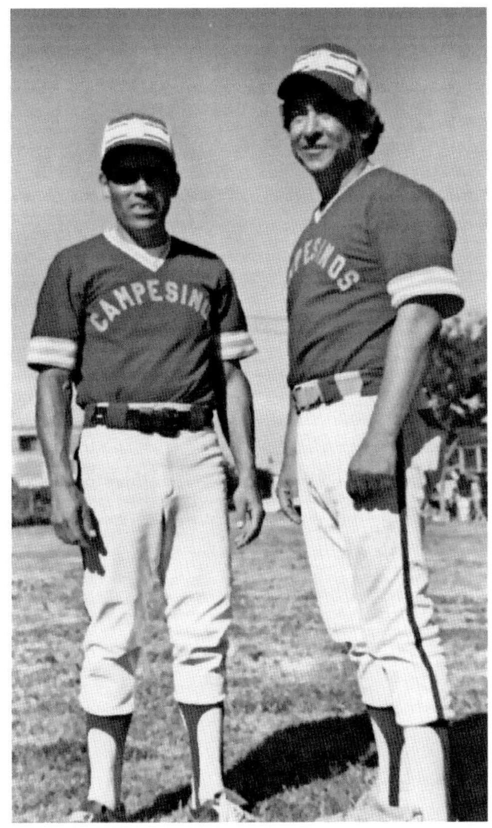

Cat Hernández (left) and John Garza of the Dinuba Campesinos are pictured in 1976. Hernández was known for his defensive prowess and quick hands at shortstop. He remains involved with baseball, instructing Little League players in Dinuba and Reedley. The Campesinos were composed of players from nearby towns outside Dinuba, such as Reedley, Selma, Fresno, London, and Orosi. After games, teams held festive barbecues. (Courtesy of John Garza and Linda Garza Ávila.)

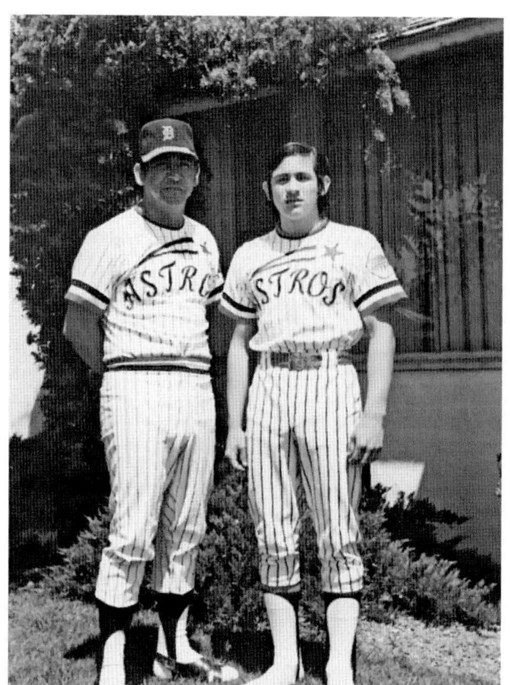

The talented father-son pitching duo of John Garza (left) and John "Ringo" Garza Jr. played for the Dinuba Astros in 1978. Other Dinuba teams during this era included the Dinuba Tigers and Dinuba Lobos. Players on these teams included Alex Montañez, Joe Mendoza, Manuel Hernández, Cat Hernández, John Delgado, Ray Ortega, Eddie Martínez, Nato González, Chico Real, Amado Díaz, Mickey Martínez, Pete Corona, Richard Medina, Frank Treviño, Pete Cervantes, and Adam Real. Garza Sr. still plays, pitching for senior softball teams such as the Porterville Patriots and Tulare Barks. He has competed in the Huntsman World Senior Games in softball, held in St. George, Utah. (Courtesy of John Garza and Linda Garza Ávila.)

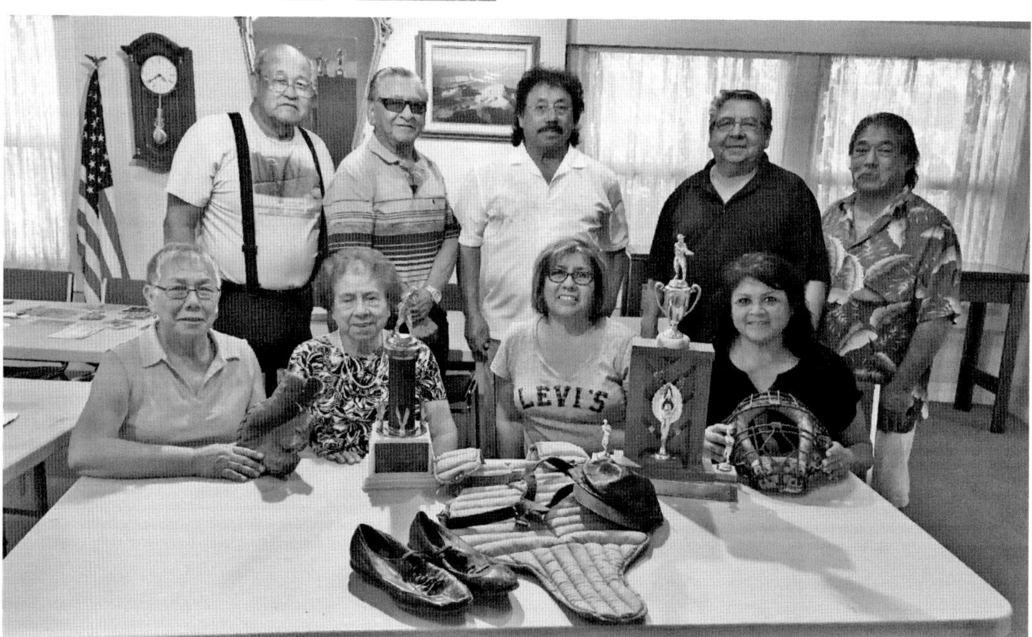

In August 2017, members of historical Dinuba baseball families met at the Alta District Historical Society. From left to right are (first row) Anita Delgado Betancourt, Isabel Delgado Ybarra, Margie Delgado Carrillo, and Linda Garza Ávila; (second row) Rudy Trejo, John Garza, John Delgado, Richard Delgado, and Danny Delgado. Displayed on the table are the baseball equipment and awards belonging to Félix Delgado, the foremost baseball pioneer in Dinuba. Betancourt currently serves as mayor of Reedley. (Courtesy of Christopher Docter.)

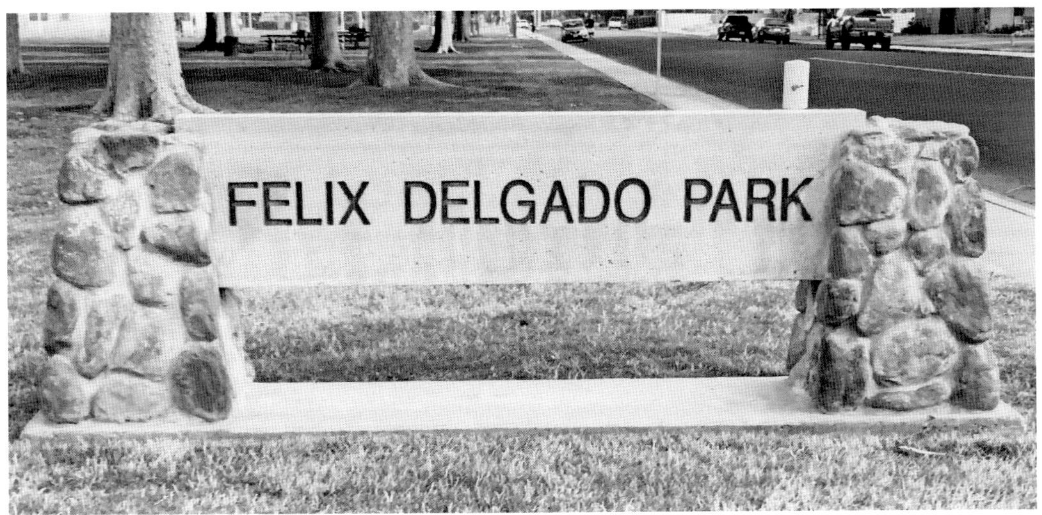

On July 19, 1997, the city of Dinuba dedicated the local baseball field to Félix Delgado, a respected baseball mentor in the community. The field was originally named Tortilla Flats and was the center for baseball activity among the Mexican American teams in the region. Born in 1916 in Lindsay, California, Delgado started playing baseball in the 1930s for the Dinuba Dons. He later formed the Dinuba Redskins and spearheaded the formation of Dinuba Little League and Dinuba Babe Ruth League. Thousands from the community attended the dedication ceremony. (Courtesy of Christopher Docter.)

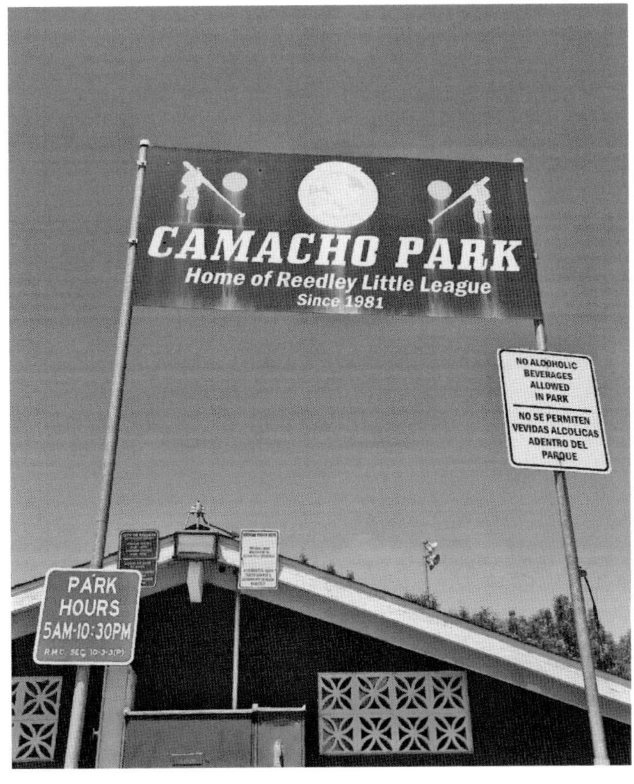

Camacho Park in Reedley is named after Frank Camacho. Known as the "Quiet Man," he selflessly dedicated his life to baseball and softball in the Reedley community. Camacho was born in 1900 in Jalisco, Mexico, and immigrated to the United States through El Paso in the early 1920s, moving to Reedley shortly thereafter. He formed some of the earliest teams in town and used his own money to buy balls, bats, and other equipment. Not only did he support his children's involvement in baseball, he also made sure that all neighborhood kids had the opportunity to play. His son John Camacho served as mayor of Reedley. (Courtesy of the Camacho family.)

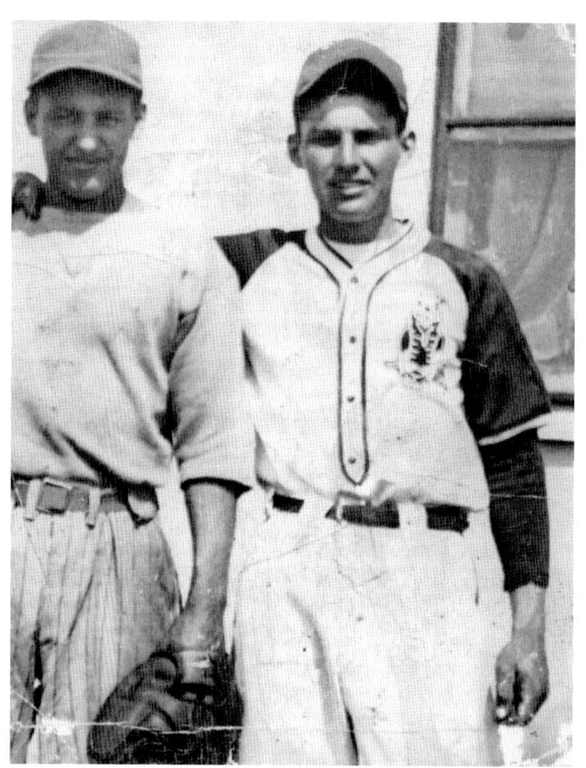

Brothers Oscar (left) and Eddie Chapa pose for a picture before playing baseball in 1950. Eddie is wearing his Madera Owls softball uniform. Born in Laredo in 1930, Eddie Chapa grew up in the highly competitive atmosphere of Texas baseball. He played shortstop on American Legion and various all-star teams, traveling for tournaments in Corpus Christi and Austin. Chapa moved with his family to Madera, California, in 1947 and worked at Madera High School in the athletic department for 35 years. Oscar Chapa played catcher and worked at Safeway in Fresno for 45 years. (Courtesy of Eddie Chapa.)

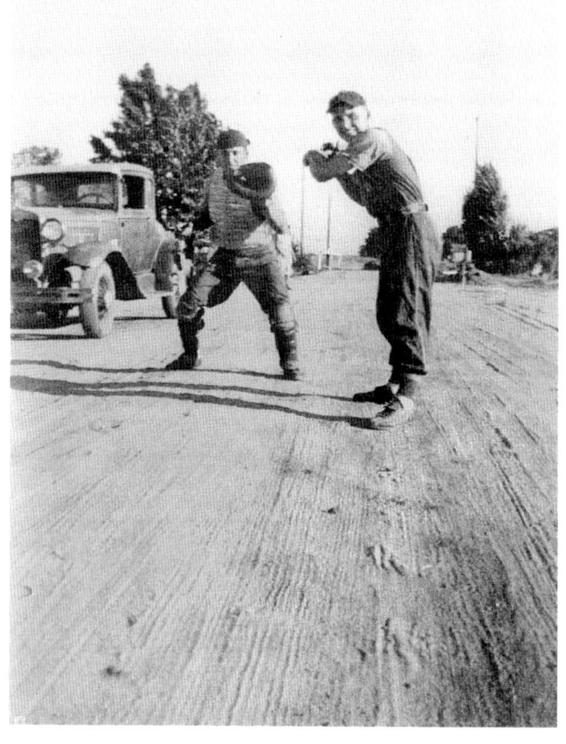

Oscar Chapa (catching) and Eddie Chapa (batting) practice on the dirt roads of Madera. The brothers played all over the state, including in Fresno in the California Mexican League. They moved to Madera from Laredo, Texas, with their father, Teodoro, in 1947. The Chapas worked in the fields of Madera, picking peaches, grapes, and potatoes. In 1950, Eddie founded the Madera Merchants, a summer-league baseball team for high school boys. He coached the Merchants until 1979, when his son took over. Eddie Chapa continued his baseball journeys in later years. In 1972, he played a double-header in Tijuana. He coached his children and grandchildren, and wrote articles for the *Madera Tribune* and *Fresno Bee*. Eddie Chapa passed away in 2018. (Courtesy of Eddie Chapa.)

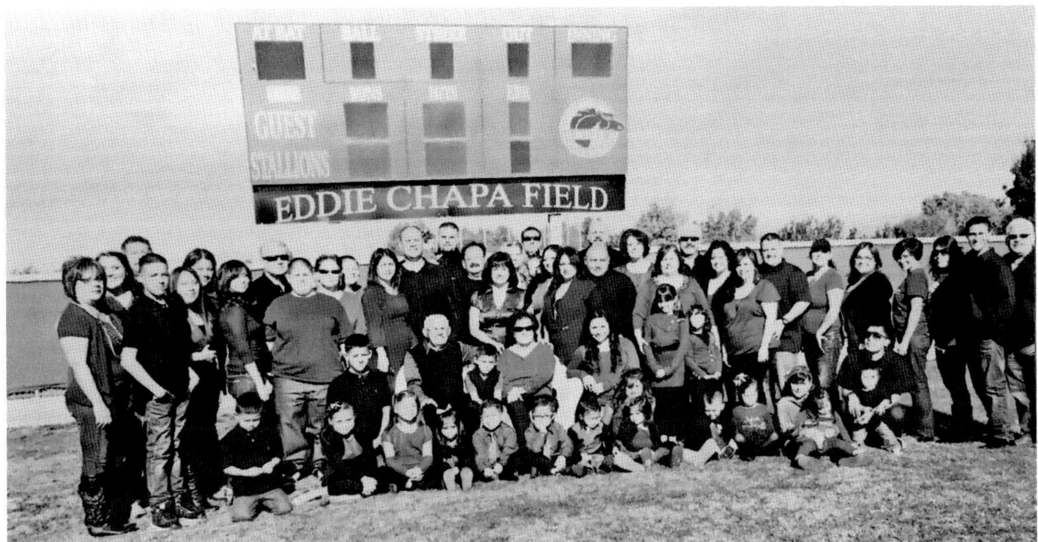

In 2012, Madera South High School named its varsity baseball field after Eddie Chapa. Hundreds of family, friends, alumni, and community members attended the dedication ceremony of Eddie Chapa Field. Chapa received plaques from Madera Unified School District and the Madera County supervisor honoring his devotion to youth sports for more than 60 years. Eddie Chapa is seated in the black vest along with his wife, Frances, their seven children and families, and numerous grandchildren and great-grandchildren. (Courtesy of Eddie Chapa.)

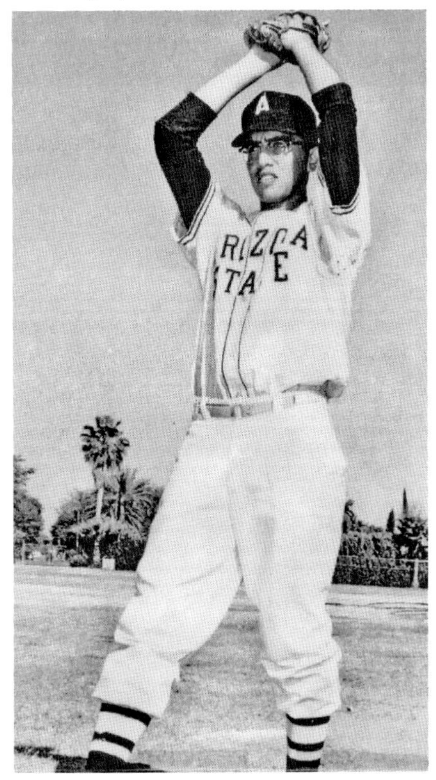

Planada native John Chávez winds up for the Arizona State Sun Devils. Chávez was a starting pitcher at Arizona State from 1957 to 1958. After receiving his bachelor's degree and teaching credentials from Arizona State in 1960, Chávez served in the Army for two years. While there, he played on numerous softball teams, including Ponce Cement when he was stationed at Fort Allen in Puerto Rico. Chávez played softball in Central California for 20 years after he got out of the service. His daughters Amanda, Luci, and Marisa played on the Le Grand High School softball team in 1985. Amanda played two years for Merced Community College. Her daughter Jessica also starred at Le Grand High for four years. (Courtesy of John Chávez.)

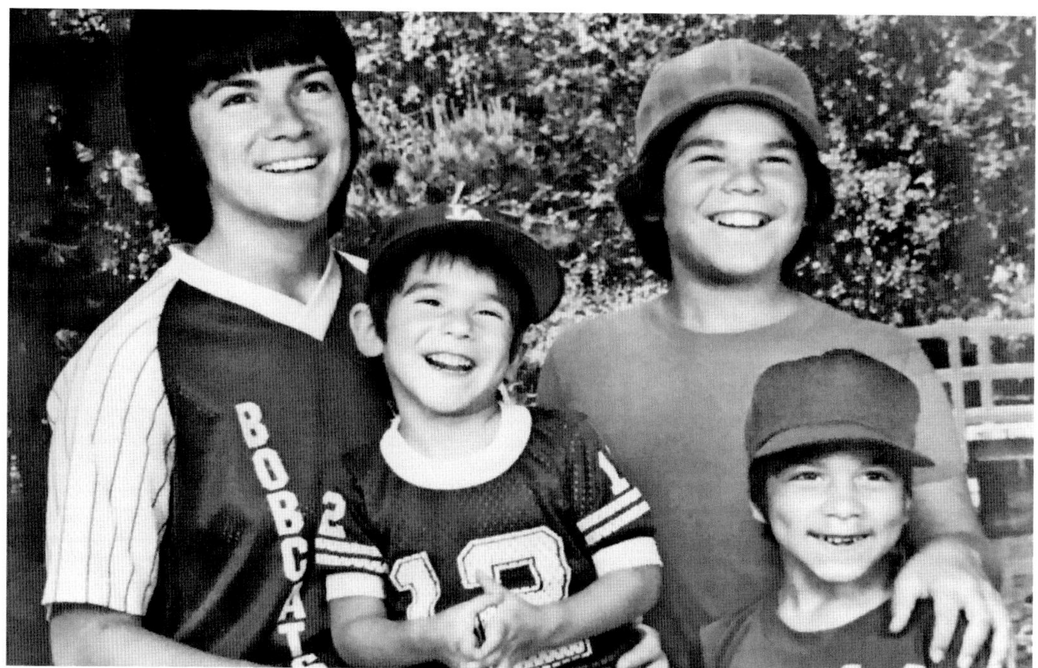

Pictured in the 1970s, Sylvia Lovato sits with her sons, from left to right, Jason Lovato Chávez (in her lap), Raymond Lovato Chávez, and Frank Lovato Chávez. She is wearing her Modesto Bobcats jersey; Jason was the batboy. Sylvia pitched, played left field, and batted cleanup for most of her softball career. Born in East Los Angeles, Lovato is descended from New Mexico Spanish Mexican settlers who lived there for centuries. She started playing baseball and softball in grade school. At Le Grand High School, she became Girls Athletic Association president and won the High Point Senior Award in 1966. (Courtesy of Sylvia Lovato.)

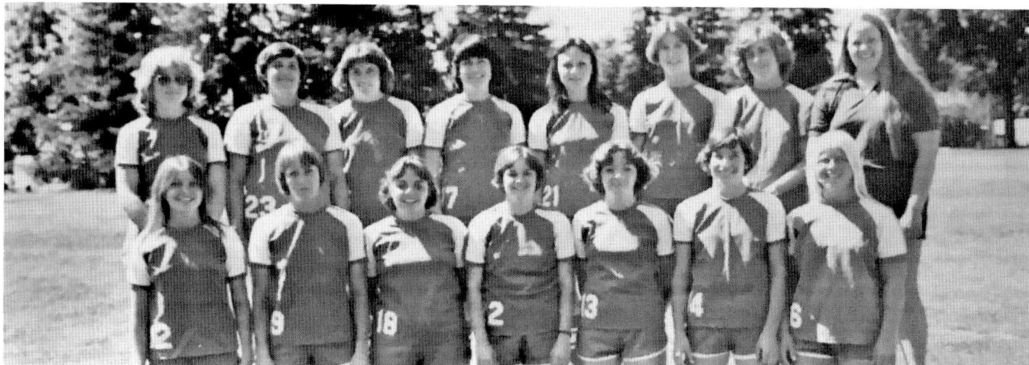

The 1977 Modesto Junior College women's softball team featured Sylvia Lovato (second row, fourth from left). Other players include Cindy Cunningham, Cindy García, Mary Lou Grossi, Julie Hofmann, Jackie Munn, Carol Peters, Joan Watson, ? Roest, ? Lyman, ? Twyman, ? Jordan, ? Lynch, and ? Oden. Lovato led the team in hitting that year with an astonishing .458 batting average. She also played for the Planada Chevronettes, Bob Kleins (Modesto), USA Team, Stockton Raiders, Ceres Bobcats, and Modesto Bobcats. An all-around athlete, she also played tennis and basketball. (Courtesy of Sylvia Lovato.)

Field of Dreams

From its humble beginning, the Mexican American Baseball series has concluded each book with a chapter entitled "Field of Dreams." This chapter is designed to showcase the day-by-day events and activities taking place in countless communities paying tribute to these magnificent players, glorious teams, and legendary managers. These photographs and testimonies include spellbinding exhibits, memorable luncheons, exciting book signings, impressive symposiums, unforgettable parades, riveting local hall of fame inductions, emotional renaming of parks and ballfields, and first pitch ceremonies. These and many other ongoing forms of recognition convey to the players and coaches that their achievements on and off the field have not been forgotten by their neighborhoods and communities and that their extraordinary accomplishments will live on forever through books, newsletters, oral interviews, film, and other forms of documentation by the Latino Baseball History Project at California State University, San Bernardino.

Besides highlighting sponsored events and organized activities saluting these players, teams, and coaches, this chapter includes very special photographs—family photographs of three or four generations of players; individual players in their 80s and 90s in a batting stance or holding a mitt; group photographs of players at the ballfields where they played so long ago; players with their elderly managers and coaches; players with their wives; players holding old trophies, aged letterman jackets, and worn-out uniforms that have survived decades; family members holding bats, gloves, uniforms, trophies, and plaques of players who have gone on to the big diamond in the sky; brothers and sisters who played ball during the golden age of Mexican American baseball and softball; high school and college rivals who, despite their adversarial matches on the field, have remained close friends for over 60 years; and funerals with baseball themes and baseball-inspired Day of the Dead ceremonies at the gravesites of former players.

Throughout the United States, younger generations of Mexican Americans are hosting and sponsoring countless events remembering achievements, accomplishments, and contributions of those born between the early 1900s and the late 1930s. These lavish tributes highlight the preeminent military service on the battlefield and on the home front, civil and political rights leaders, influential educators, fearless labor and union organizers, gifted artists, matchless sports heroes and teams, the groundbreaking vanguard within the news and entertainment fields, and effective business leaders. Over 100 "Field of Dreams" photographs have appeared in the first 15 books. *Un gran brindis a todos los sabios y sabias en la comunidad.* (A toast to all of the wise ones in the community.)

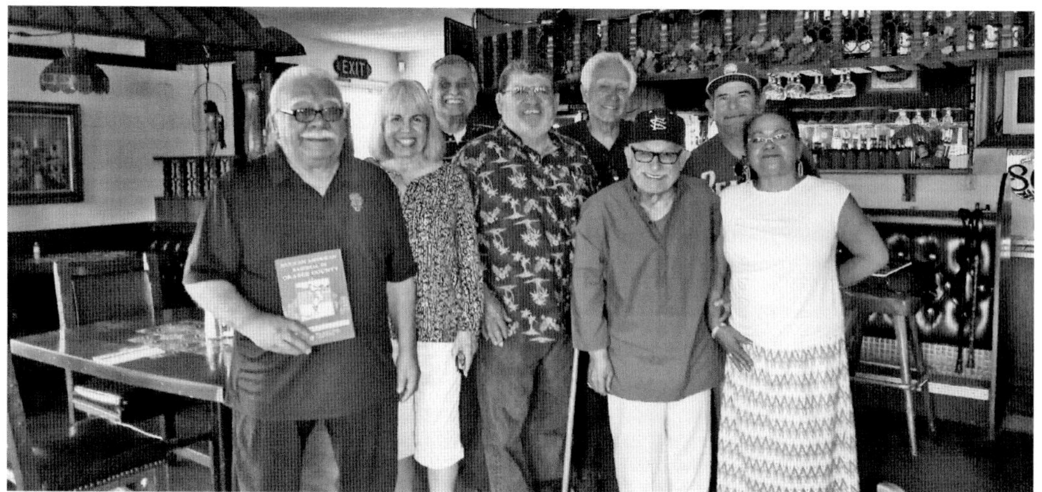

From left to right, Joe Talaugon, Teresa M. Santillán, Richard A. Santillán, Eddie Navarro, Eddie Corral, Bill Soto-Castellanos, Al Ramos, and Karen Louise Evangelista meet on June 17, 2017, in Buellton, California, halfway between Santa Barbara and Santa Maria, to discuss the progress of an upcoming book on the remarkable history of Mexican American baseball and softball in the Santa Maria Valley. Navarro and Ramos coauthored Santa Maria Valley chapters in previous books. Joe and his daughter Karen operate the Guadalupe Cultural Arts Center, promoting and preserving traditional and contemporary Latino culture through the fine arts. (Courtesy of Richard A. Santillán.)

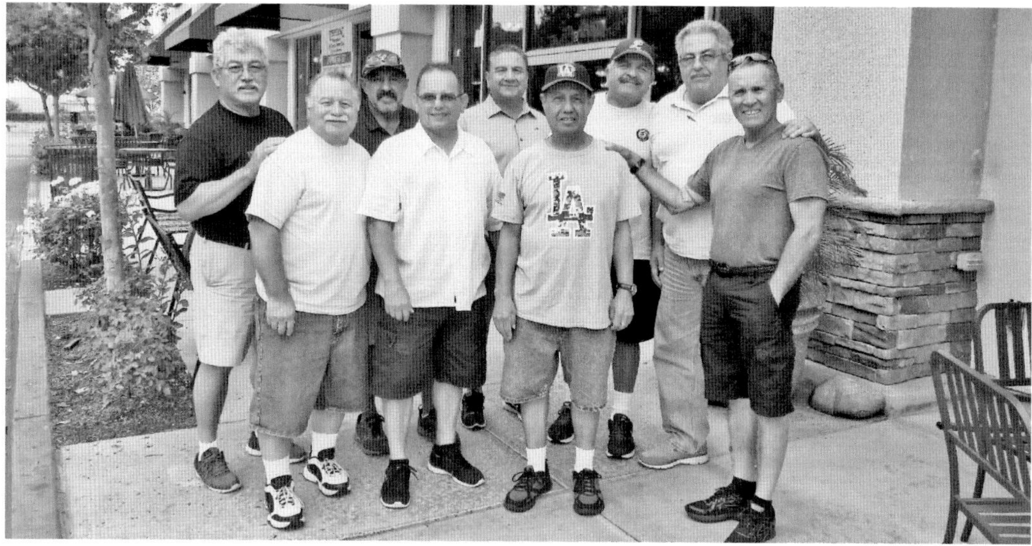

On July 15, 2017, a reunion luncheon was held in Hacienda Heights, California, to bring together several outstanding players, some of whom also coached and played college and professional baseball. From left to right are Jack Arenas, Alex Gúzman, Danny Valles, Frankie Sandoval, Al De La Rosa, Bob Durán, Bob Lavato, José Romero, and Rudy Martínez. Arenas, Valles, Durán, Romero, and Martínez attended Lincoln High School; De La Rosa and Sandoval attended Roosevelt High School; and Gúzman attended Belmont High School. Durán and Lovato's fathers, both named Robert, played ball in New Mexico in the 1950s. (Courtesy of Richard A. Santillán.)

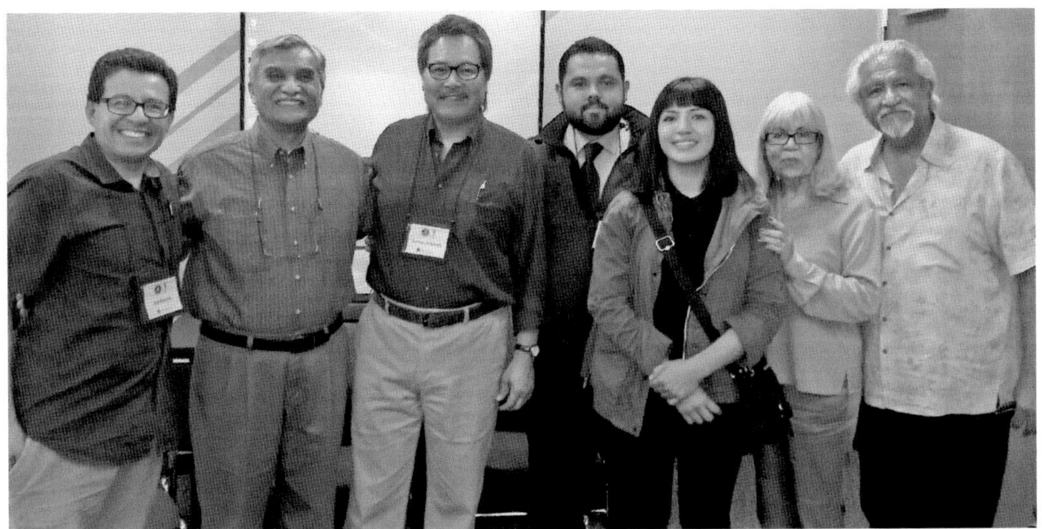

On May 29, 2017, the North American Society for Sport History held its annual meeting at California State University, Fullerton. A panel discussion entitled "The Other Field of Dreams: A Discussion on the Latino Baseball History Project" highlighted the project as a true collaboration, bringing together community historians, academic scholars, students, academic staff, players, and their families in the spirit of El Plan de Santa Barbara. From left to right are José Alamillo, Richard A. Santillán, Sam Regalado, Mark Ocegueda, Monse Segura, Teresa M. Santillán, and César Caballero. (Courtesy of Richard A. Santillán.)

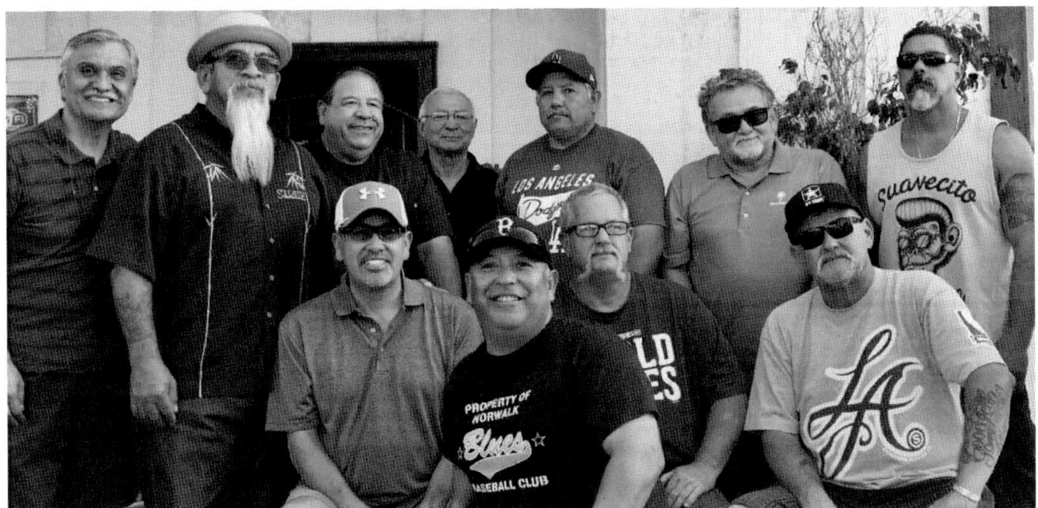

On October 21, 2018, a book signing event was held In Norwalk, California, at TNT Mexican restaurant celebrating the release of *Mexican American Baseball in the San Gabriel Valley*. Norwalk has had a rich history of baseball and softball including the Norwalk Dukes, a powerhouse team in the 1980s that won several local, regional, state, and national honors. From left to right are (first row) Steve Hernández, David Gallegos, Tommy Burgess, and Tomas Espinoza; (second row) Richard A. Santillán, John Lemos, Tony Hernández, Ramiro Gallegos, Jerry González, Joe Espinoza, and Isaac Alvidrez. (Courtesy of David Gallegos.)

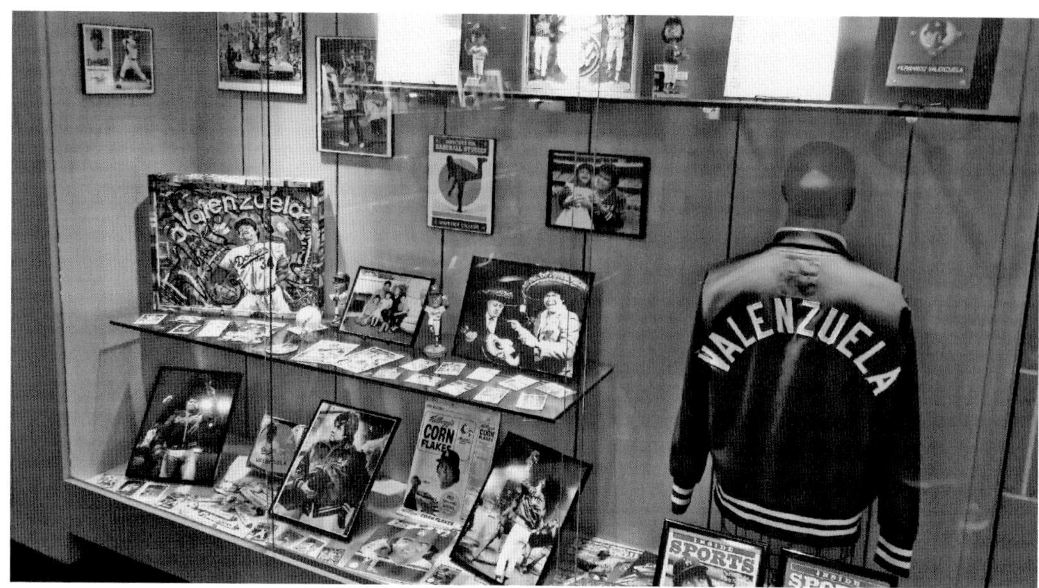

On April 4, 2018, The Institute for Baseball Studies at Whittier College, the Pasadena-based Baseball Reliquary, and the Historical Society of Southern California presented a talk entitled Major League Baseball Moves West. Andy McCue and Robert Garratt gave an outstanding presentation on the Dodgers and Giants moving to California. Guests visited the Wardman Library to view the photo exhibition on the early years of the Dodgers in Los Angeles and a display on Fernando Valenzuela. The exhibit is entitled "Eye on the Dodgers: Highlights from the Dr. Richard A. and Teresa M. Santillán Collection." (Courtesy of Richard A. Santillán.)

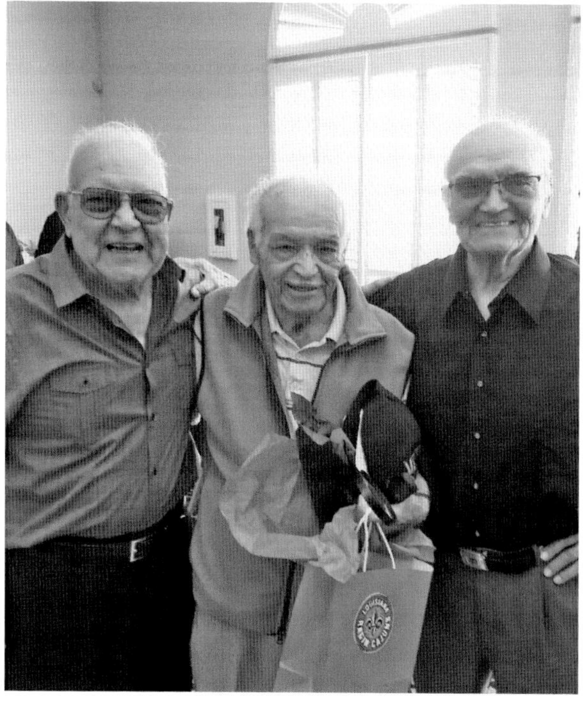

On April 15, 2018, a 90th birthday event was held for John Peña at the California Country Club in Whittier. John (left) is seen here with his brothers Pete (center) and Gabriel. At one time, there were nine Peña brothers; they were coached by their father from the 1940s until the 1960s. Collectively, the brothers played youth, high school, college, military, community, and professional ball. Their children, grandchildren, and great-grandchildren continued the long and rich history of baseball and softball. The Peña family has been a major supporter of the Latino Baseball History Project's book series and exhibits, sharing photographs and stories. (Courtesy of Richard A. Santillán.)

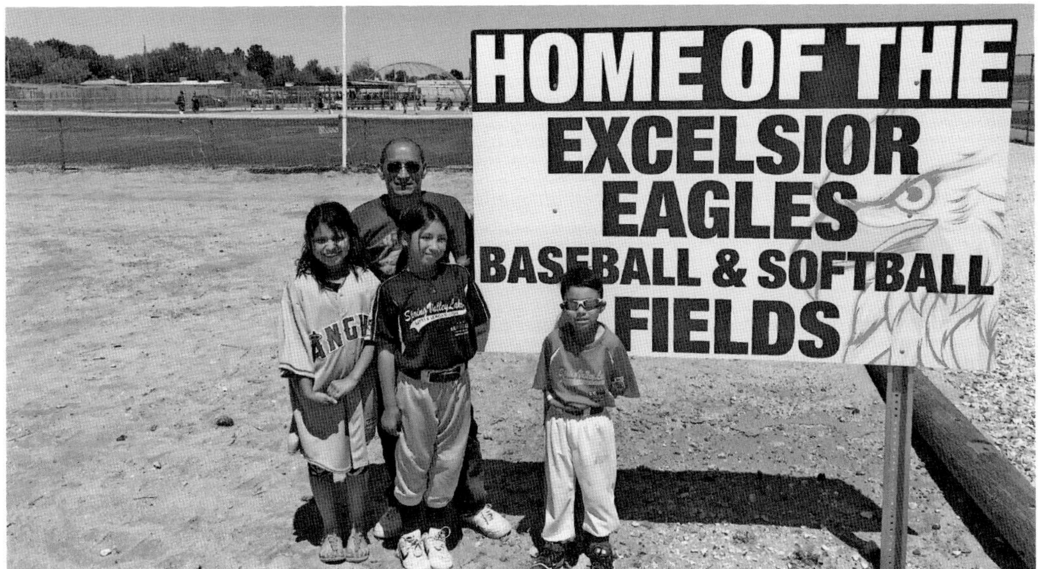

Dale Suchil is seen here with his three grandchildren, from left to right, Aleina, Valeny, and Vincent Morgutia. They are the great-grandchildren of Albert Suchil, who was an outstanding player during the 1930s, 1940s, and 1950s in the Inland Empire and also in the military during World War II. Dale Suchil grew up in Colton, California, and is a community historian of Mexican Americans. He has shared many stories with his grandchildren about Albert. The children play for the Spring Valley Lake Little League in Victorville, California. (Courtesy of Dale Suchil.)

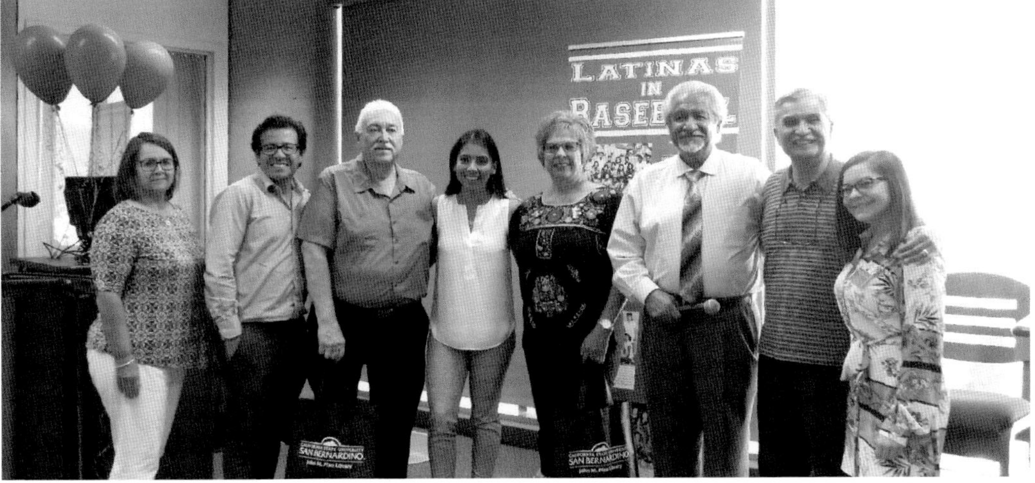

On October 27, 2018, the Latino Baseball History Project, in partnership with the Smithsonian Institution, sponsored a symposium paying tribute to Latinas who have made major contributions to baseball and softball. The all-day event included speakers, panel discussions, presentations, a film, a scanning session of vintage photos, and the donation of two uniforms by the Salazar and Cryan families to the Smithsonian. From left to right are Alicia Serra Stevens, José Alamillo, Gene T. Chávez, Angelica "Jelly" Felix, Patti Encinas García, César Caballero, Richard A. Santillán, and Margaret Salazar-Porzio. (Courtesy of the Latino Baseball History Project.)

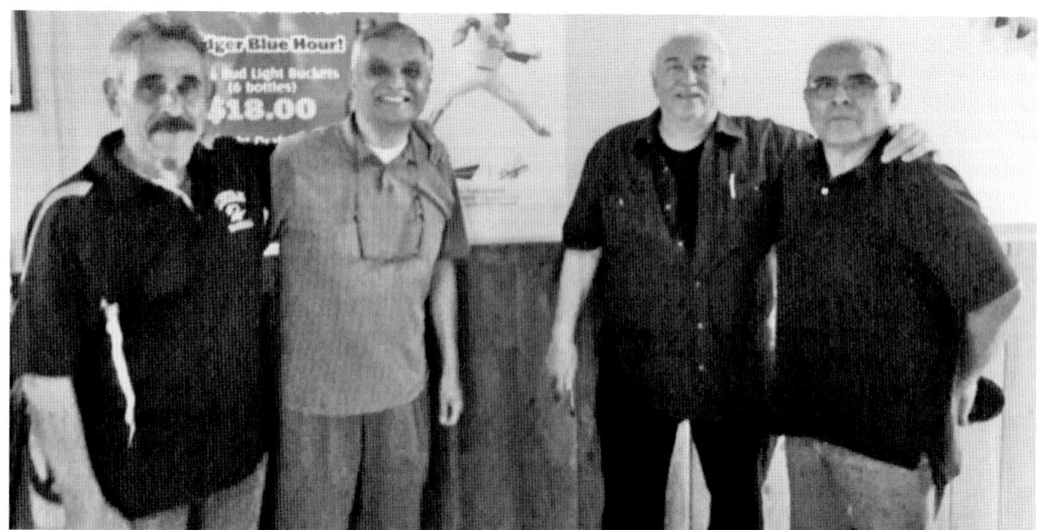

Seen here in 2018 from left to right are Ray Lara, Richard A. Santillán, Gene T. Chávez, and Rod Martínez. Santillán, Chávez, and Martínez are coauthors of *Mexican American Baseball in Kansas City*. Chávez, who lives and works in the Kansas City area, has hosted several exhibits, talks, and documentaries on the remarkable history of baseball and softball in Kansas and Missouri. Ray Lara was an outstanding player in the greater East Los Angeles region and is currently the head coach at Lincoln High School in East Los Angeles. (Courtesy of Richard A. Santillán.)

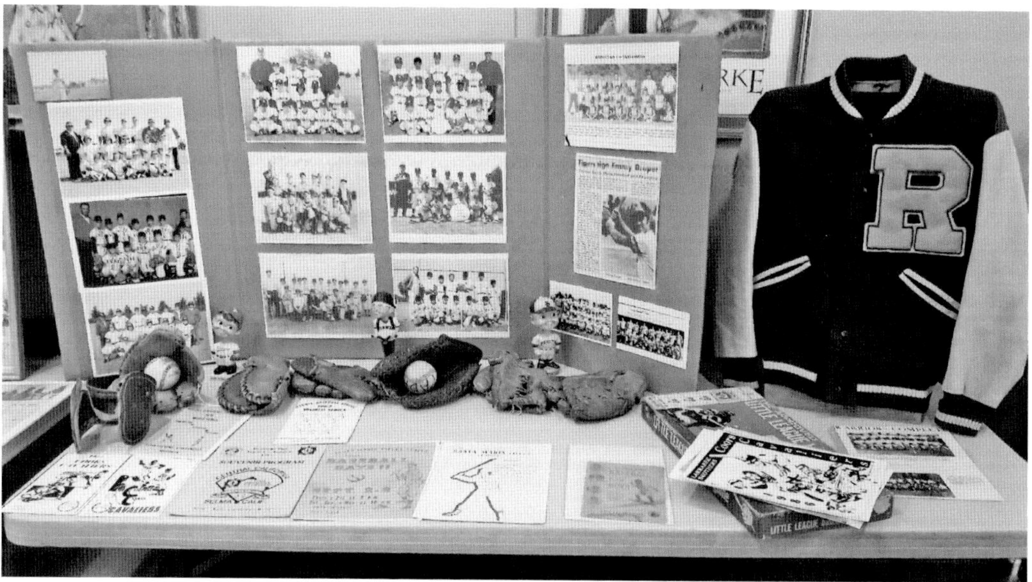

Major highlights of the January 27, 2018, event in Santa Maria, California, included many displays and exhibits showcasing photographs and rare memorabilia from the history of ball in the Santa Maria Valley. Included were game-used balls, bats, gloves, uniforms, yearbooks, programs, warm-up jackets, vintage catcher gear, newspaper articles, lettermen jackets, caps, bobbleheads, pocket schedules, posters, and much more. Al Ramos, Eddie Navarro, Ernie Corral, and Joe Talaugon have been the vanguard in keeping alive this region's sports history. (Courtesy of Teresa M. Santillán.)

Gene T. Chávez (left) is pictured with Fernando Valenzuela at the Montebello Country Club in Montebello, California, on April 14, 2018. Chávez, a coauthor of *Mexican American Baseball in Kansas City*, was in Los Angeles promoting the book and the current initiative with the Smithsonian Institution on the contributions of the Latino community to baseball and softball. Valenzuela has generously lent support for the initiative by appearing at one of the Smithsonian–Latino Baseball History Project events at California State University, San Bernardino in 2017, and signing baseballs for several exhibits. (Courtesy of Gene T. Chávez.)

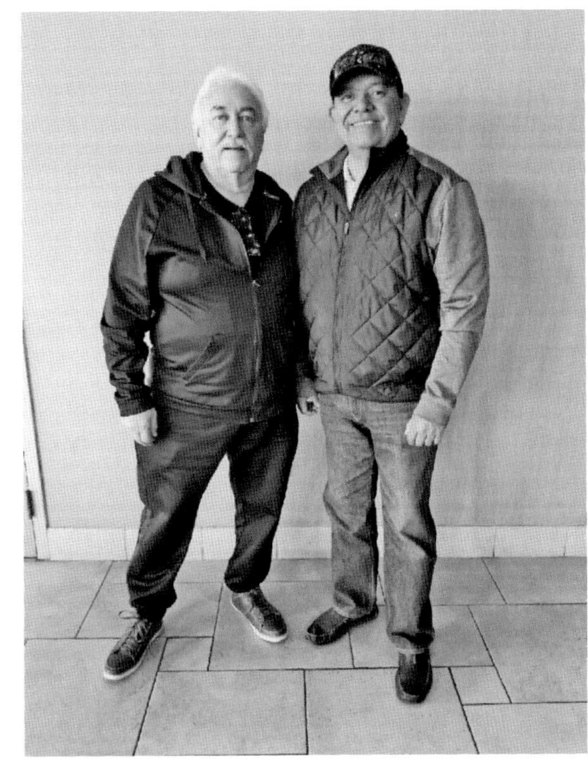

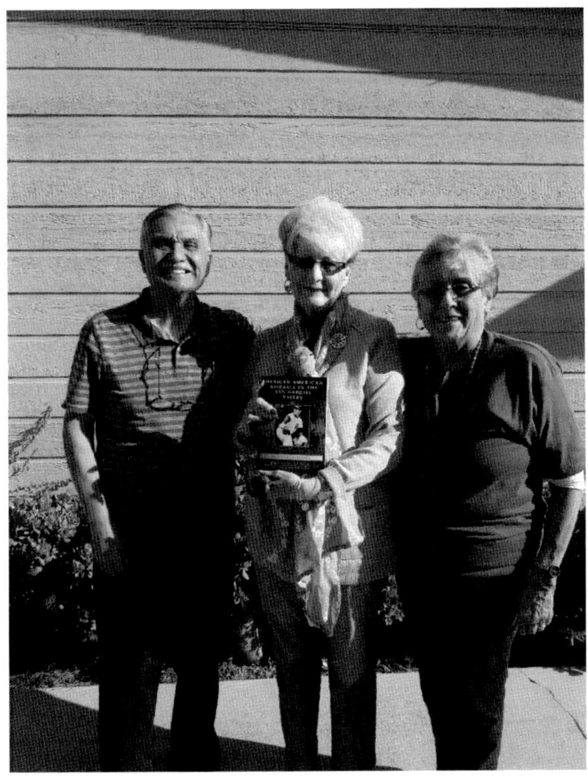

On November 11, 2018, the San Gabriel Historical Association sponsored a book signing event for *Mexican American Baseball in the San Gabriel Valley*. From left to right are Richard A. Santillán, Irene Aguirre Juarez, and Camila López. Santillán and López are coauthors of the book. Irene is holding the book with her brother, Hank Aguirre, on the cover. Hank was raised in the San Gabriel Valley and played major league baseball for 16 years with the Tigers, Cubs, and Dodgers. After retirement, he became a successful businessman and generous philanthropist. He died at a young age in 1994. (Courtesy of Richard A. Santillán.)

LATINO BASEBALL HISTORY PROJECT ADVISORY BOARD

James Henninger Aguirre
José M. Alamillo
Eduardo B. Almada T.
Richard Arroyo
Gabriel "Tito" Ávila Jr.
Francisco E. Balderrama
Cuno Barragán
Tomas Benítez
Anna Bermúdez
Juan J. Canchola
Terry A. Cannon
Juan Carrillo
Ben Chappell
Gene Chávez
Ernie Cervantes Jr.
David Contreras Jr.
Juan D. Coronado
Raúl J. Córdova
Christopher Docter
Peter Drier
Robert Elias
Luís F. Fernández
Donna Galvan
Maria García
Mark García
Gregory Garrett
Jorge Iber
Rumado Z. Juárez
William Lange
Alfonso Ledesma
Camila Alva López
Enrique M. López
Jody L. and Gabriel A. López
Susan C. Luévano
Amanda Magdalena
Rod Martínez
Douglas Monroy
Carlos Muñoz Jr
Eddie Navarro
Victoria C. Norton
Mark A. Ocegueda
Alan O'Connor
Raymond Olaís
Monica Ortez
Al Padilla
Richard Peña
Al Ramos
Samuel O. Regalado
Vicki L. Ruíz
Anthony Salazar
Richard A. Santillán
Teresa M. Santillán
Marcelino Saucedo
Mikaela Selley
Ray P. Serra
Monserrath Segura
Alicia S. Stevens
Joe Talaugon
Joseph Thompson
Carlos Tortolero
Sandra L. Uribe
Elisa Grajeda-Urmston
David Vargas
Alejo L. Vásquez
Angelina F. Veyna
Alfonso Villanueva Jr.
Robert Zamora

BIBLIOGRAPHY

Cabral, Rick. "The Long Journey of Facundo Antonio 'Cuno' Barragán." www.baseballsacramento.com.

Dhillon, Jagdip. "Cal Mex Baseball League Still Strong at 50." *Stockton Record*, August 9, 2011.

Díaz, Ella Maria. *Flying Under the Radar with the Royal Chicano Air Force: Mapping a Chicano/a Art History*. Austin, TX: University of Texas Press, 2017.

Finch, Lynda, and Rachel Arias. *150th Anniversary Kern County Mexican Settlement: Pioneers from the South*. Self-published, 2016.

———. *150th Anniversary, Kern County, California Mexican Settlement 1866–2016, Volume II: The Legacy*. Self-published, 2016.

Flores, Lori A. *Grounds for Dreaming: Mexican Americans, Mexican Immigrants, and the California Farmworker Movement*. New Haven, CT: Yale University Press, 2016.

Galarza, Ernesto. *Barrio Boy*. Notre Dame, IN: University of Notre Dame Press, 2011.

———. *Merchants of Labor: The Mexican Bracero Story*. San Jose, CA: Rosicrucian Press, 1964.

Garland, Frank. "Tracy's Mr. Baseball." *Tracy Press*, August 22, 1977.

Hagaman, Gwen. "Club Mercedes Celebrates 70 Years of Service." *Merced County Times*, September 14, 2017.

Jacobs, Martin, and Jack McGuire. *San Francisco Seals*. Charleston, SC: Arcadia Publishing, 2005.

Loza, Mireya. *Defiant Braceros: How Migrant Workers Fought for Racial, Sexual, and Political Freedom*. Chapel Hill, NC: University of North Carolina Press, 2016.

Nakagawa, Kerry Yo. *Japanese American Baseball in California*. Charleston, SC: The History Press, 2014.

Mandt, Edward. "Latin American All-Stars: Los Niños de Otoño." *Society for American Baseball Research Journal*, 1988.

McPoil, William D. *Sacramento Baseball*. Charleston, SC: Arcadia Publishing, 2017.

O'Connor, Alan. *Sacramento's Great Baseball Players: Gold on the Diamond*. Sacramento, CA: Big Tomato Press, 2008.

Rosas, Ana Elizabeth. *Abrazando el Espíritu: Bracero Families Confront the U.S.-Mexico Border*. Berkeley, CA: University of California Press, 2014.

Santillán, Richard A., Christopher Docter, Anna Bermúdez, Eddie Navarro, and Alan O'Connor. *Mexican American Baseball in the Central Coast*. Charleston, SC: Arcadia Publishing, 2013.

Consistent with our mission to preserve history on a local level, this book was printed in South Carolina on American-made paper and manufactured entirely in the United States. Products carrying the accredited Forest Stewardship Council (FSC) label are printed on 100 percent FSC-certified paper.

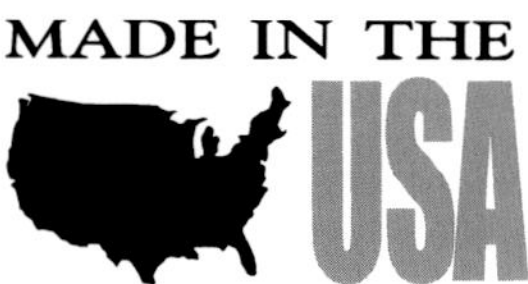

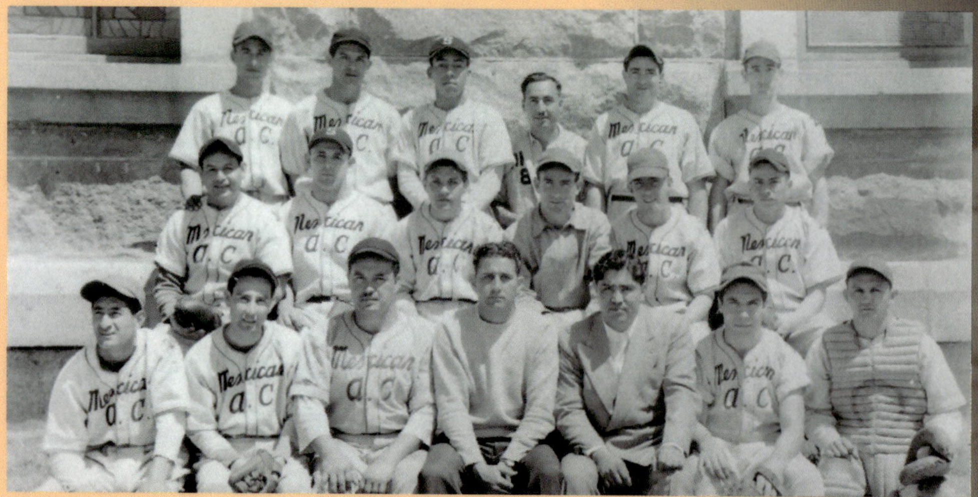

Mexican American Baseball in Sacramento explores the history and culture of teams and players from the Sacramento region. Since the early 20th century, baseball diamonds in California's capital and surrounding communities have nurtured athletic talent, educational skills, ethnic identity, and political self-determination for Mexican Americans. The often-neglected historical narrative of these men's and women's teams tells the story of community, migration, military service, education, gender, social justice, and perseverance. Players often became important members of their communities, and some even went on to become professional athletes—paving a path for Latinos in sports. These photographs serve as a lens to both local sports history and Mexican American history.

Mark A. Ocegueda is an assistant professor of US and Mexican American history at California State University, Sacramento. Christopher Docter is a baseball researcher and professional in museum, library, and archival fields. Richard A. Santillán is professor emeritus of ethnic and women studies at California State Polytechnic University at Pomona. Ernie Cervantes Jr. is a member of Sacramento's Mexican American Hall of Fame Sports Association and was inducted in 1989. Cuno Barragán is a former major-league baseball player with the Chicago Cubs and inductee to the Sacramento Mexican American Hall of Fame Sports Association.

ISBN-13 978-1-4671-0269-8 $24.99
ISBN-10 1-4671-0269-5

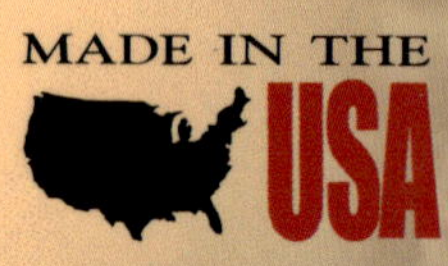

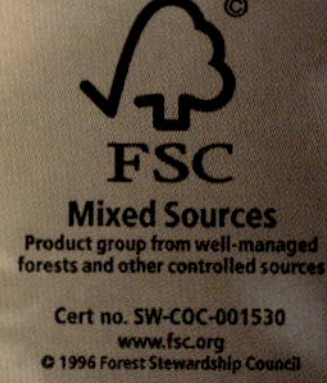

www.arcadiapublishing.com

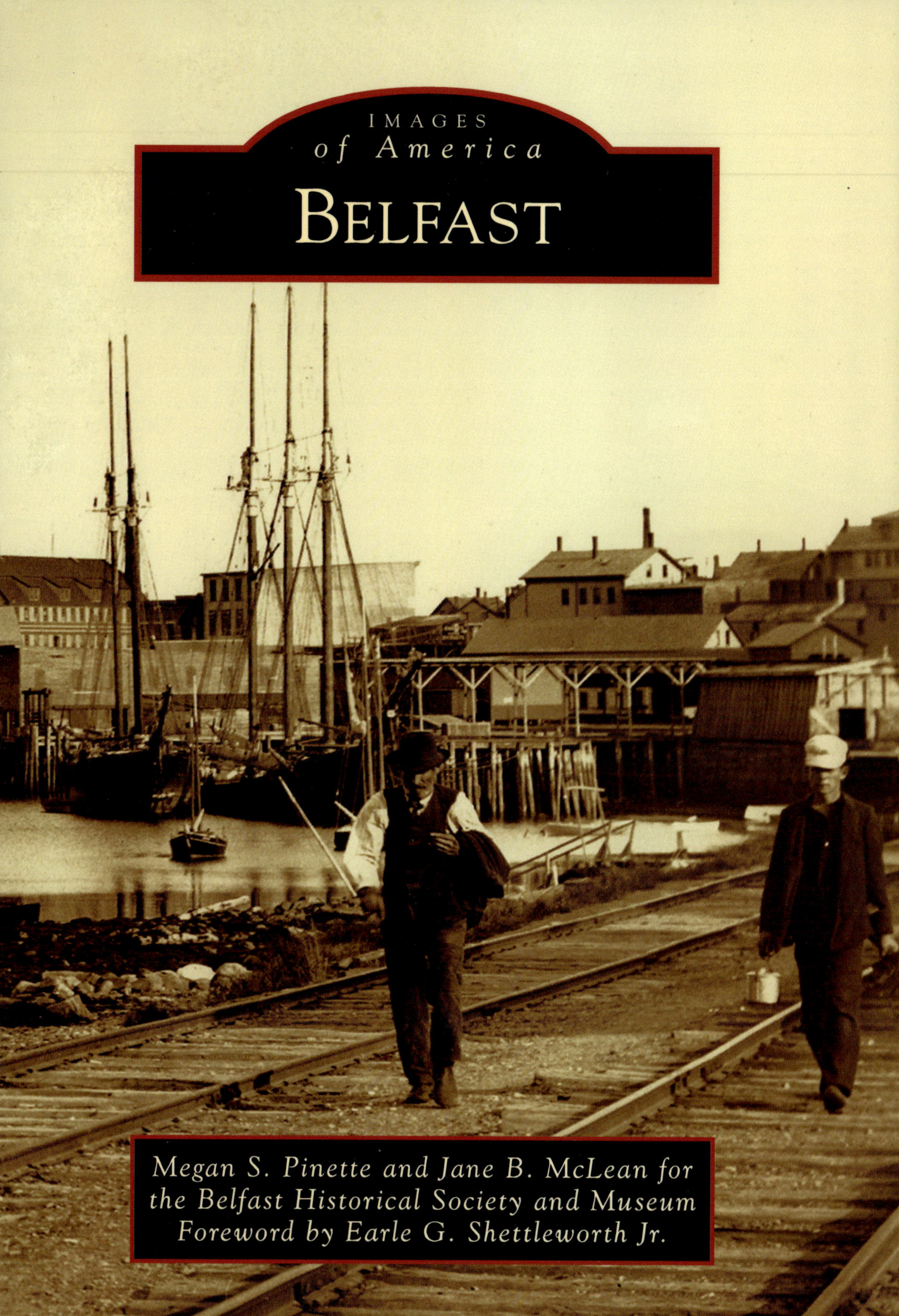
IMAGES
of America
BELFAST
Megan S. Pinette and Jane B. McLean for
the Belfast Historical Society and Museum
Foreword by Earle G. Shettleworth Jr.